Back to Back

By Leonard Baker

THE JOHNSON ECLIPSE
A President's Vice Presidency

BACK TO BACK
The Duel between FDR and the Supreme Court

BACK TO
BACK *The Duel between*
FDR and the Supreme Court

Leonard Baker

The Macmillan Company
New York

The Macmillan Company, New York
Collier-Macmillan Canada Ltd., Toronto, Ontario

Printed in the United States of America

To my parents,
Charles and Bess Baker

Contents

Part One

Pack the Court!

1

THE LIMOUSINES began arriving at the White House a few minutes before ten o'clock in the morning, bringing the worried, nervous men to the session in the Cabinet room. The chairmen of the Senate and House Judiciary committees entered first. "Why are you here?" each demanded of the other. Neither could answer except to say the obvious: a telephone call late the previous evening had summoned him.

The others followed quickly—the Secretary of State, the secretaries of war and Navy, the Attorney General, the secretaries of interior, labor, agriculture, and commerce. The Vice President came. He would sit silently through this meeting, the first such session with the President and the Cabinet in which he does not speak.

Next came the Senate Democratic leader, then the Speaker of the House of Representatives and the Democratic majority leader in the House. This last person would later say of this meeting and the subsequent events: "I regret this . . . more than anything else."

They moved quietly about the room, making small talk with each other or not talking at all. Some lounged in the leather chairs that surrounded the conference table, glancing occasionally at the door leading to the President's office.

In that office sat the most powerful man in the nation. There were some—some even in this Cabinet room now—who considered him a dangerous man, some who watched the danger grow as he increased his power. And so toward this man, their

President, these men had conflicting attitudes: admiration for his obvious ability, a certain dread of his plans, mixed with an apprehension of the purpose of today's sudden and unexplained session.

One man present could have told why they had been summoned. The Attorney General. From the beginning he had been in on the events leading to today's meeting and had helped shape them. "I am bursting with ideas," the Attorney General had told the President several weeks earlier, beginning the procession of conferences, plans, drafting of legislation, speech writing, and politicking that had led to today's meeting. But the Attorney General did not tell. The drama of that moment—the moment of telling— belonged to the President and to him only.

Then the door opened. Those in the Cabinet room turned. Quickly they quieted, stubbed out their cigarettes, moved to their chairs, and peered intently toward the oval office that was the nerve center of the American government.

Franklin Delano Roosevelt, the thirty-second President of the United States, entered. In any delineation of an American aristocracy, the Roosevelt family of Hyde Park belonged among its leaders. But this Roosevelt, ironically, in his character and manner the embodiment of such an aristocracy, did not show allegiance to that elite group. His allegiance, instead, was to the mass of people. Only a few months earlier, in November of 1936, these people had marched to the voting booths in their miners' hats, farmers' overalls, and housewives' aprons to give this scion of Hudson Valley patroons the biggest popular vote a Presidential candidate ever had received. FDR interpreted that vote as a call, one conferring upon him both a power and a responsibility. He planned to use the first to fulfill the second.

He guided his wheelchair to his accustomed place at the center of the Cabinet table as the others hustled to their chairs. Immediately he dominated the room, but not merely by virtue of his office. There was something else about him. The massive shoulders, the strong jawline, the air of self-assurance—all suggested a man who had accomplished much in his life, as Franklin Roosevelt certainly had. They also suggested a man who will accomplish much more, as Franklin Roosevelt was certain he would.

As he grew up in the big Roosevelt family home overlooking the wide Hudson River Valley, Franklin Roosevelt had developed a panoramic view of life. With this perspective one can see problems from their early development to their ultimate end. More importantly, one visualizes solutions and sees himself as part of those solutions, as one selected by destiny, perhaps, for service. Roosevelt—tall, handsome, witty, and charming in an almost overwhelming way—moved early to the area of public service. He ran for the New York State legislature and was elected. At the outset he battled the bosses of his own party. During the First World War he was Assistant Secretary of the Navy. Then, in 1920, he became his party's nominee for Vice President.

During these years a small band of supporters began to associate with Roosevelt, attracted by his courage, his style, and his concern for the common man. After his unsuccessful bid for the Vice Presidency, disaster struck. Polio turned Franklin Roosevelt into a helpless cripple. But then Franklin Roosevelt turned that helpless cripple into a powerful, active, mature, and tough man. Never again did he walk, except for a few steps, and then holding on to someone, usually one of his sons. But always he moved. Twice he was elected to two-year terms as governor of New York. Then, in 1932, Franklin Roosevelt was elected to the Presidency. He took office in a time of national despair, determined, single-handedly if he must, to banish that hopelessness from the nation.

Now as he began to speak to those sitting in the Cabinet room, he was a curious picture. The shoulders, distorted by his having walked so much with crutches, suggested power, not only physical strength but the power of a man determined to succeed against personal and national afflictions, to succeed where others fail. FDR had a handsome face, barely marred by a line although he had just observed his fifty-fifth birthday. His full head of wavy dark hair was just beginning to gray. His face, his whole manner, sparkled as if he were enjoying himself immensely, even though he was obligated to a job that other men would find killing.

He nodded pleasantly to each of the persons sitting around the table, calling them by their first names. A secretary had followed him into the room and placed a pile of papers at each seat. Those papers contained a message to the Congress from the President. The thirteen men and one woman—Frances Perkins, the Secretary of Labor—glanced through the papers, wondering what the message was about.

The President wasted no time. He had scheduled a news conference and did not wish to be late. He reminded the group before him that some weeks earlier he had sent a message to Congress recommending reorganization changes in the executive branch of the federal government. Today, the President continued, he was sending to Congress a message on the reorganization of the judicial branch. Slowly the people sitting around the Cabinet table realized the import of the President's action. He was taking on the Supreme Court of the United States.

For two years Franklin Roosevelt had watched, helpless, while the Supreme Court destroyed the legislative program he had tried to build. The anger had grown in him as one New Deal measure after another was declared unconstitutional by a Court that Franklin Roosevelt considered a political body hiding behind a reputation for being above politics. Now FDR was striking back, determined to pull the Supreme Court from its lofty perch and engage it in a political duel.

Friday, February 5, 1937, the day of this meeting, began a struggle to determine if the Presidency, the Congress, and the judiciary were indeed equal branches of the federal government, as the people understood the Constitution to say, or whether one branch, the Presidency, was supreme.

At stake was not a question of constitutional law for college professors and lawyers to argue over during the coming decades. Involved was the question of people. How and by whom would they be governed? What future did they have? Which course would the United States of America choose? This day began events that would shape American politics for decades, determining the course of the American Presidency. "If we can pass the legislation," Roosevelt said of his bill, "the whole country will move forward."

Before FDR's duel with the Supreme Court would end, all the powers in the United States would be called on to be seconds. The bankers and industrialists would contribute funds. Newspaper and magazine publishers, owners of radio stations, would allow, sometimes direct, their media to be used as weapons. The powers at City Hall and the powers in Congress would barter their support for patronage, a dip into the pork barrel, and votes. The labor unions and the farmers, as well as the businessmen, would play the same sleazy politics. A former President would hopefully seize the issue as a ticket back to the White House. Others would grasp it as a way to fulfill personal vendettas. But there were some who would see not the votes and the pork barrel, neither the personal glory nor the rewards of history, but only the good of the nation. All who were involved, however, no matter what their motive or their side, would bear wounds when the duel ended. Sometimes the pain of those wounds would ease. Never would they heal.

The Roosevelt message was lengthy. An hour was required for him to read it to the Cabinet members and Congressional leaders. He also ad-libbed a bit. At one point he held up a draft of his proposed bill, calling it something "into which Henry and Hatton can sink their teeth." He was referring to Senator Henry Fountain Ashurst of Arizona, the chairman of the Senate Judiciary Committee, and to Representative Hatton Sumners of Texas, the chairman of the House Judiciary Committee. These two men were a check on the President. Because their committees must consider, then rewrite if they desired, the President's legislative proposals, they and the entire Congress, which then must vote the bills up or down, balanced the President's enthusiasm, if they chose to. The two men, Hatton Sumners and Henry Ashurst, did not respond to FDR's remark. Even as the President rushed on with his proposal, these two were severing themselves from the Roosevelt band. In their minds formed the word "No."

Sumners made no secret of his feelings. At this moment, as he

listened to the pleasant, cultivated voice of the President, Sumners
did not speak. Roosevelt was not asking for comments, and
Sumners did not feel obliged to offer any. But later, when he was
with his friends, he announced: "Boys, here's where I cash in my
chips." And to others he called the proposal "infamous" and gave
it "Hell, specifically and generally." Henry Ashurst, suave and
courtly, never used such words, either publicly or in the privacy
of his own diary. But he had similar sentiments. On two previous
occasions Ashurst had advised Roosevelt not to launch the type
of attack he now was beginning. The Senator appreciated FDR's
vexation at not having had one appointment to the Supreme
Court, at not being able to place men on the Court amenable
to the New Deal philosophy. But age, Ashurst had said, must
eventually take its toll, creating, either through death or through
retirement, vacancies on the court which Roosevelt then could fill.
"It will fall to your lot to nominate more Justices of the Supreme
Court than any other President since General Washington. You
will nominate four, possibly five, Supreme Court Justices," Ashurst had predicted to Roosevelt a year earlier. "Father Time, with
his scythe, is on your side," Ashurst had said in 1936. "Anno
Domini is your invincible ally."

Roosevelt, however, gave no sign that he remembered Ashurst's
earlier advice. In February, 1936, he had sent Ashurst a memorandum discussing a proposal for removing some of the older justices from the court. Ashurst had replied then that the time was
not appropriate for such a move. This day in February, 1937, one
year after that exchange, Roosevelt scrawled a note to Ashurst to
go along with the proposed legislation. "Dear Henry, here it is,"
FDR said in reference to the 1936 memorandum, "back again!"

In the coming weeks and months of 1937 Henry Ashurst would
not be so open in his opposition as would Hatton Sumners, but
he would be as effective, perhaps more effective. The checks on
Franklin Roosevelt already were beginning.

The FDR plan was simple. The Supreme Court had nine members. Six were over seventy years of age. For each member of the
Court who declined to retire at age seventy, Roosevelt proposed

that a co-justice be appointed to the Court to serve alongside the older justice. If his bill became law, Roosevelt immediately could make six appointments of co-justices to the Court, and the Court would jump in size from nine to fifteen members. If one of the six justices over seventy chose to retire, the President still would be able to make an appointment to fill his vacant seat on the bench as well as naming five co-justices, but the Court would go up only to fourteen members. If all the justices over seventy retired, FDR could then fill their vacancies, and the Court would stay at nine members. Either way, through the appointment of co-justices or through the retirement of justices over seventy, Roosevelt would have the authority to place on the Supreme Court persons whose philosophy agreed with his.

The President based his case, in the message he now read, on the argument that the older judges were unable to carry a full share of work. He used a supporting quotation that judges were so often unable to acknowledge their infirmities that they "seem to be tenacious of the appearance of adequacy." It was Roosevelt's joke. He refused to identify the author of the quotation, knowing that it would be quickly recognized. The words had been said years before by Charles Evans Hughes. When FDR used them, Hughes was seventy-four years old. He also was Chief Justice of the United States, the presiding officer of the Supreme Court, one of the nine men now under attack by Roosevelt.

The Roosevelt proposal could be compared, as a political cartoonist did compare it, to that of a football coach who insists on changing the lineup of his team but without taking any men off the field. Anticipating an obvious objection, Roosevelt conceded at the meeting that he could have proposed instead a constitutional amendment requiring the justices to retire at age seventy. But amendments must be approved by state legislatures. And FDR, a former governor of New York, knew state legislatures. They could be influenced or bought.

Already, he said, his opponents in the conservative-oriented Liberty League had collected "a large sum of money in New York" to use at the state legislature level against any amendment. "Give me ten million dollars," Roosevelt said to the meeting in the Cabinet room, "and I can prevent any amendment to the Constitution from being ratified by the necessary number of states." Later he cut that estimate down to five million dollars.

Although the argument in the message was based on physical age, everyone in the room understood there was another motive. Franklin Roosevelt had entered the White House in March of 1933 promising a "New Deal" to the "forgotten man." He had followed through. He had whipped the Congress into obeying him and had created a federal bureaucracy to distribute the federal government's largesse. At each turn, however, the Supreme Court stood in his way, blocking him, jeering him, challenging him. At each turn a majority of the Supreme Court spoke out in behalf of the wealthy, the privileged, the aristocracy—that same aristocracy that Roosevelt had deserted.

Franklin Roosevelt could not permit this to continue. "When I retire to private life on January 20, 1941," he explained, "I do not want to leave the country in the condition Buchanan left it to Lincoln. If I cannot, in the brief time given me to attack its deep and disturbing problems, solve those problems, I hope at least to have moved them well on the way to solution by my successor. It is absolutely essential that the solving process begin at once."

The problems were many. Eleven years after the First World War, a great depression, caused in part by that war, had swept across the world. Nations reacted differently. Most European powers skittered back and forth between governments. One, Germany, chose a totalitarianism that already was threatening the peace of the world as well as man's view of himself as a civilized being. In the United States the social and economic ills of generations were culminating in fights, sit-down strikes, and lockouts. The poor and the rich were fighting each other in a thousand skirmishes across the United States. Hoping to avoid both the indecisiveness of some nations and the dictatorship of Germany, Franklin Roosevelt resolved to bring peace to a troubled United States.

The distance between the Supreme Court building at one end of Pennsylvania Avenue and the White House at the other end is not two miles. In the 1930s, however, it had become eternally long, a journey from what some men visualized as the nineteenth century to what others conceived as the twentieth, from what some men considered worth preserving to what others believed must come. The journey was the hardest that man ever is called upon to make, from the past that has left him to the future that is imposing itself upon him.

Roosevelt intended to force the Supreme Court to make that journey. Those six new members of the Court he sought would create a Roosevelt majority of ten on the Court. No longer would New Deal legislation be called unconstitutional by the Court. And there was more. If Roosevelt won—and that "if" was a tantalizing question that February morning—the symbolism of his victory would be understood. Don't challenge the President, it would say. To do so is to risk a fight and a defeat. It would also say something else: Don't attack the New Deal, that collection of laws and ideas that were FDR's tools for helping the forgotten man, or you risk political destruction. That was a message not only for the Supreme Court but also for the Democratic party, which still was only loosely tied behind the Roosevelt and New Deal banners. It would be a message for anyone interested in entering politics, for a Roosevelt victory over the Supreme Court would be a victory of the mass of people over the few who were wealthy. It would determine whether the role of government was to help the people or to protect property. A Roosevelt victory would give direction to political careers not yet commenced.

Of those in the room, not all would become involved in the fight. The secretaries of state, war, the Navy, and commerce had no political leverage they could bring to bear. They became spectators to a duel that greatly influenced history's assessment of an administration in which they served. The Secretary of Labor, Miss Perkins, had power available to her—contacts and influence with the politically potent American labor leaders. But in the coming months she would become so involved with the labor riots and

and sit-down strikes that threatened to divide the country that she could not join the struggle between FDR and the Supreme Court. As Secretary of the Treasury, Henry S. Morgenthau, Jr.. had no role either, but as an old friend of Franklin Roosevelt's, he would be a sympathetic listener.

FDR did expect several members of the Cabinet to play influential parts. One was the Secretary of Agriculture, Henry A. Wallace, who, it was hoped, could bring the farm leaders behind FDR's plan. Another was Harold Ickes, the Secretary of the Interior. He had numerous contacts with influential liberals around the country; certainly he would bring them into line. Also, Ickes had a considerable amount of political plums to hand out in return for support of the Court plan. There was never a question of where Ickes stood. All his life the "Old Curmudgeon," as he was called, had fought for the reforms that Roosevelt was trying to impose on the nation and which the Supreme Court was blocking. Although Ickes did not speak at this February 5 meeting, he did talk to Roosevelt about the Court plan a few days later. "He insisted that he would win his fight," Ickes said of that discussion with Roosevelt about the Court plan, "and I told him that he simply had to. I said to him that unless he won he might as well resign, because he could not hope to realize the objectives that he has in mind or to accomplish what the people elected him to accomplish."

The Postmaster General, James A. Farley, who was not at the meeting, was expected to be the most helpful. Big, bald, and Irish, Farley was the prototype of the professional politician. Once he understood the political objective, he then determined the means necessary to achieve that objective. He did so in the Court fight— and, curiously, the man who had always before been so successful at politics this time would fail disastrously.

One Cabinet member expected to be a valuable team player in the coming months. This was Homer S. Cummings, the Attorney General, the man who six weeks earlier had produced the specific plan now before the Cabinet members. Like Roosevelt, Cummings was a man of an aristocratic and well-educated background. Like

Roosevelt too, Cummings believed the law and politics were means of helping the poor who did not understand how they could help themselves. Cummings was a tall, lean man who suggested a teacher searching for an errant pupil to crack over the knuckles. He was actually an astute and knowledgeable politician. An old acquaintance of FDR's from the Wilson Administration, Cummings also had been national chairman of the Democratic party in the 1920s. He knew many of the people on Capitol Hill—those members of Congress who could block or delay Roosevelt's Court plan if they desired. Cummings could speak their language, deal with them as they wished to be dealt with, with the respect and deference for their position they believed they deserved. As the weeks passed, however, Homer Cummings saw the younger men in the Roosevelt Administration take over the Court battle and squeeze him out. This February morning his face practically shone in anticipation of the coming political duel. But later he saw himself ignored as the strategy was mapped out and as the politicking took place. "If that's the way they want to do it," he finally said in disgust, "let it go."

FDR expected his Vice President to back him up. John Nance Garner of Texas was a man of the Congress; he had been Speaker of the House when he became Roosevelt's running mate in 1932. He also was a southerner. At the Democratic party's convention in 1932, he had sought the Presidential nomination as the candidate of the South. FDR had dealt with him as one deals with a potentate, as with a leader of a separate nation: Challenge him, defeat him, offer him terms. With Garner the terms offered were the Vice Presidency. Garner—"Cactus Jack" as he was nicknamed—had accepted, and that acceptance was understood to mean that he had bound his loyalty to the Roosevelt Administration. Now that he was in his fifth year as Roosevelt's second man, he was expected particularly to ride herd on the southern congressmen, making certain they did not lose their FDR brand.

But Cactus Jack Garner was motivated by something more than his loyalty to FDR. He believed a greater loyalty was to the needs of his country as he understood them. To him the Supreme Court was not the menace but the savior. He was a conservative. He did not like big government spending and he did not like big labor; he did not like what Franklin Roosevelt was doing. Garner was seen later this day expressing his opinion of the Court plan in a most forceful manner. At one time he held his nose and turned his thumb down. At another moment, when he was alone with some friends, he slammed his fist down on a table and charged Roosevelt with being "the most destructive man in all American history." Garner would not be part of Roosevelt's army; he would become the traitor within.

FDR was forced to rely on the Congressional leaders. In addition to Hatton Sumners and Henry Ashurst, there were the Senate Democratic leader Joe T. Robinson of Arkansas, Speaker of the House William Bankhead of Alabama, and the newly elected House Democratic leader, Sam Rayburn of Texas. Of these last three, the brunt of the fight would fall on old Joe Robinson. Robinson had misgivings about the Roosevelt plan, but he was a loyal party member. "My task is to meet the situation as it is," he explained to a friend a little later. "I am trying to work it out fairly and with due regard to every right and interest involved."

The Cabinet meeting ended. The session demonstrated Roosevelt's approach to his job. He simply had announced what he wanted from the Congress, explained the bill that he wanted passed, and then anticipated that the Congressional leaders, aided by the members of the executive branch, would produce that bill. Generally the approach had worked in the past. Roosevelt had first been elected in a time of economic crisis, and the Congress had rushed to give him every opportunity to end that crisis. After the Congressional session during Roosevelt's first year in office in 1933, Henry Ashurst had written:

President Roosevelt, during the Special Session, sent Congress so many messages that we grew dizzy. Before we could analyze one message from the White House, swiftly upon that message would come another and yet another, and so on, until Senators and Representatives became Whirling Dervishes. Each house had from ten to twenty committees in session by day and by night. We ground out laws so fast that we had no time to offer even a respectful gesture toward grammar, syntax and philology. We counted deuces as aces, reasoned from non-existent premises and, at times, we seemed to accept chimeras, phantasies and exploded social and economic theories as our authentic guides.

But the feeling of crisis had begun to pass. On Capitol Hill the members of Congress felt slight stirrings of independence. These stirrings would become a crucial factor in Roosevelt's duel with the Supreme Court, but FDR would be at a disadvantage. Never a member of Congress, he did not understand it. Nor did he have the honest advice about such stirrings to warn him to protect that flank on Capitol Hill. As the meeting ended at approximately eleven o'clock the morning of February 5 and Franklin Roosevelt wheeled himself back to his office, where he would meet the press, the opening through which his enemies could move already existed.

The excitement had spread. The newsmen felt it first. They waited expectantly to be called into the Presidential office, guessing at what was up, pumping each other for information that none had. There were more of them than usual this Friday. By some alchemy that always has been part of Washington the reporters had heard that this morning's session would be more than the usual routine announcements and friendly repartee, that this morning would be a good time to be at the White House. Something big, the word had quickly spread, is going to break.

Steve Early, FDR's press secretary, had emphasized to Roosevelt that in announcing "the subject," as Early called it, the President should stress its confidential nature. The reporters must understand that they should not publicize "the subject" until the message actually reached Capitol Hill. "This is a precaution to prevent newspapermen from going to the Capitol and begin collecting comments and opinions, or interviewing members of the Court or others in advance of the release." Early added to Roosevelt: "Please request that no one leave the conference until it is over."

When the newsmen had formed a semicircle around the President's desk, he smiled at them, explained that copies of his message would be available when the news session ended, "and don't anybody go out until that time." The reporters laughed and one shot back: "We brought our lunches." FDR joined in the laughter. "That is all right," he said, "I am glad you did."

A politician and the press are natural enemies, or should be. The politician must worry because the press, by revealing information not planned for publication, or by overemphasizing a point that the politician would prefer not mentioned at all, or by coloring a development with a personal bias, can ruin a political action, even destroy a politician's career. The press, on the other hand, must always be alert for hidden meaning in the politician's words and actions—the possibility of nepotism, of graft, of legitimate power reaching out in illegitimate ways. The reporter, of all members of the public, is closest to the politician; the reporter stands watch for all the public.

But when Roosevelt and the press met, there was more relaxation than is usual between a politician and the press. The two liked each other. Each treated the other with a respect, a respect born of admiration for the job that the other had to do and for the manner in which the job was performed. At these twice-weekly sessions the President spoke frankly. Even when he dodged a question as he frequently did, he did not fall back on the political prerogative of pretending to answer by offering a maximum of words and a minimum of information. The reporters knew where FDR stood, even if the stance was betwixt and between. The reporters, in turn, did not quote him directly unless he specifically authorized them to; they used the information he gave as the basis for stories about trends in government, developments in the Presidential program, or changes in Roosevelt's thinking.

FDR talked to the newsmen of his Court plan with an air of boyish enthusiasm. His purpose—humbling the Supreme Court—was cloaked in a series of jokes and asides to the reporters which produced frequent laughter. Roosevelt read his message to them, a message which already was being carried up to the Capitol by special messengers. There were few questions; the reporters were too busy writing. One reporter recalled: "I made notes on every piece of paper I had in my pocket, borrowed all I could and even used the back of a Tulsa *World* pay check for notes. Every reporter in the room was out of note paper before the press conference ended." When the session was over, a reporter asked if it had been the cause of the special Cabinet meeting. FDR replied that it had. "Can you tell us what the reaction was this morning?" Roosevelt answered: "I did exactly what I did here. As soon as I finished I came in here. There was no discussion." Those last four words could mean much to an attentive and thoughtful reporter. "There was no discussion." Those words were Franklin Roosevelt's public announcement that this was to be his fight. The others involved would be his aides, he was saying. He would tell them his plans and issue his orders. He would expect them to obey. The major test would be on Capitol Hill.

2

CONGRESS CONVENES at noon. It convenes slowly. The members saunter into the chambers, nod to each other, make a quick check on the day's schedule, then ascertain that the first hour will be taken up, in the Senate, by pro forma speeches in favor of free enterprise, motherhood, Boy Scout troop number thirteen, and other virtues to which politicians must bow; and, in the House, by a ritual in which clerks read a collection of material required by parliamentary procedure but which the House member can better leave unheard. Assured that the coming hour is safely relegated to the nonessential, the member then goes to lunch.

On Friday, February 5, 1937, the members of the House knew immediately that this was going to be a different day. Microphones had been set up in the chamber; something was going to be broadcast. What? A Presidential message, about, the word quickly spread, the Supreme Court. The members postponed their lunch. They came to the chamber from their offices, from the hidden nooks and crannies the senior members had for privacy. A reading clerk droned out the words into the microphones, his voice carried across the nation by radio even as the assembled representatives heard it for the first time.

On the Senate side of the Capitol the chamber quickly filled. Members came to Vice President Garner, to Joe Robinson, Henry Ashurst. What did this message mean? they demanded to know. Why didn't the President tell anyone? they asked. They gathered in their small knots on the chamber floor, then withdrew into the cloakrooms to ask and argue again. An Administration official, known as a lobbyist for the White House on Capitol Hill, happened to be in the cloakrooms that afternoon. The senators lurched at him, demanding that he speak about the President's sudden proposal. He could not; he knew nothing of it.

Consideration of a bill by Congress is a formal procedure. It begins with the introduction of the bill by a member of the Senate and of the House. Then the proposal is referred to the proper committees in each chamber for consideration. These committees can ignore the bill, hold or not hold hearings on it as they choose, report to their parent bodies—the Senate or House—the original bill, a bill partially or completely altered, or no bill at all. Then the House and Senate each vote on the proposal. If either the House or the Senate defeats the bill, it is dead no matter what the other does. If they approve different versions of the bill, these versions must be reconciled. If this reconciliation is far different from what the House or Senate voted on originally, then another vote may be called for, and the members are given a second opportunity to vote the bill up or down. It is a lengthy and complicated process, purposely so. If it were not, Congress would not be a check and a balance on the President. It would not even be a check and a balance on some of its own members who on occasion have used the power available to them as congressmen to advocate legislation hazardous to the nation.

It was this process that the President's proposal to reorganize the judiciary was starting on. In the coming weeks and months almost anyone who wished to speak would be heard, whether for or against the bill. The members of Congress would have, if they wished, the counsel of the nation's most esteemed constitutional lawyers, its most concerned social workers, its outstanding business leaders, its most zealous union men. The members of Congress would have the time; if they chose to use it, to test the reaction among their constituents. Democracy would have the opportunity to function.

In the Senate, the FDR bill was introduced by Henry Ashurst in his capacity as chairman of the Judiciary Committee, to which the proposal certainly would be assigned for hearings. On the House side, however, there was trouble over the bill's introduction. Hatton Sumners, who should have done the job because he was chairman of the House Judiciary Committee, was not inclined to do so. He already had decided to cash in his chips; he didn't like playing the political poker dealt by Franklin Roosevelt. But there were plenty of New Deal zealots in the House. One, Representative Maury Maverick of Texas, quickly sensed Roosevelt's intention. Maverick grabbed a mimeographed copy of the bill, scrawled his own name on its top, and then dropped it into the House hopper. The bill—now formally known as H.R. 4417—was referred to Hatton Sumners' Judiciary Committee.

Gauging an immediate Congressional reaction to a proposal such as FDR's was difficult. There were 435 members of the House and 96 members of the Senate. Each was an individual, and no matter how much he followed a party line previously, it could not be assumed that he would follow it again. Each man reacted differently to each situation he met. This was clearer at the end of the Court fight than it was the first day.

Turner Catledge of *The New York Times* reported that the immediate reaction was favorable. There were ample reasons for that assessment. The members of Congress, like FDR, were angry at the Supreme Court. They also continued to have faith in Franklin Roosevelt's liberalism and to respect his political prowess; many were in Washington as riders on his political coattails. A

month earlier, at the beginning of January, the President had appeared before a joint session of Congress to read his State of the
Union message. Roosevelt did not reveal then his specific plan of
attack against the Court or even that such an attack was coming,
but he made clear his anger with the Supreme Court and with the
drift of its decisions against the New Deal.

"The Democrats cheered," Catledge wrote then, "practically
every [Presidential] remark which they could interpret as aimed
at the Court." This response to the State of the Union message
led Catledge and most other observers to conclude that "President
Roosevelt appeared in complete control of the new Congress."

Rarely had a State of the Union message been received as that
one had been in January. When the President had entered the
House chamber at two o'clock in the afternoon, supported by his
son James, the reception was thunderous. The members of Congress and the public galleries joined in the prolonged applause and
cheering. Sitting with the Cabinet, Harold Ickes "found myself
yelling on one occasion, and that is something that I do not often
do." As FDR read his message, each sentence that could be interpreted as an attack on the Court was read slowly and with de-
liberation so his listeners would clearly hear his implied threats.
Those remarks about the Court had been Roosevelt's attempt to
find out if the Congress was behind him. He had no doubts when
his speech was finished. On his return to the White House, FDR
joined in a poker game—the best means he had for relaxation.
"The President," Ickes recalled, "was plainly pleased over the reception that he had at the Capitol."

There had been a noticeable absence in the House chamber as
FDR had read his State of the Union message, however. The
members of the Supreme Court, who traditionally attend such
ceremonies, did not show up. Apparently they did not intend to
sit for insults. The President could only guess at their reaction.
It was not a difficult guess to make.

The Republicans tried to find solace in historical comparisons.
Although FDR's comments about the Supreme Court in his State
of the Union message may have been as blatant in their intent as

those of Theodore Roosevelt, the Republicans said, the remarks were not as vicious as those of Andrew Jackson about the Court. That FDR felt antagonistic toward the Supreme Court surprised no one; his feelings were well known. But the fact that he had come so close to an open declaration against the Court did cause some shock and was a main reason for the undercurrent of suspicion in January that a Presidential move against the Court was in the offing. If FDR did attack the Court, Republicans agreed in January, he would succeed. His power over Congress was too great for him to fail, they believed.

When the Court plan went to Capitol Hill on February 5, that impression of wide Congressional support was heightened as prominent Democrats fell in line behind FDR. Party stalwarts like Alben Barkley of Kentucky and James F. Byrnes of South Carolina joined with young New Dealers like Harry S. Truman of Missouri to back the President. As Truman explained some years later: "I knew from my study of history that there was nothing sacrosanct about the number nine, that the membership of the Supreme Court had fluctuated during our history from five to ten. President Lincoln wanted to enlarge the Supreme Court to eleven. I saw no reason why the number of the justices could not be increased so that the nation would have, within Constitutional bounds, a more forward looking approach to changing times and conditions."

The impression of Congressional acquiescence, however, was erroneous. The surprise and the immensity of the Roosevelt action caught members of Congress off guard. "We were shocked," recalled one House member, Emanuel Celler of Brooklyn. And Speaker Bankhead lamented to another House member: "Wouldn't you have thought that the President would have told his own party leaders what he was going to do?" And the Speaker added: "He didn't because he knew that hell would break loose." Even Joe Robinson, the old Senate workhorse and party loyalist, was dismayed at being given such a controversial measure with neither advance warning nor any opportunity to plan a campaign.

Most congressmen were taking a noncommittal attitude. They

wanted to study the proposal, investigate its ramifications, survey the public reaction. The members of Congress might have cheered Franklin Roosevelt when in the State of the Union message a month earlier his words indicated he might act against the Court. But now that he suggested that the members of Congress do something, they decided to wait until their astonishment and that of the public faded before deciding whether to resume their cheering. "The President would have done well to have advised more frankly with his friends before precipitating this issue," said Joe Robinson, adding: "In the failure to do so, some believe that he made a mistake."

A couple of days later, Jim Farley, just back in town, asked Roosevelt directly why he hadn't given anyone advance information. "Anyone" included Farley himself. He had seen the President on Thursday, the day before the Court plan became public knowledge, but FDR had not said a word to him about it. Roosevelt answered Farley's question by saying he did not want to tip off any of the congressmen beforehand because "more than once when I've had groups of Senators and Congressmen down here, reporters have gathered a detailed account of what went on within forty-eight hours. I didn't want it to happen again." Actually, three weeks earlier a member of the Senate had nearly revealed prematurely the possibility of such an attack. On Monday, January 18, Sherman Minton of Indiana, an ardent New Dealer, had visited with Roosevelt at the White House. When the meeting ended and Minton emerged from the President's office he immediately was surrounded by reporters searching for a story. Politicians enjoy being interviewed in the White House lobby; the publicity gives them an image of importance before their constituents. The President, Minton said, was planning a conference on plans to limit the power of the Supreme Court. "I think that something can be done to limit the power of the court," said Minton, "by requiring unanimous decisions or decisions by two-thirds of the members of the court." But, said Minton, he would not introduce any legislation himself until the President's plan was unveiled. Would there be a Presidential plan to limit the power of the Supreme Court? the reporters persisted. "Legal aides of the administration," Minton answered, much to the later concern of the White House, "have been studying the possibility of legislation and the President has been kept informed of the progress of these studies."

The word was out, too soon. Quickly the White House moved to squelch it. The next day, Steve Early issued a formal denial. According to Early, Senator Minton had come by to talk with the President and to seek his endorsement for Minton's anti-Court proposals. FDR had replied, according to the White House statement, that Attorney General Cummings had been studying the problem and suggested that Minton discuss it sometime with Cummings. "The White House also announced," the newsmen dutifully reported, "that the studies discussed were undertaken long since, in an effort to find some way to attain the objectives of the New Deal program under the law, without recourse to amendment of the Constitution. These studies have been unsuccessful thus far in pointing the way to that objective." When on January 19 the newsmen wrote that the studies were "unsuccessful," Roosevelt definitely had decided on his plan of attack.

FDR could not bring himself actually to lie to newsmen. Three days later, at a news conference, a reporter, with the Minton statement obviously in mind, asked: "Can you tell us whether you will join or support any legislation seeking a change of practice of the Supreme Court?" Roosevelt dodged by replying: "That is sort of an 'iffy' question."

Not all the speculation ended. One of FDR's opponents, Senator William E. Borah, a Republican of Idaho, remained suspicious. In the Senate chamber on February 1, he spoke of possible pending attacks on the Court and then found a quote from George Washington to suit his purpose: "If, in the opinion of the people, the distribution, or modification, of the constitutional power be in any particular wrong, let it be corrected by an amendment in the way the Constitution designates; but let there be no change by usurpation."

Even outside Washington there was speculation about a possible

Presidential attack against the Court. A day or so before Borah made his speech one of his friends wrote to him that "it would seem that a drive is to be made upon the Supreme Court with the thought of destroying its place in our constitutional system with the resulting destruction of the mutual independence of the three great branches of government. . . . I surely hope that you will devote your great abilities to the defeat of any such plan."

Borah's reply indicated he not only was eager for such a fight but had also given it considerable thought. He wrote back:

> I say to you with no sham of modesty that I do not feel equal to the task which you assign to me. But I hope to be of some service in that respect. There is one phase of this matter which I think must be taken up. Not sufficient literature from our viewpoint is reaching the great body of people throughout the United States. The other side is constantly pouring in material, to my mind, most misleading, and we need not be surprised if such propaganda bears fruit. I have been wondering if it would be possible, without any display or ostentation, to really work up some plan to get a more thorough distribution of our side of the question. The situation may be imminent.

That exchange had come four days before the plan was unveiled, meaning that FDR's concern about secrecy was legitimate. Not only had his sense of drama insisted that he keep an airtight lid on any information about his plan, but his political acumen told him that to permit his plan to come out in dribs and drabs from the mouths of members of Congress would have tipped off his opposition—and FDR was hated almost as fiercely as he was loved—to begin a campaign against the plan. He then would not have been able to launch an offensive against the Court on February 5. He would have been, instead, thrown on the defensive. That was a position Franklin Roosevelt did not enjoy.

And so because of his emphasis on secrecy, he did achieve a certain degree of surprise with his plan. "I was flabbergasted," said Burton K. Wheeler. Burton Wheeler, the Yankee from the West, the Massachusetts-born senator from Montana, the liberal Democrat and old Roosevelt supporter; Burton Wheeler, the man of the Congress who had watched with growing alarm as the

Presidency, as filled by Franklin Roosevelt, had overshadowed the Congress; Burton Wheeler, who had felt a deepening anger as he believed the men of the New Deal were turning against the old Democratic politicians who had done so much to assist Franklin Roosevelt achieve the Presidency—this man would assume leadership of the forces arrayed against the Roosevelt Court plan. And because he knew the Senate so well—its members and their habits, its peculiarities, its parliamentary procedures—he would be a giant of an opponent.

This was the first serious rift between two politicians whose comradeship was of long standing. "As I look around for a general to lead the Democratic Party . . . I ask to whom can we go?" Wheeler had said in 1930 when the race for the 1932 Democratic Presidential nomination was wide open. "I say that if the Democratic Party of New York will elect Franklin D. Roosevelt governor, the West will demand his nomination for President and the whole country will elect him." That was one of the first public endorsements of Franklin Roosevelt for President by a prominent Democratic politician outside of New York State. FDR responded in kind, writing to Wheeler: "I was made very happy by your reference to me at the Democratic club dinner, for the very good reason that I have always thought of you as one of the real leaders of the progressive thought and action in this country." FDR and Burton Wheeler were good friends.

They continued that way. After Roosevelt was elected to his first term in the White House, Wheeler became one of his ardent supporters; other members occasionally chided him for being so much an Administration man. In the 1936 contest for a second Roosevelt term, FDR had written to "My dear Burt" that "I do want to take this opportunity to tell you how deeply I appreciate the very real help you gave me on our recent western trip. It is good to know in these busy days that I have fine friends like you." And Wheeler shot back a telegram. "Since leaving you in Chicago," it said, "have been in Iowa, Minnesota, South Dakota, Nebraska, Kansas and Wyoming. Feel certain you will carry every one of these states and every state west of Mississippi River not because I've been there but because the people believe you are on their side against the overlords of finance."

The public impression was that Franklin Roosevelt and Burton Wheeler were compatible, that they had the same political objectives. This belief was so widespread that when a news story predicted that Wheeler would oppose FDR on the Court plan, an editor of a Montana newspaper refused to print the story. It just could not be true, he thought, that Burt Wheeler would go against FDR on this issue. Not everyone was that surprised. Wheeler's split with FDR could be foreseen, it was said. The more intriguing question involved the causes of that split. Wheeler had spent thirty years in public life, long enough to make many friends and the same number of enemies. His friends argued that Wheeler was forced to act against Roosevelt because of his uncompromising integrity. "If you knew Burt, you wouldn't be surprised" was a familiar refrain. According to this argument Wheeler sincerely believed the Roosevelt plan was a threat to the nation.

There was another side, however. Burton Wheeler long had been the champion of the underdog in the West, fighting against the mining and railroad interests that had tried imposing an economic feudalism in the areas of the country where they held power. In recent years, however, some members of Congress believed they saw a lessening of that zeal for the underdog in Wheeler's politics. It was debatable whether that assessment, which became general in another decade, was the result of accurate insight into the political shiftings of a one-time liberal or the result of political pique against a man who had been in politics so long that he had made many enemies. It was less debatable that Wheeler's discontent with the President was growing. The Senator believed that he and other local political powers had been instrumental in getting Franklin Roosevelt elected President. Instead of thanks, Wheeler and his fellow political barons were receiving another kind of treatment. The late Huey Long of Louisiana, for example, had fought for FDR back in 1932; for thanks, as Wheeler understood it, the Administration had Long's income tax investigated. Even Wheeler suffered under FDR's brand of thanks. If nothing else,

Wheeler believed he should have been recognized as the political power in Montana. That was his state; he had the political seniority there. His early support of FDR should have earned him recognition of that. Instead, Wheeler was bypassed on patronage. The Administration funneled it through one of his political enemies in the state. To make matters worse, the man in the Administration who had influenced Roosevelt to turn the patronage over to a Wheeler enemy was Homer Cummings, who also was the author of the Court plan. Burton Wheeler had never trusted Homer Cummings, considering him "a cheap politician." Wheeler well remembered the 1932 Democratic convention, when Homer Cummings wanted to speak out against the rule requiring a Presidential nomination by a two-thirds vote of the delegates rather than by a majority. That two-thirds rule was the device used by the South to dominate the convention; a candidate for the nomination could get a majority but not a two-thirds vote without the support of the South. If Cummings had made that speech against the two-thirds rule, Wheeler reasoned, the result would have been the alienation of the southern delegates from FDR because Cummings was one of FDR's men at that 1932 convention. Wheeler always believed this had been Cummings' intention—to deprive FDR of the nomination and throw it open to a dark horse with appeal to all the nonsouthern delegates, perhaps even Homer Cummings, just as William Jennings Bryan had united the dissidents years earlier with his "cross of gold" speech. The Roosevelt difficulties with the Supreme Court never would have developed, Wheeler believed, if Cummings, as Attorney General, had been a better lawyer and wasn't always trying to make a "political" case against the Court.

So Burton Wheeler's opposition was not quite the surprise the Montana newspaper editor thought. Wheeler would have help, inside and out of the Senate. One such assistant was vacationing in Miami when the Court plan was announced. "Listen to this!" said Frank Gannett to his wife when he read an Associated Press story about FDR's Court message on the front page of the Miami *Herald*. "This is the worst yet." Gannett was the publisher of a chain of newspapers. He also had substantial contacts among the nation's businessmen and bankers. He would use not only the communication media at his disposal but his wealthy associates to finance and distribute a message to the American public against the Court plan.

Another opponent was ensconced in a Waldorf-Astoria tower suite in New York City. From those Olympian heights former President Herbert Hoover charged that ". . . it is now proposed to make changes by 'packing' the Supreme Court. It has the implication of subordination of the court to the personal power of the Executive. Because all this reaches to the very depth of our form of government, it far transcends any question of partisanship." Perhaps so. In the coming weeks, however, Herbert Hoover, who had left the White House in disgrace as Franklin Roosevelt entered it in triumph, could be seen using the FDR Court plan and the emotions it created as a means for personal aggrandizement. Another Presidential election was coming up in 1940. No Republican yet had a clear lead for the nomination. With his attack on "court packing," Herbert Hoover was running.

There was another kind of opposition that Franklin Roosevelt did not anticipate. From New York came a letter, almost as painful for the writer as for the one to whom it was written. "I feel," wrote Herbert H. Lehman to Franklin Roosevelt, "that the end which you desire to attain does not justify the means which you recommend." Herbert Lehman not only was an outstanding liberal of his day, he also was FDR's political protégé and comrade. When his position against the FDR plan became known, Roosevelt was in a position of a battlefield commander who finds that one of his most loyal generals has suddenly defected.

One of the severest attacks on Roosevelt came from the typewriter of a small-town newspaper in the Middle West. "Adroitly President Roosevelt is proposing to pack the Supreme Court," wrote William Allen White, editor of the Emporia, Kansas, *Gazette.* "And because he is adroit and not forthright, he arouses irritating suspicions, probably needless, about his ultimate intentions as the leader of his party and the head of his government." Through the brilliance of his writing, of his insight into the minds and emotions of his fellow midwesterners, of his ability to reflect the thinking of the Midwest, William Allen White had attained a reputation as a political oracle whose impact reached far beyond the limits of Emporia. The words poured from his typewriter in increasing bitterness: "This Presidential adroitness, this uncanny capacity to avoid the direct joining of issues in full, fair, and free debate, this seemingly instinctive lack of candor, this smiling assumption of courage while avoiding all danger, this elaborate stage play to flatter the people by a simulation of frankness while denying Americans their democratic rights of discussion by suave avoidance—these traits are not the traits of a democratic leader. These are tricks which have been played in the new game wherein other people have lost their democratic liberties in other lands." And the editorial ended: "How long will the people be fooled?"

William Allen White is best known to the American public as the author of "Mary White," a touching tribute to his daughter, written in the form of an obituary. Every American high school student has read it in literature class. White is also thought of as the prototype of the small-town newspaper editor, sitting at his desk, wearing a green eyeshade and pecking out homilies and all-American editorials with two fingers on an old typewriter. This he was, but he was much more. A Republican and an old liberal, White had solid contacts both within the New Deal camp and outside it. He advised both. He also was a politician of skill, having been one of the engineers of the Republican nomination for President of Governor Alf M. Landon of Kansas the previous year. That feat shocked a good many professionals; the Landon people had ripped control of the GOP from the eastern seaboard Republicans who believed they held it firmly. William Allen White would be one of FDR's more effective opponents.

There would be many others. Before the fight was finished the nation would have an example of what the President can do in the face of the combined opposition of those who control the nation's wealth, its communication media, its religious and secular organizations. The nation would know how strong the President can be—or cannot be.

3

ON THIS FRIDAY, as the word of the Presidential message percolated through Washington, the subject of that message—the Supreme Court of the United States—was in session. The Chief Justice of the United States and the eight associate justices—"The Nine Old Men" as a pair of columnists friendly to the New Deal had called them—were holding forth in their courtroom, apparently oblivious to the excitement eddying around them. This courtroom had been their home only for two years. Previously they had met in cramped quarters in the Capitol. Their new chamber was a small one but possessing great dignity, appropriate to the nation's highest tribunal. The public entrance is at the west end and the justices sit at the east, directly across from the entrance. They sit enthroned on a high platform at a table of dark wood. Behind them rise pillars of colored marble and between the pillars, curtains of rich velvet.

In the center of the nine sits the Chief Justice. In 1937 he was the seventy-four-year-old Charles Evans Hughes. A former associate justice of the Supreme Court who resigned to run against Woodrow Wilson for the Presidency in 1916, Hughes was reappointed to the Court as Chief Justice by President Herbert Hoover in 1930. A stocky man with gray hair and a large beard, Hughes was the picture of the wise man, the Solomon one hopes for as a judge. Some thought he even looked more than merely wise. According to a story that Hughes found amusing, a Negro passed a Washington photography studio with a picture of the robed members of the Supreme Court in its window. "They's de grandest lot of men Ah ever saw," he thought. "And that Chief Justice Hughes—he jes looks lak De Lawd Hisself!"

A creature of habit, Hughes was a punctual man; people along Massachusetts Avenue in Washington set their clocks by his early morning walks. On days the Court was in session Hughes was in the robing room ready to assume the cloak of his office a few minutes before noon. At precisely twelve o'clock he led the other Court members to their seats. In his own philosophy, however, Charles Evans Hughes was not quite so exact. He had been, in addition to a Republican Presidential candidate fighting the New Freedom of Wilson, a fearless investigator, a progressive governor of New York, and an advocate of civil liberties. He also had been a lawyer for some of the wealthiest economic interests in the nation. Perhaps his philosophy was best summed up by one of his own lines. "It is well," he once remarked to a law professor, "to be liberal but not messy."

Hughes was protective of the Supreme Court. Nine years earlier, when he was not yet Chief Justice, he had given a series of lectures at Columbia University on the Supreme Court. In those lectures he had demonstrated his understanding that "the Court has found its fortress in public opinion." When the Court moves contrary to public opinion, Hughes had asserted then, it is in error; then he cited three instances when the Court has "suffered severely from self-inflicted wounds." The first time was the Dred Scott decision when the Court refused to free a Negro slave who had crossed from slave to free territory. The decision was reversed by the Civil War. The Court's action in that case was "a public calamity." Many years were required before the Court "was able to retrieve its reputation," according to Hughes. The second instance was the legal tender cases following the Civil War. At issue was whether the War could be paid for. The Court first declared the Legal Tender Act unconstitutional, but President Ulysses S. Grant "packed" the Court. The case was reopened and the act declared constitutional. This, said Hughes, "shook popular respect for the Court." The third occasion was the Court's overturning of the income tax law which "gave occasion for a bitter assault" and which later was reversed by a constitutional amendment.

With this understanding and his own background as a politician, Charles Evans Hughes realized in 1937 that there was a great deal of public discontent with the Supreme Court. He had tried to prevent that discontent. In the preceding years, as the Court and the President had become locked in struggle, Hughes had shifted his influence from one bloc to another within the Court in an attempt to keep the Court within that "fortress" of public opinion. That he had failed was evidenced by the Presidential message being read before the House of Representatives.

And because Charles Evans Hughes had failed, he and Franklin Roosevelt now entered into the strangest duel of American politics. "My personal relations with President Roosevelt have always been agreeable," Hughes said later. "In his occasional letters and whenever I have seen him, he has shown the utmost cordiality and friendliness." This may have been true about the personal relations between the two men. But there was more involved than a personal relationship. Charles Evans Hughes led a group of men who had joined the Court before Franklin Roosevelt became President. The oldest member of the Hughes Court in seniority donned his robes in 1911; the youngest in 1932. FDR had been unable to tip the Court's majority to a New Deal philosophy by making appointments to the Court. The justices—in a reverse form of "packing"—had refused to retire. And so Roosevelt believed he had no other choice than to begin the duel between the two institutions: the Presidency and the Supreme Court.

There had been a hint of the pending fight two weeks earlier when FDR was sworn in for his second term. Charles Evans Hughes had administered the oath. That day, January 20, had begun formally for the inaugural party with ten o'clock services at St. John's Church across from the White House. "Politics may make strange bed fellows," Harold Ickes cracked, "but this event proved that it also makes strange co-worshippers." Roosevelt then had gone to the Capitol for the inaugural ceremony. The Cabinet members and various government officials came out onto the covered platform at the East Front of the Capitol. The Supreme Court came next. The justices, robed in their long black gowns, were all present, except Associate Justice Louis D. Brandeis, the oldest member of the Court, who always avoided ceremonial occasions. Another associate justice, James C. McReynolds, one of the three oldest men on the Court, left the platform after only a few minutes. The day was a cold, rainy one—the kind of day men in their seventies avoid.

When the Chief Justice administered the oath to Roosevelt, he spoke the words about protecting and defending the Constitution slowly and with great emphasis. FDR repeated the words in the same manner. "The whole incident," thought Ickes, "was quite significant . . . [for] what was the Constitution to the Chief Justice was not the Constitution to the president."

But the significance of that moment was not easily defined. "It has been a long time," wrote an old friennd of Hughes's to the Chief Justice, "since I have had anything which has given me more pleasure and satisfaction than listening yesterday to your administering the oath of office to the President and requiring him to swear, right before your face, to 'support the Constitution of the United States.' This must have been a bitter pill to him, after the sarcasm and contempt which he has seen fit to try to bestow upon the Constitution and the Supreme Court."

FDR had a different reaction. As he later related to an associate, when Chief Justice Hughes read to him the oath about supporting the Constitution, "I felt like saying: 'Yes, but it's the Constitution as I understand it, flexible enough to meet any new problems of democracy—not the kind of Constitution your Court has raised up as a barrier to progress and democracy.' " To make certain no one misunderstood his intentions, Roosevelt said in his inaugural address that Americans "will insist that every agency of popular government use effective instruments to carry out their will."

That scene on the rainy inaugural day had been the warning from the President to the Chief Justice. Now this Friday, February 5, at approximately one o'clock in the afternoon, the marshal of the Court passed among the justices sitting in the open courtroom and distributed to them copies of the President's message.

One member of the Court was not surprised. Earlier that day a Presidential assistant named Thomas G. Corcoran—"Tommy the Cork" as he was called because of his ebullience—armed with

FDR's approval had come to Brandeis to inform him of the impending proposal. Because Brandeis was the oldest member of the Court in years, he seemed the one against whom FDR was taking direct aim. Brandeis, in Corcoran's opinion, must be made to understand that this was incorrect, that FDR meant to exclude Brandeis from his attack on older justices. There was a special reason for this.

Among New Dealers, among almost any group of liberals in the country in the 1930's, the name of Louis Dembitz Brandeis was hallowed. To them he was their philosophical father. Almost alone twenty and thirty years earlier he had forced the courts to acknowledge that law was not only a matter of precedents grown musty from their tenure in the law books of the previous century but that law was a means by which society secures for itself a better and more meaningful life; Brandeis fought to make the law as much a tool for the poor and oppressed as it was for the wealthy. When he had been appointed to the Court in 1916 by President Woodrow Wilson, the Senate fight on his confirmation became one of the great struggles in the history of Congress. Much of this fight appeared to be because Brandeis was Jewish and would be the first of that faith to sit on the Court. But these echoes of anti-Semitism masked the basic reason for the opposition: The wealthy interests in the nation massed against him because they feared he would oppose them from the Supreme Court.

That fear was accurate. In the 1930s Brandeis—"Old Isaiah" he was called affectionately among the White House and New Deal people—still retained his credentials as an outstanding liberal, still spoke for the individual against the organization. The "original New Dealer," he often was called. The young New Dealers, like Tommy Corcoran, understood that any plan by FDR that seemed to offend Brandeis would immediately run into trouble with the liberal community. And that was why Corcoran, who considered himself Brandeis' protégé, had secured permission to give Brandeis advance notice of the plan. Corcoran caught up with Brandeis in the robing room where the justices don the robes that cloak them in the power of their office. Corcoran and Brandeis then moved to the hall between the robing room and the Court chamber. They talked softly as the other justices filed by them. Quickly Corcoran explained the President's plan. Brandeis told Corcoran to thank the President for the advance knowledge. Then "Old Isaiah," and he was seventy-nine years old, told Corcoran that he was completely opposed to the Roosevelt plan to enlarge the Court and said also that he believed FDR was making a serious mistake. Much that should have been avoided could have been avoided if Franklin Roosevelt had heard those words and considered them seriously. But he did not hear the warning; nor, probably, would he have paid any attention to it if he had.

As far as is known, Louis Brandeis never spoke again of his reactions to the Roosevelt plan, nor did he write of them. But he felt them deeply. Although he agreed with much of the New Deal and regretted to see a majority of his fellow justices declare it unconstitutional, Brandeis even more resented an attack on the independence of the Supreme Court and on his fellow justices. It was widely known in Washington, for example, that one justice, Willis Van Devanter, was so physically feeble that he could barely write a decision and obviously was not doing a fair share of the Court's work. But when this was mentioned to Brandeis, he quickly defended Van Devanter as being very helpful on jurisdictional matters. Brandeis was a liberal; Van Devanter, a conservative. But as far as Brandeis was concerned, that dispute ended at the marble walls of the Court building. Beyond those walls, before the American public, he was united with Van Devanter; both were associate justices of the Supreme Court.

One New Dealer who understood Brandeis well said of him later: "He would have no hands laid upon the institution from the outside. It mattered not that the outside hands would in the main uphold his views and would rebuke those with whom he had long and often disagreed. Brandeis valued its independence of decision even more than rightness of decision." In the duel between the Court and the Presidency, Brandeis would take only one action. It would be sufficient.

Brandeis' defensive attitude toward the Court was not unique among the nine justices. Among and between those nine men were all the passions and ambitions, all the hates and the hopes that men can feel toward each other. There were men on that bench who did not speak to others on that same bench except to make the most offensive remark. There were men on that bench who coveted the position of the man at their side. But these emotions generally were held inside the private chambers of the Supreme Court. Outside those chambers the Court appeared a fortress, solid and impregnable.

This Friday afternoon, for example, when the Court members realized the enormity of the attack that was being made on them, they showed no reaction. As always happens with such a moment, some persons later spoke of a murmur of excitement sweeping through the courtroom. At the moment itself, however, there was nothing about it to distinguish it from any other moment. Nothing, that is, that could be seen.

The justices refused public comment. Chief Justice Hughes spoke of the Roosevelt plan as being "justly regarded as an assault upon the independence of the Court." But this came later, not during the fight. When the National Broadcasting Company telegraphed Chief Justice Hughes that its facilities "are available for any member of the Supreme Court to discuss the proposal to Congress made by the President today," a secretary to the Chief Justice wired back that "he thanks you but he does not care to take advantage of it." Later, Edward R. Murrow of the Columbia Broadcasting System wanted to come from New York to see Hughes, obviously hoping to persuade the Chief Justice to make a radio address on the Roosevelt plan. "I gave your message to the Chief Justice," Hughes's secretary wrote to Murrow. "He does not wish to put you to the inconvenience of coming to Washington if the matter about which you wish to see him is one which he could not in any event consider."

Pathe News found a 1931 newsreel film clip of the Chief Justice speaking about the Court. The newsreel company distributed it as part of their newsreel dated February 13, 1937, without mentioning that it was six years old. Hughes correctly realized that this film segment would be interpreted by the viewing public as an answer to FDR. He sought help from J. Edgar Hoover, the energetic head of the Federal Bureau of Investigation. Hoover handled the matter promptly. He told the Chief Justice that he had persuaded Pathe News to withdraw the offending film clip. "It was a pleasure to be of assistance to you in this connection," said Hoover, "and if at any time this Bureau can be of any service, please do not hesitate to call upon me." But Hughes, although reluctant to become involved in a public scrap with Roosevelt, refused either to acknowledge or to accept defeat. Behind the scenes, he became a formidable opponent.

For the remainder of that day and the weekend that followed, the members of the Court betrayed no reaction. They declined to discuss the proposal with reporters and did not speak of the plan with their friends, at least with friends who might repeat their words. Newsmen watched them as they filed into the Conference Room for their regular Saturday afternoon closed-door session on the cases of the past week. The justices seemed friendly, not outwardly concerned, certainly not nervous. The next Monday, however, during the first public Court session after the plan was well publicized, some observers detected an unusual self-consciousness on the part of the justices. Even the Chief Justice made a few procedural errors, primarily handing down some orders out of turn. It was barely significant, or would have been barely significant any other day.

In *The Washington Post* the morning of Friday, February 5, there had appeared a story, buried on page nine, about "an organized fight to clip the powers of the Supreme Court." The story reported efforts by a group of senators and representatives to enact legislation requiring a seven-to-two vote on the Supreme Court to declare a law unconstitutional rather than the traditional five-to-four majority. The story, which had appeared before those long black limousines had begun arriving at the White House a few minutes before ten o'clock, was not considered very important. There are too many members of Congress for the actions of a small bloc to rate more than passing mention on page nine. If

that small bloc includes the party leadership, indicating that the
stand will be a party position, that is another matter, perhaps a
front-page story. There is no question, however, of the news value
of a Presidential action in a controversial matter. The Roosevelt
plan made the front pages that Friday afternoon, the next morning, and would dominate the news for the coming six months.
Henry Ashurst summed it up in his diary:

Much excitement over the President's proposal to reorganize the
Judicial Branch of the Government. This excitement may simmer down
to a billow, even to a bubble, but an angry ocean of adverse opinion
is now rolling over Eff Dee. Some observers believe that he has been
toppled from his dizzy peak of popularity and that his prestige is gone.
He is denounced as attempting to "pack the Court" in order to validate
New Deal laws. His proposal is condemned by the press as "indirect,"
"immoral" and "too clever."

Claude D. Pepper, a young New Deal senator from Florida,
wrote in his diary the night of February 5 the most accurate pre-
diction. "The President sent down a message," wrote Pepper,
"which I daresay will cause some controversy."

Part Two

One-third of a Nation

4

To SUCCEED with his Court plan Franklin Roosevelt had several weapons. First, there was himself. An exciting and magnetic person, FDR convinced people he cared, that he was concerned about their problems and wanted to do something to help them. Roosevelt appreciated this power. At one point when the Court fight looked bleak, Farley recalled, FDR proclaimed happily that "all we have to do is to let the flood of mail settle on Congress. You just see. All I have to do is deliver a better speech, and the opposition will be beating a path to the White House door."

To one who disliked him, FDR was an outrageous egotist; but to one who admired him, he had a fabulous sense of self-assurance. To the admirer, FDR was friendly and smart; to the critic, he was one who manipulated his friends for his own purposes and who was much too smart. His friends and enemies agreed he was often too clever and too persuasive for them. Representative Emanuel Celler, a New Deal supporter, has said that when he left a meeting with Roosevelt, "I found that he had committed himself to no point of view. At the end of each visit I realized that I had been hypnotized." And Gerald P. Nye, a Republican senator from North Dakota during the 1930s, recalled that "I've never encountered anyone in public life more difficult to say 'No' to than Franklin Roosevelt."

But the people believed in Franklin Roosevelt. As they crowded around their radios to hear his famous fireside chats, they paid careful attention to each word. These were the poor. The children waited in food lines; as soon as they received their breakfast, they returned to the end of the line to wait for food for lunch and supper. The widows dodged the landlords because they could not pay the rent. The fathers watched their families grow cold because they had no money to pay for electricity, gas, or coal. These were the people who feared they were restricted to the perpetual drabness of poverty—until Franklin Roosevelt's New Deal with its make-work projects and welfare programs scattered some of the dark shadows of insecurity and unemployment. These were the farmers. They watched the dust storms and the droughts constantly diminish the fertility of their fields. They watched their cattle grow too lean. And they waited for the foreclosure notice on the land their fathers had turned from wilderness into homes—until Franklin Roosevelt's New Deal said it was the role of the federal government to plant the trees and build the dams and pipe the water. These were the people become callous in an uncaring society—until Franklin Roosevelt gave them hope by forcing society to notice them and to act.

For many of these people the dreams they now dreamed had not yet come true, and for many these New Deal dreams would never come true. But that perhaps was not as important as that they now did dream, that they could see beyond tomorrow and think in terms of weeks and months and years. The fact that someone cared was enough to make them resume caring about themselves. And this was important for it gave them self-respect. Franklin Roosevelt had reached down to a desperate people, turned almost into animals by deprivation, and pulled out human beings.

It was this impression that he cared, more than anything else, that made Franklin Roosevelt so popular at the polls. And in 1936 when he had been reelected to a second term he was very popular. Roosevelt interpreted that vote as a popular mandate, rightly so. In an article appearing in *Collier's* magazine after that election George Creel had written: "It was the nation that spoke through the voice of an overwhelming majority and [Roosevelt] holds that what this voice declared and imposed was the national will." The words, appearing under Creel's byline, had been dictated by Roosevelt himself. It was his way of announcing that he considered this national mandate as a tool to be used.

He had ample reason to believe that this mandate he had received in November allowed him an attack on the Supreme Court. He himself had not publicly mentioned the Court during the entire campaign. But then FDR had campaigned on the basis of only one real issue: Franklin Delano Roosevelt. He barely mentioned his political party during the entire campaign, no more than three times by one count. He jettisoned Democrats if he believed they were not as loyal to the New Deal and to FDR as another party's candidates. He turned the 1936 campaign into a personal crusade; the voter either was for or against FDR. If the voter was for him, then anything the President would do, within constitutional bounds, must be acceptable.

Other Democrats in 1936, however, did not hesitate to make the Supreme Court an issue in the election. "Is the Supreme Court beyond criticism?" a sweating Alben Barkley roared at the Democrats attending the convention that was to nominate Roosevelt for a second term. "May it be regarded as too sacred to be disagreed with? Thomas Jefferson didn't think so. Abraham Lincoln did not think so. Theodore Roosevelt did not think so." The cheers of the assembled Democrats as Barkley continued to attack the Court in his one-hour keynote address showed clearly they did not think so either.

This attitude by a political party toward the Court surprised no one. In May, 1936, as the Supreme Court was about to recess for the summer, Arthur Krock wrote in *The New York Times* that the Court was going "more or less on trial in a Presidential campaign for the first time in years." He continued: "This is the natural result of dissents to the Court's majority's invalidation of certain New Deal laws. . . . The Court knows itself to be on trial. . . . [The justices] are sure to be interested in observing, if they can be observed, the political effects of Republican arguments that a vote against the President is a vote to prevent the Court's future majority from being more sympathetic with his attempts than is the present one."

As the Krock column suggests, it was the Republicans who made the Supreme Court a major issue in the election. Among the most important actions a President takes is appointing justices to the Supreme Court. Because a justice may stay on the Court for many years, the philosophy he holds, his understanding of the role of government, his conception of civil liberties, will long be part of the nation's judicial fabric. In 1936 the Republicans were well aware that the aged justices on the Court could not hold out much longer. Either death or forced retirement would claim several of them during FDR's second term, if there was a second term. "Does any man or woman within the sound of my voice," said one Republican to a conservative Liberty League dinner early in 1936, "doubt that the President hopes, if reelected, he will have the opportunity within the next four years to place upon the Supreme Court enough judges holding his own Constitutional views to change the whole current of constitutional construction in this country?"

This then was a prime point of that campaign—the future of the Supreme Court. "This election," said Frank Gannett, the newspaper publisher, "will determine who shall appoint perhaps a majority of the Supreme Court." In calling for the election of a Republican, specifically the old liberal William E. Borah, Gannett warned: "These justices to be appointed as vacancies occur must not be advocates of any new ideas concerning our Federal government."

The use by the Republicans of the Supreme Court as a campaign issue was not accidental. Shortly after he was nominated to carry the GOP banner, Governor Alf M. Landon of Kansas met with an adviser to map out strategy for the coming months. When the adviser "thought the Constitution and gold standard were the winning issues," Landon has recalled that "I said, No. As Senator Borah said after the '34 campaign, 'You can't eat the Constitution.' " Landon, instead, insisted: "We've got to try to make the President say what his policies will be in the way of any new legislation. I think he'll dodge us."

The Republicans had good reason to believe that one of FDR's efforts, if he was reelected, might be an attack of some kind on the Court. Not only was FDR's anger at the Court evident through much of 1935 and early 1936, but he had dropped several hints. As Paul Block, the publisher of the Toledo *Blade,* told it to Landon early in 1936, he and Roosevelt were having lunch together on the back porch of the White House. The Court had just handed down one of its anti-New Deal decisions. "The President was railing at the Court," Block told Landon and related that he finally said to FDR: "Mr. President, why spoil this delicious lunch? There isn't anything you can do about it." Roosevelt replied: "There isn't anything I can do about it! There isn't anything I can do about it! I might respond with what Gladstone told Queen Victoria when the House of Lords had rejected his home rule bill after the House of Commons had passed it. He told her he could appoint enough new members to Lords so that they would ratify it!"

So, suspecting that FDR did contemplate an attack of some kind on the Court if he was reelected, and also believing that forcing FDR to confess such plans against a revered institution was good politics, the GOP pressed hard on the Court issue. "The integrity and authority of the Supreme Court have been flaunted," said the party platform; the Republicans pledged themselves to "resist all attempts to impair the authority of the Supreme Court." Local politicians also considered the Court a good issue. State Senator George R. Fearon of New York, an old Republican foe of FDR's, made an unsuccessful try for his party's gubernatorial nomination that year by campaigning against what Roosevelt might effect if reelected—"amendment of the United States Constitution by indirection through appointments . . . of new members of the United States Supreme Court."

Perhaps motivated more by hope than by reality, *The New York Times* tried to eliminate the Court from the campaign. In an editorial on August 4, the *Times* said that "it is true that what appeared six months ago to be fiercely debated issues have been sterilized, or at least set aside for the time being. One of these was the proposed attack on the Supreme Court." The "time being" did not last long. "One of the great issues of the campaign is the sanctity of the Supreme Court," cried one Republican orator the next month. The party leaders took up the cry. "Why not tell the American people before the election what changes he proposes?" said Herbert Hoover of Roosevelt. "Does he intend to stuff the court itself?" And the GOP candidate, Governor Landon, told seven thousand cheering GOP stalwarts in a major speech in Phoenix, Arizona, that "we are left in no doubt that the present administration regards [the Court's actions against the New Deal] not as an end to their efforts but only as a minor barrier to be circumvented if it can't be hurdled."

Roosevelt refused to be baited by such traps, however. He was seeking a blank-check endorsement from the American people in the 1936 election year, and he did not believe it wise politics to offer an itemized shopping list. Whether the American people did intend to give FDR that blank check when they gave him their votes was locked in the heart and mind of each individual voter. The results of that 1936 election gave FDR almost twenty-eight million votes out of forty-four million cast and 523 electoral college votes to his opponent's eight. It was a stunning victory. And no matter how it was intended by the voters, Franklin Roosevelt interpreted it as a blank check, not only as a personal mandate for himself but also as an endorsement for whatever action he chose to take against the Court.

Robert H. Jackson, then an assistant attorney general in the Justice Department, later Attorney General of the United States, and still later an associate justice of the Supreme Court, has written of that 1936 campaign and election: "The Republicans lost no opportunity to identify themselves with the Court and the Court with themselves. Although the Court was helpless to prevent being thus publicly embraced, it had . . . at least encouraged the advances. . . . The election had gone against the Court quite as emphatically as against the Republican Party, whose bedfellow it had been." And so Franklin Roosevelt had begun his duel with the Supreme Court in 1937 believing that he personally carried the strongest weapon—the overwhelming support of the American people.

The immediate public reaction to his Court plan, however, was not favorable. "The President has a first-class fight on his hands," Harold Ickes was obliged to acknowledge. "I do not think," lamented Henry Morgenthau ten days after the Court plan had gone to Capitol Hill, "that he has better than a fifty-fifty chance of getting [the Court plan] today. . . . Certainly the sentiment is rolling up against him. I hear it on every side. I have not met anybody who thinks well of it. Certainly the only person who can save it is the President himself."

Morgenthau did not inform FDR of this estimate "because I do not want him to think that I think he only has a fifty-fifty chance." As the Court fight continued, more and more of FDR's friends and political aides showed that same lack of candor with their chief, that same hesitancy to be bluntly honest with him. What was developing was one of the worst situations an executive, whether he be in politics or business, can face: a lack of correct information.

Actually FDR had begun his Court fight clumsily. Five years earlier, when he was first campaigning for the Presidency, a supporter had written him: "Everyone now understands what you stand for. Be careful not to confuse the issue." FDR's political technique was in line with this advice. When he announced a policy, proposed legislation, took on a political fight, everyone knew what he was doing and why. With the Court fight, however, Roosevelt had lapsed. His emphasis in his message of February 5 on the inability of the older justices to carry their fair share of work misrepresented the issue and confused the people. He had been too tricky. The people worried if perhaps there was not some hidden meaning to his plan. His political enemies were quick to suggest one.

The 1930s were the era of Benito Mussolini and Adolf Hitler. The charge of "dictator," when hurled against Franklin Roosevelt, may have been unwarranted; but the concern with the possibility that dictatorship would come to America was genuine. "Even many persons who believe in President Roosevelt opposed his bill," said Henry Ashurst, "because they were haunted by the terrible fear that some future President might, by suddenly enlarging the Supreme Court, suppress free speech, free assembly and invade other Constitutional guarantees of citizens."

Not all commentators were so kind to Roosevelt. "I wish I could recover the belief that the President really is interested in democratic reforms and not in the establishment of irresistible power personally directed," wrote Walter Lippmann in his syndicated column. "My feeling is that if Mr. Roosevelt's attempt to enhance his power by the judiciary bill, the reorganization bill, and the wages and hours bill is not checked here and now, we shall see actions that will astonish us even more than the scheme to pack the Court." Such charges angered New Deal stalwarts. "When Chief Justice Taft and Chief Justice Hughes suggested compulsory retirement of the Supreme Court Justices, it was regarded as evidence of their patriotism and wisdom," snapped James Byrnes sarcastically. "But when President Roosevelt suggests a plan to accomplish the same purpose, the safety of the Republic is threatened, the very liberties of the people are endangered."

Roosevelt had grasped a great deal of power for the Presidency. But he wished to do a great deal. He realized as Presidents such as Abraham Lincoln, Theodore Roosevelt, and Woodrow Wilson had realized, that if a President is to succeed in establishing his goals, he must grasp power, hold it firmly, use it wisely—and surrender it at the end of his four-year term if the people so decide in the voting booths. But the people of the United States had forgotten about strong Presidents. Franklin Roosevelt had been preceded by three Presidents who in their combined dozen years in office had either surrendered power or failed to take it when it was available. For this reason there was an undercurrent of suspicion directed against Franklin Roosevelt's personal ambitions.

Some of this suspicion was childish, such as this telegram sent to a prominent Republican the night Roosevelt was reelected to a second term. "Would it be possible," read the telegram, "for Roosevelt through Congress or vote of the people to abolish the Constitution and Supreme Court of the United States? If so, is there not something that can be done about it before it is too late?

Could not Roosevelt and his entire Cabinet be impeached and re-
moved from office before entering another term?"

But much of the suspicion was based on more carefully considered fears. An old friend of FDR's named Jerome D. Green pointed
up the dilemma for the intellectual who favored both Roosevelt
and an independent Court. In the "Letters to the Editor" column
of *The New York Times* he wrote that "if the Court as guardian
and umpire is to be destroyed, let us not pretend that we are doing
anything else. Let us frankly abolish the Constitution and adopt a
system of parliamentary absolutism or its only alternative, a dictatorship. For one who knows the President it is impossible to believe that he is aiming at a future dictatorship; but it is also
impossible not to recognize the packing of the Supreme Court as
exactly what a dictator would adopt as his first step. The President
may not know where he is going, but he is on the way."

Green sent a copy of his letter to the President with a note saying he regretted having felt compelled to write it. FDR answered
him:

You have, of course, every right to feel as you do, and, in spite of
what I construe to be your fear in regard to the future of our nation,
I think you will have a right to send similar letters to any paper
twenty-five years from now just as you do today. There are some of
us who believe, however, that unless this nation continues as a nation—
with three branches of government pulling together to keep it going
—you might find yourself unable to write to the papers a quarter of
a century hence. You see that I am seeking to save your freedom of
expression!

Those two letters, Green's and the President's, correctly summed
up the problem. Green was accurate when he insisted that the
Court plan had overtones of dictatorship. The whole purpose of the
plan was to insure that FDR could dictate a legislative approach
to the problems of the country and also dictate the political direction the nation would take in coming decades. This purpose created fears which FDR understood, but he believed these fears had
to be accepted if the United States was to survive.

The possibility that a President, without resorting to military force, could ever become a dictator in the sense that Adolf Hitler and Benito Mussolini were dictators—they held power that could not be taken from them without their consent—is not a real one in the United States. A President, his political heirs, his party, can remain in office only if they continue to enjoy the support of the American people; the Constitutional requirement of Presidential elections guarantees that power can be stripped from American Presidents without their consent.

Roosevelt scoffed at the fears of his becoming a dictator, sometimes even joked about them. Once, when an assistant was going to the race track, FDR directed him to place a Presidential bet if the assistant could find a horse running whose name "smacked of the sea." The assistant bet a total of six dollars on a horse named "Naval Cadet," two dollars each to win, place, and show. The horse came in third, paying $6.70. "It gives me great pleasure," the assistant told the President in a note, "to enclose seventy cents." Franklin Roosevelt replied: "You are hereby appointed Chief Bookmaker to the Dictator."

Despite the jokes, the fear that Roosevelt would become "too strong" persisted. The President did not seem to resent it. Certainly he would not permit it to undermine his determination to do the job of moving the country forward, a job he believed had to be done. Convinced in his own mind that he would never become an Adolf Hitler or permit the destruction of individual freedoms, Franklin Roosevelt was not deterred by others' fears that he might.

At first this obscured to his vision and that of those closest to him a point obvious to others: There was something "too tricky" in his plan to enlarge the Supreme Court. The original emphasis was on age, but age was a cover for the real issue. Brandeis was the oldest judge and considered the greatest liberal, while Owen J. Roberts was one of the youngest judges and had fast been moving into the conservative bloc. The problem was philosophy, not age.

There also was another facet. If FDR could humble the Supreme Court, an independent branch of the federal government, and the victory of his bill would have that effect, then his leadership of the Democratic party could not be challenged. Even in 1936, when he seemed so popular, FDR could not command the allegiance of all the Democrats. The conservatives in the party—and the party when Roosevelt assumed its leadership in 1932 had been more conservative than liberal—were not willing to go along with him.

During the 1920s the Democratic party had been dominated by conservatives, men like Al Smith, Jouett Shouse, and John Raskob. Many Democrats were concerned by this conservatism at the top of the party's leadership. In 1928 a young member of the Florida state Democratic executive committee named Claude Pepper wrote Roosevelt: "For one, I want the Democratic Party genuinely to become the liberal party of this nation. I want it not to compromise upon that matter, because we cannot go to the people with conviction in our eyes unless we are sincere in our liberalism. . . . To do that it shall be necessary that we so declare ourselves, that we shall lose some of those who are now with us. They are appreciated; they are as noble as we, but they cannot go with us in a straightforward policy of liberalism in politics. We must stand for principle and not election always." In 1932, when the Democratic party had been doing preliminary work aimed at setting up its Presidential nominating convention, FDR acted behind-the-scenes to make over the leadership of the party. "In a great many sections of the country among our own Democrats there has been a good deal of opposition to what has been very inaccurately called the Raskob-Smith-Shouse control of the party machinery," he suggested to Governor Harry Flood Byrd of Virginia. "I know you will recognize this and that is another reason for suggesting 'new blood.' "

The split between the Roosevelt wing of the Democratic party and the conservative wing became very evident during FDR's first term. Years later one of these conservative Democrats, Representative Howard W. Smith of Virginia, reminisced about Roosevelt with a reporter. His comments reveal why many Democrats in the 1930s felt free to oppose their party's national leader. "I remember when we were a conservative people," Smith said. "I dug out a copy of FDR's 1932 platform the other day and read it through. It was a conservative platform. Harry Byrd used to say he was the last of the New Dealers, because he supported that platform. But Mr. Roosevelt turned a somersault after he was elected to office."

That "last of the New Dealers," Harry Byrd, who became a United States senator in 1933, and Virginia's other senator, Carter Glass, paid FDR little attention in the 1936 campaign. Glass, in effect, declared his independence of the New Deal, saying he had no apology for his anti-New Deal votes during FDR's first term and promising, "I shall continue to vote against any and every measure that I regard as either unsound or unconstitutional." During the 1936 campaign Senator Glass had been asked to make a pro-Roosevelt speech in Baltimore, but he refused, explaining that he had made a speech for Roosevelt in 1932 but "within a few months after his inauguration he had repudiated every word of it and almost made me feel ashamed for having made the speech. . . . When he personally asked me three weeks ago to make two radio addresses for him, I suggested that I feared he might later repudiate them as he had done my speech in the last Presidential campaign."

Nor did Roosevelt's overwhelming election victory impress Glass. He considered it only a demonstration that "it is well nigh impossible to beat a five million dollar campaign fund." Franklin Roosevelt was well aware of this attitude. In 1937 when Virginia was having some primaries, Roosevelt worked to build up support for those opposed to the Glass-Byrd machine. Harry Byrd told Glass that "apparently [FDR] is actively supporting in Virginia all the forces hostile to us."

This developing split between the New Dealers and the southern conservatives in the Democratic party became a matter of concern to those Democrats more interested in party organization than in philosophy. Many thought the Court dispute should be reconciled with some kind of compromise before the party was destroyed. Representative John W. McCormack, a young Democrat from Massachusetts, voiced this concern:

I think that the time has arrived when a compromise should be arrived at. I think that I bespeak the minds of most Democrats when I say that it is their opinion that a compromise should be arrived at. A head-on collision of powerful groups of our party is to be avoided. . . . As we view the situation today we see two apparently irreconcilable forces preparing for a great battle that will in all probability leave scars that will take years to heal up in the Democratic Party. . . . Before the collision that is apparent arrives—when it might be too late to talk compromise—such an effort [at reconciliation] should be made.

But such appeals did not carry weight at the White House. There the belief was that a Roosevelt victory over the Supreme Court guaranteed that the Democratic party would become the party of the New Deal, that the conservatives either must come around to FDR's brand of liberalism or drop off the party's rolls. A Roosevelt victory would assure that in 1940 the Democrats would unite behind a presidential candidate who would carry on FDR's liberal policies, not revert to conservatism.

Conversely, and this was not realized in the opening days of the battle, a defeat for Roosevelt would mean the further splintering of his party along liberal and conservative lines and would jeopardize the chances that a Roosevelt liberal would be nominated in 1940.

Probably because there was so much involved of importance to Roosevelt, he felt reluctant to be as open as he usually was in his dealings with the American people, and so he fell back on the age gimmick. Homer Cummings had produced it. In December of 1936, as he was trying to find the best means of fighting the Supreme Court, Cummings came across a bill proposed twenty-two years earlier by Woodrow Wilson's first Attorney General. Under this proposal, when a federal judge failed to retire at age seventy, the President would "be required, with the advice and consent of the Senate, to appoint another judge who would preside over the affairs of the court and have precedence over the older one. This will insure at all times the presence of a judge sufficiently active to discharge promptly and adequately the duties of the court." The Attorney General in 1914 excluded justices of the Supreme Court from his proposal, but it seemed logical that if it was wise policy to appoint a second judge for every federal judge over seventy below the Supreme Court, it was wise policy to do the same for judges over seventy on the Supreme Court. It was from this that the FDR plan developed.

Making it even more palatable was the identity of the Attorney General who made the proposal in 1914. His name was James C. McReynolds. In 1937 that same James McReynolds, then seventy-four years old—four years beyond the retirement age he himself had suggested for federal judges, sat on the Supreme Court, where he was one of the bitterest foes of the New Deal.

The day after Christmas 1936, Cummings came to the White House with his proposal that the McReynolds bill of 1914 be revised to include Supreme Court justices in 1937. The beauty, he and Roosevelt thought, of using McReynolds vintage 1914 to attack McReynolds vintage 1937 was the belief that the public would accept the plan as having merit above any motives FDR might have. Roosevelt considered the idea the "answer to a maiden's prayer."

No man can be perfect in all his choices. Many of FDR's aides, once February 5 came and they learned of the plan, believed he had not been perfect in his choice of dueling weapons against the Court. The maiden's prayer really had not been answered, they believed. The Court could have been attacked directly. Many persons, even outside the circle of New Deal zealots, believed the Court in its devotion to preserving the past had overstepped its proper bounds. Even some members of the Court itself had hinted publicly that the institution had gone too far in its attack on the New Deal.

By the end of February, Roosevelt himself agreed with this estimate, that the subterfuge of the age argument had not caught on with the public and had aroused needless suspicion. He decided to turn to the real issue—the need for support of the New Deal by the Supreme Court. Roosevelt chose a Democratic victory dinner scheduled for March 4 at the Mayflower Hotel in Washington as the occasion for a speech to rally the people behind his plan. The speech became one of Roosevelt's most famous and most quoted, certainly one of his greatest. "His peroration was one of the best that I have ever heard," said Harold Ickes of that address.

Perhaps no one prepared a speech more carefully than did Franklin Roosevelt: there were twenty-one drafts of the March 4 talk. Roosevelt knew that when he discussed complicated and sophisticated governmental problems, he had to discuss them in such a manner so that it could "go over with Moses Smith," the man who ran the President's farm in Hyde Park.

For his March 4 speech the President was seeking a particularly dramatic approach when Stuart Chase, a liberal economist, sent him a copy of a letter he had written to *The New York Times* for that paper's "Letters to the Editor" column. In his letter, which defended FDR's Court plan, Chase said he personally preferred a constitutional amendment but argued that the ratification process was too lengthy. "The Child Labor Amendment has been kicking around State Legislatures for thirteen years," Chase wrote, continuing: "And here are all these farmers and workers. Now. Here are women laboring forty-eight hours a week in New Bedford Mills for $5. Now. Here is the Dust Bowl beginning to blow again. Now. Here are millions of landless tenants progressively sliding to economic perdition. Now."

Roosevelt liked the emphasis on the "Now," on the pressing problems demanding immediate solution. The letter had not yet been published by the *Times*. At FDR's request Chase stopped publication, and then FDR adopted the format as his own. A political party's victory dinner usually is a time for thanking the faithful and gloating over the defeated. But Franklin Roosevelt used the March 4 dinner as a reaffirmation of his intentions.

He reminded his audience—including the thirteen hundred guests at the Mayflower and most party members across the nation through a hookup by telephone lines to eleven hundred other Democratic victory dinners—that in the 1936 campaign he had warned that the fight against the "economic royalists" had far to go. "Did some people really believe we did not mean it?" he demanded of the Democrats the night of March 4. And he answered: "Well—I meant it, and you meant it." After outlining the New

Deal efforts to meet the crisis of the 1930s and pointing out how
the judiciary had blocked those efforts, FDR warned: "If we do
not have the courage to lead the American people where they want
to go, someone else will." Then he delivered what was intended
as a call to crusade:

> Here is one-third of a nation ill-nourished, ill-clad, ill-housed—NOW!
> Here are thousands upon thousands of farmers wondering whether
> next year's prices will meet their mortgage interest—NOW!
> Here are thousands upon thousands of men and women laboring
> for long hours in factories for inadequate pay—NOW!
> Here are thousands upon thousands of children who should be at
> school, working in mines and mills—NOW!
> Here are strikes more far-reaching than we have ever known, costing
> millions of dollars—NOW!
> Here are spring floods threatening to roll again down our river
> valleys—NOW!
> Here is the Dust Bowl beginning to blow again—NOW!
> If we would keep faith with those who had faith in us, if we would
> make democracy succeed, I say we must act—NOW!

Robert La Follette, Jr., a Wisconsin senator and supporter of
FDR's, told the President the next day that the speech was "inspiring. . . . I feel certain the overwhelming majority of the people
will answer by coming to your support with renewed determination to win the battle you are waging to save our fundamental institutions of democracy." And others told FDR the same thing.
Over and over again all that he heard was that he had delivered
a great speech, certain to pull a large public response favorable to
his plan.

Five days later, the night of March 9, he delivered one of his
famous fireside chats. Again speaking on the Court plan, he sought
to assuage fears of his becoming a dictator. He ended the address
with: "You who know me will accept my solemn assurance that
in a world in which democracy is under attack, I seek to make
American democracy succeed." At the last moment he scrawled
a new final line: "You and I will do our part." Franklin Roosevelt could not permit an opportunity to go by without expressing
his determination to win.

5

IN ADDITION to his own personality and his use of what he considered a public mandate to move against the Court, Franklin Roosevelt had another weapon: patronage, political favors, the public works projects otherwise known as the pork barrel, the federal subsidies, the deals—all the ruthless and behind-the-scenes machinations, the skulduggery, every dirty trick available to a person with political power.

Washington was filled with many reports of such happenings. According to one, two senators who had not announced either for or against the Court plan came around to Roosevelt's side after patronage plums had been handed them. There was talk that several Presidential appointments were being held up as insurance against any Congressional backsliding. The talk became so rife that several members of Congress complained openly of the tactics.

Another political tactic, widely discussed, was exemplified by what happened to one Democratic senator who spoke out against the President's Court plan. FDR retaliated by sending one of his supporters to the opponent's home ground to make a speech in favor of the Court plan. In addition Cabinet officials were sent around the country to speak in behalf of the Court plan, particularly Cabinet members like Ickes of the interior, who had charge of public works, and Wallace of agriculture, who, it was hoped, would be influential with the farmers. The belief in Washington was that Roosevelt was taking the position that whoever was not with him was against him and that the President intended to "crack down" on any who disagreed with him.

Gerald Nye had to face this situation directly. Although a Republican, Nye was considered a liberal who had given the New Deal much support. White House strategists actually anticipated at first that he would support the Court plan and carry some other western senators along with him. But Nye's inclinations were against the plan. He met one night with a small group of senators who opposed the plan; all except Nye were lawyers. They suggested that Nye make a speech against the Court plan the coming Sunday afternoon. When Nye protested, saying he was not a lawyer, he was told that a nonlegal argument might be the best one for what would be one of the first protests against the Court plan. The real purpose of having Nye speak first was to insure his commitment against the Court plan. Shortly after the newspapers appeared with a brief reference to Nye's scheduled appearance on radio, he received a telephone call from a White House aide. "The Chief would like to see you," said the aide. Nye had answered such summons before and he went this time. FDR was at his most persuasive.

At first the President suggested that Nye not speak publicly on the Court plan because he was not a lawyer and did not understand the issues involved. Then Roosevelt began to speak of the various federal projects in Nye's state of North Dakota. Because of the breakdown in the economics of agriculture, "We were one hundred and ten per cent dependent on the federal government out there," Nye has recalled. Although no specific threats were made, Nye understood that he faced the possibility that federal assistance to his state would be curtailed or slowed down if his opposition to the Court plan continued. "I'll think it over," he told the President.

He went home, thought it over, and continued preparing his speech. Sunday morning, as he was going over a final draft, a farm leader from his state appeared at his house. Nye asked the farm leader to come in, hear the speech, and time it to make certain it was within the allowed fifteen minutes. The farm leader said he did not wish to hear the speech and made a comment that demonstrated to Nye where the farm leader had been first. During Nye's session at the White House Roosevelt had suggested that Nye could get out of making the radio address by pretending to sprain an ankle. FDR had even offered to help Nye get into a military hospital where he could hide out for a few days. This Sunday morning the farm leader said to Nye: "Why don't you go out and sprain an ankle and get into the naval hospital?" Nye delivered the speech.

There was talk in Washington that many members would oppose Roosevelt on the Court plan except that they did not have the financial resources to suffer a defeat at the polls. Senator Pat Harrison, Democrat of Mississippi, was cited as an example. Then fifty-five years old and a member of the Senate for nineteen years, Harrison had no outside income and no profession. If he believed the people of his state would back him in opposing FDR on the Court issue, he would have gone against FDR; but he was not sure and he feared defeat.

Another story in Washington concerned a lobbyist, a former official in the Woodrow Wilson Administration, who told his friends that he opposed the Roosevelt plan but could not say so publicly. To do so, he explained, would block him from getting any consideration for his clients from Administration officials and agencies.

On February 12, Charles Brooks Smith, Washington correspondent of the Wheeling, West Virginia, *Intelligencer,* wrote a story suggesting that a patronage appointment of Senator Matthew M. Neely, Democrat of West Virginia, might not be cleared by the White House. "Signs of uneasiness" was the phrase the reporter used to describe the situation. The same day he wrote that story, Smith wrote a letter to Senator Borah, tipping him off to the political situation regarding the Court plan in West Virginia. Of Senator Neely, Smith reported to Borah that his "hope of being assigned more patronage [is] probably the strongest binding tie in the case of the Senator." That exchange not only speaks of the power of patronage, it also suggests the wide-ranging intelligence system which the FDR opponents had. Neely supported the Court plan, and his patronage appointment went through.

The power of patronage was not a minor power. A senator trying to secure a patronage appointment needed political clearance. One senator, in February, 1937, telephoned Secretary of the Treasury Morgenthau about an appointment of a party stalwart as Collector of the Customs. "Well, I understand that Mr. Farley is working on it, see?" the secretary told the senator, "and is trying to locate a place for him but they haven't been able to do it yet. Now, the President spoke to me about it himself. And, as I understand it, they're trying to make some kind of a swap up there. But the matter is really in Farley's hands and hasn't come to me yet." The senator then spoke about how his man had personally been responsible for his state's supporting FDR in 1932—the first time the state ever had gone Democratic in a Presidential election. But Morgenthau could do nothing even though the appointment was in his own department. "I am waiting," he said to the senator. "I don't like to pass the buck, but I am waiting to hear from the Democratic organization. . . . And the next move is up to them."

There were other ways in which patronage could be used. If the FDR bill went through, there would be six additional appointments to the Supreme Court—the most prestigious spot a lawyer can aspire to. After the plan was announced, reporters found Administration officials willing to speculate on possible appointments. One name mentioned prominently was that of Joe Robinson, the Senate Democratic leader. Then sixty-four years old, Robinson was a Democratic workhorse. A former member of the House, briefly governor of Arkansas, and then senator, Robinson was known for his loyalty to the Democratic party. In 1928 he had become Al Smith's running mate because the Democratic party hoped Robinson's ties to the South would blunt some of the anti-Catholic sentiment there. Robinson fought for his party that year in his usual valiant manner even though it was a lost cause. He had a dream of many years' standing, a not surprising dream considering the political realities of the time. He wanted to end his career in public life with a seat on the Supreme Court. He considered such an appointment a fitting reward for his years of service to his country and to his political party. He had many friends in the Senate who wished to see his dream become a reality. Robinson, motivated then by his loyalty to party and by his personal ambitions, would use all his power and influence as Senate Democratic leader as well as his personal friendships to help push the Court plan through. He had much to gain from the Court plan's success. But he would come to the most tragic end.

Another name frequently mentioned as a possible Court appointee was that of Felix Frankfurter, the Harvard Law School professor. In the liberal lineage, Frankfurter was the direct descendant of Brandeis. Many of the young men staffing the New Deal offices were known in Washington as "Felix's Hot Dogs," so many of them having come to Washington on his recommendation. The mention of Frankfurter's name, as well as that of Senator Robert F. Wagner of New York, a liberal Democrat, was expected to help keep the liberal section of the Democratic party behind FDR's plan.

And two names mentioned frequently at first were those of Senator Ashurst and Representative Sumners, the chairmen of the judiciary committees which made up the first obstacle to the Court plan. The minor Administration officials who dropped these last two names apparently hoped that greed might encourage the two committee chairmen to think positively about enlarging the Court. Roosevelt himself did not speak of the possibility that either Ashurst or Sumners would join the Court. When Sumner's opposition became known, his name was quickly dropped from the speculation about possible nominees. Ashurst's name faded more slowly.

With all of this, however, patronage was not used as much as reported. After Burton Wheeler's opposition became known, a White House aide met with the Senator and expressed hope for a reconciliation between the Senator and the President, saying something to the effect that Franklin Roosevelt would enjoy having Wheeler's advice on new appointees to the Supreme Court. This story made the Washington rounds and was transformed into a White House offer to allow Wheeler to name some of the new appointees to the Court if he would withdraw his opposition; in the story's most common version, Wheeler could name two of the new justices. The deal had not been that specific nor that blatant; Wheeler himself understood he was not offered a bribe.

Jim Farley recalls that the President, just a few days after announcing his Court plan, threatened to hold up judicial appointments in states where the Congressional delegation was opposing

the President, make the appointments quickly in states where
the delegation supported the plan, and funnel the appointments
through those members of Congress siding with the Administration where the state delegation was divided. In line with this, it
was widely believed that Senator William H. Dieterich of Illinois,
a Democrat and a member of the Judiciary Committee, went along
with Roosevelt on the Court plan in exchange for a patronage
appointment he sought—that of District Judge J. Earl Major to be
United States Judge for the Seventh Circuit.

This exchange was not quite the bartering arrangement that it
seems. With any appointment that requires Senate confirmation, as
a judgeship does, the senator whose state is involved has more
impact on the appointment than does the President, who makes
the formal appointment. The Senate has a practice known as "senatorial courtesy." The Senate will not confirm an appointment if
the senator whose state is involved raises an objection on the
Senate floor. Franklin Roosevelt never could name any person to
a judgeship in Illinois without William Dieterich's express approval. The appointment could have been delayed, as Farley recalled FDR threatened to do in some cases, but Dieterich was in
a better position actually to block an appointment than was FDR.

Dieterich's support of the Court plan had another origin. He
was from southern Illinois, tended toward conservatism, and disliked the Court plan. But he needed political support from the
city of Chicago, a Democratic stronghold under the control of the
"Boss Kelly" machine. This machine was heavily dependent upon
the federal government because only the federal government could
provide the welfare funds that were keeping the people of Chicago
from starving and the Kelly machine in power. In a situation like
this no one has to go from the White House to the Chicago powers and threaten them with a reduction in federal assistance unless
the Chicagoans lean heavily on Dieterich. And in a situation such
as this a senator like Dieterich does not have to wait until "the
boys" come to see him with their threats of political retaliation.
The people involved are all sophisticated adults. A senator like
Dieterich understands that if his votes vary sharply from the sen-

timents of the city overlords, he cannot expect those powers to continue supporting him. The people who ran Chicago understood that if their Congressional delegation did not support the Administration, then the Administration either would be thrown out of office or else rely on other sources of political strength. The New Deal was probably the first time that a national administration was concerned with the economic plight of the people in the cities. If the people in the cities did not support the New Deal, that Administration and its concern would be short-lived. The Kelly machine understood this. William Dieterich understood this.

In other areas the Administration could be more direct—public works, for example. The federal government had a great deal of public money to dispense for dams, post office construction, flood control projects, and the like. The Administration could be extremely effective politically by the careful timing and placing of these funds. In connection with the Court plan the most well-known example of such a strategy was the visit of the Governor of Kentucky, A. B. "Happy" Chandler, to the White House in search of some flood control money. Kentucky's Democratic Senator Marvel M. Logan had been recalcitrant about the Court plan. Senator Logan became a supporter of the plan. Kentucky got its flood control projects.

This worked both ways, however. An otherwise strong Administration supporter could raise the possibility of withdrawing his support unless more federal money flowed into his Congressional district or state. Joe Robinson, a canny politician who understood that kind of game very well, had a talk with Tommy Corcoran shortly after the Court plan was announced. Robinson made clear that he was not altogether satisfied with the public works funds coming his way. Corcoran immediately urged Harold Ickes, who was in charge of dispensing that money, to take remedial action.

Another form of political pressure available to FDR was the legislative process itself. Senators and representatives all have favorite legislation they want passed. The senators who have many union members among their constituencies are interested in a bill concerning the minimum wage. Senators from farm states are concerned with legislation protecting the farmer from the vagaries of nature. If such legislation was held up pending the disposition of the Court bill, an uneasiness would grow among the legislators. They would want the dispute over the Court bill ended so they could get on with their own pet legislation. They also would not wish to be recorded as being too strong against the Administration on the Court bill. They might always need some White House aid when their own project was before the Congress. One Senator who felt under this kind of pressure was Robert Wagner of New York. His primary interest was a housing bill. He needed both White House and conservative Congressional support. An old professional, Wagner played both sides. To Roosevelt privately he gave assurances of going along on the Court fight. He also appeased the conservatives by keeping unusually quiet publicly about the issue.

With all these possibilities for political pressure before him, Roosevelt showed himself to be a competent practitioner of his art. He never went quite all the way, however. Playing politics roughhouse style—delaying judicial appointments, bartering with other appointments, using public works funds as bait—implies that the final blow will be landed if it is required. This is the blow that completely crushes your opponent. This much FDR declined to do. Alben Barkley recalled once saying to Roosevelt, "Mr. President, you play with men like a cat plays with a mouse." Barkley continued that Roosevelt laughed and said: "Well, I don't devour them in the end." Henry Ashurst is an example.

Sixty-two years of age, Henry Ashurst had risen to the powerful position of chairman of the Senate Judiciary Committee through the seniority system. This is the system that gives a committee chairmanship to the member with the greatest tenure on the committee whether or not he is otherwise qualified. Often the system has produced chairmen of only mediocre abilities, or even less. In the 1930s many in Washington considered Ashurst to be such a chairman. Often he was. He had been in Washington as a senator since 1912, and, with its sophisticated people and their charming parties, Washington was a heady place to be for a man who had grown up on the Arizona frontier. But there still was a little of the frontier deep within Henry Ashurst, a trace of stubbornness, a hardness. It would not show very often, but it showed occasionally. The Court fight was such an occasion.

Ashurst's crucial position was not understood at first. Roosevelt originally intended that the House take up the Court bill, pass it, and send it on to the Senate, where it would then come under Ashurst's care. But Sumners' opposition jinxed that. This was a blow to the White House strategy. Because all House members run for reelection every two years, the Administration believed that FDR's political coattails had most impact on that side of the Capitol, that the House members would be anxious to rush the Court plan through. Also, Roosevelt supporters in the House said that the President could count an immediate strength of 100 of the 435 members, a good foundation for a controversial piece of legislation. It was here that the White House first did its work. "I suggest you call and talk to Zeb Weaver of North Carolina, a member of the House Judiciary Committee," the House Democratic leader, Sam Rayburn, told FDR. "He is going along." And Speaker of the House Bankhead suggested to Roosevelt that it was "quite important for you to ask Hatton Sumners, chairman of judiciary, to see you alone at as early a moment as possible."

But Sumners remained obdurate, and also vocal in his opposition. His many "off-the-record" comments to newsmen about the Court plan were the basis for stories that the bill was in serious trouble in the House. Also, Sumners had strong ties to Rayburn, the House Democratic leader. Both were Texans, close politically and philosophically, and also Rayburn had once been married to Sumners' sister. Suspicion developed at the White House that perhaps Rayburn was not sufficiently zealous in urging Democrats to swing into line behind the President's proposal. The decision then was made at the White House to push the bill through the Senate first. A strong victory there would build up enough momentum to sweep the Court plan through the House.

That decision was sealed at a White House meeting February 23 between the President and the House leaders—Speaker Bankhead, Sam Rayburn, and Hatton Sumners. Because Washingtonians habitually say in public other than what they mean, the White House announced after that session that the House leaders assured the President that the House would approve his Court bill. However, it was explained, the House leaders also had informed the President of their belief that the Senate should act first. The leaders did not feel that the House members, all of whom would be up for reelection in 1938, should be asked to go out on a political limb on such a controversial question unless they were assured that the Senate, with only one-third of its membership up for reelection in 1938, would also approve it. So now it was up to the Senate, and that first meant Henry Ashurst.

"I am a fountain," Henry Ashurst said of himself, "not a cistern." This former cowboy who was called a "word wrangler" and who affected the cutaway-coat garb of the statesman was indeed a word spouter. Even in 1937, when the era of the great Senate orators still was in full sway, Henry Fountain Ashurst could hold his own with the very best of them. When he spoke, his tall, lean figure straightened, his index finger rose toward the sky, or a hand waved his pince-nez for emphasis. His voice rumbled when angered, almost sang when happy. He said he was for the Court plan. One day in the Senate one of his fellow Democrats, but an opponent of the plan, stood up and directed this question at Ashurst:

I wish to ask the Senator if, as reported in the newspapers, he spoke the following words: "And among the unjust criticisms which have been uttered, or printed, rather, about President Roosevelt was that he intended at some time—nobody knows when or where—to increase by some legerdemain—nobody knows when or where—the membership of the Supreme Court of the United States, so that his policies might be sustained." I desire to ask the Senator from Arizona whether that is an accurate quotation from the newspaper of his remarks?

It was an embarrassing position for Ashurst. Several weeks before FDR had announced his plan to enlarge the Court, Ashurst had indeed said those words, publicly denying that the President would attempt to enlarge the Court. Embarrassing, yes. But difficult? Not for the superman of the vocal cords. Ashurst rose and answered:

> It is obvious from the rhetoric that that is my utterance. My faults are obvious. There can be no doubt I have my full share. I suffer from cacoethes loquendi, a mania or itch for talking, from vanity, from morbidity, and as is obvious to everyone who knows me, an inborn, an inveterate flair for histrionics.
>
> But there never has been superadded to these vices of mine the withering, embalming vice of consistency. Whoever in his public service is handcuffed and shackled by the vice of consistency will be a man not free to act as various questions come before him from time to time; he will be a statesman locked in a prison house the keys to which are in the keeping of days and events that are dead. Let me quote Emerson: "A foolish consistency is the hobgoblin of little minds, adored by little statesmen."
>
> I spoke of my vice, cacoethes loquendi. There is another vice called cacoethes carpendi, the mania to find fault, to carp against everything that somebody else proposes, but never suggesting a remedy yourself. Such is cacoethes carpendi, a vice not wholly unknown in this Senate chamber!

None of Henry Fountain Ashurst's Senate colleagues referred to the Senator's earlier statements again. Few also doubted his allegiance to the Administration on the Court matter. At the White House, however, there was not quite so much certainty.

The first Monday after Roosevelt had announced his Court plan, February 8, he invited some of the Congressional leaders to discuss over lunch the prospects of the Court bill. The President carved the baked pheasant and served it to the congressmen on warm trays that came in an electrically heated oven. FDR did not eat much himself. He spent most of the hour talking about his Court bill. Ashurst also spoke at the session. He did not criticize the Court bill, but he did speak in behalf of another proposal. This was Hatton Sumners' bill to allow Supreme Court justices to retire at age seventy with full pay. Under the system then in effect, if a justice did retire, he had no assurances of a full pension. When Oliver Wendell Holmes had retired in 1932, Congress had cut his anticipated pension in half. The Sumners bill would prevent that kind of penny-ante tactic against a Court member. It was widely believed in Washington at the time that if the Sumners bill had been law, at least two of the justices on the Supreme Court would have retired, making the FDR attack unnecessary. Although Ashurst did not spell out that he was favoring the Sumners bill as an alternative to the Roosevelt plan, that was the understanding. The first suspicion against the Arizonan had been lodged.

A few days later Tommy Corcoran called Ashurst and asked him to come to the White House to meet with the President. At that meeting, FDR complained that Ashurst had postponed committee hearings. "I replied," recorded Ashurst, "that I would avoid haste, would go slowly and give the opponents of his bill ample time and opportunity to explore all its implications. He received this statement with disrelish. I then went on to say that the opposition was searching avidly for some shred of evidence tending to show that he was hurrying the bill."

When the meeting ended, Joe Robinson, who also had been summoned, told newsmen: "There was a conference and discussion of the Court reorganization bill. It is believed that the matter is progressing in a satisfactory way. I do not care to discuss any further details." His abruptness indicated that the bill was indeed finding trouble.

Henry Ashurst was working against the bill in the best way he could—by the tactic of delay. It was a deliberate slowdown, a sly trick. Publicly he spoke in favor of the President's bill; actually he sided against it by letting the steam behind it slowly escape and dissipate.

Henry Ashurst also was vulnerable to a Presidential attack. His state, Arizona, was almost ninety per cent federal property. Washington controlled the state's water, its public works, its employment, everything. All FDR had to do was turn off some of the faucets, or even threaten to, and a great political juggernaut would have pressed down on Henry Ashurst. Roosevelt was advised to do this. Corcoran, for one, told him to be ruthless, to crush Ashurst.

Roosevelt, however, refused. He told Corcoran that such an act would be too brutal, that to expose the rawness of the political power of the executive was bad politics. FDR was correct about this. Congress would have united behind Ashurst rather than permit one of its own to be destroyed by a President. Also, FDR was an optimist. He hoped that an easier method, one with less letting of political blood, would eventually become available. There also was a third reason. FDR and Henry Ashurst had been political comrades. One just did not turn so ruthlessly against an old fellow soldier. Franklin Roosevelt often toyed with being completely ruthless. At one time he knew of a politician, a Democrat opposed to the New Deal, who lived a hidden life as a homosexual in the dark shadows of society. To replace this politician with a New Deal supporter, Franklin Roosevelt readied an exposé of this man's shadow life. Before FDR used it, however, the politician died. Roosevelt then was able to avoid the choice of whether or not to expose the politician. If the choice had been forced upon him, however, he probably would have decided not to. He threatened occasionally—and as happened to Ashurst in the coming months, FDR's aides threatened in his name—but he was not a ruthless person. "I don't devour them in the end," he had told Barkley.

6

IN THE FIRST WEEKS after the Court plan was announced, the public arena was the radio. In the 1930s Americans had few distractions and little money to afford those few they had. But every family had a radio or access to one. The young radio networks still felt a sense of responsibility to the public which owned the airwaves, and the networks did not hesitate to make their facilities available to any public official who wished to speak on a major topic. More than one hundred speakers broadcast for and against the Court plan in the six weeks following its announcement. One network alone used up seventeen hours of broadcasting time. These speeches were usually broadcast early in the evening so that most American could hear them.

That these speeches were broadcast is a tribute to the radio industry. Sometimes there were slipups. On one occasion Burton Wheeler believed he had a national audience for a radio speech against the Court plan. Then he found out he had been broadcast only in Washington and in Montana. Wheeler suspected that the networks bowed to Presidential power to shut out the opposition. Fortunately for Wheeler he had some power himself. He was chairman of the Senate Interstate and Foreign Commerce Committee, which had jurisdiction over legislation affecting broadcasting. He complained to the networks, and they promised to do better.

That the speeches were listened to is a tribute to the American people, for most of these speeches were thoughtful, sophisticated, intelligent examinations of the subject. On February 14, Homer Cummings spoke slowly and carefully about the subject:

In our federal courts the law's delays have become intolerable. Multitudes of cases have been pending from five to ten years. . . . Closely allied with this problem is the situation created by the continuance in office of aged or infirm judges. . . . Attacks upon the Constitutionality of measures enacted by Congress have burdened the courts. . . . If the Constitution is to remain a living document and the law is to serve the needs of a vital and growing nation, it is essential that new blood be enfused into our judiciary. . . . That the freedom of our people to direct their own destiny has been hampered, especially of late, by judicial action is scarcely open to debate. . . . What then is the real objection? It is simply this: Those who wish to preserve the status quo want to retain on the bench judges who may be relied upon to veto progressive measures.

The President kept a close watch on what his Administration members were saying publicly about the Court fight. Early in March, Harold Ickes was scheduled to give a speech in Boston in which he planned to speak of Chief Justice Charles Evans Hughes as "a justice of the Supreme Court who resigned to become a candidate for President, waged a partisan fight, following which he accepted retainers from the biggest corporations in the country to plead their causes before the Supreme Court, and then went back to the Supreme Court as Chief Justice." This was an accurate, if not comprehensive, description of Hughes's career. Roosevelt asked Ickes to change the speech because "it is not wise to come even this close to a personal reference to a member of the Court."

The speeches across the nation for and against the Administration's Court plan did not just happen. They were organized and often the result of a personal plea by a leader of one of the sides. Roosevelt himself did not hesitate to seek out supporters. In 1937 there was only one former Supreme Court justice living. This was John Hessin Clarke, who had filled Charles Evans Hughes's seat in 1916 when Hughes had resigned to run against Woodrow Wilson. Clarke himself had resigned in 1922 to campaign for United States entry into the League of Nations.

Roosevelt called Clarke to ask him to speak on radio in behalf of the plan. Roosevelt concluded that Clarke had agreed to speak over radio, and this caused Clarke "more distress and embarrassment than ever before in my long life." Clarke said he supported the New Deal but explained he could not speak in behalf of the New Deal and against the recent Supreme Court decisions "however unsound and unwise I might think them to be" without sounding partisan. As a former Supreme Court justice, "I found myself limited by my situation to a discussion of the constitutionality of the program, which is now really scarcely denied." This would be so repetitious, Clarke told the President, that "it seemed to me clear that for me to speak would not only not be of value but positively harmful to the cause which, I assure you my dear Mr. President, is very close to my heart."

The President, however, wanted the support of the only living ex-Supreme Court Justice—and wanted the public to know he had it. He pressed again, and Clarke did speak over the radio the next week. The address, however, was limited to a discussion of the

Constitutional issues—Clarke said FDR was perfectly within his Constitutional rights to seek an enlargement of the Court—and the speech did not have the impact that FDR had hoped it would have.

The opposition was perhaps even more zealous in seeking out speakers. John Callan O'Laughlin, a prominent Republican and publisher of the *Army-Navy Journal*, wrote William Allen White, the Emporia *Gazette* publisher, that "Senator Borah is very anxious to have William Hirth, the farm leader and editor of the *Missouri Farmer*, make some addresses on the President's Supreme Court proposal. It is understood here that Mr. Hirth is against the President in this matter, and that in his next issue will assail the President's plan to pack the Court. I am writing to ask you if you think you could communicate with Hirth and urge him to talk at some farm meetings, which would be most helpful to the activities of the Senator here." Hirth was a former Roosevelt supporter, and the intricate way in which the opposition approached him to speak against the Court plan indicates the carefulness with which a case was built up against Roosevelt before the public. There could be no slips.

O'Laughlin had written White because Republicans in Washington believed there would be a better response from Hirth if the first approach to him came from a midwesterner like himself. White thought it a good idea, but he was not operating alone in the Midwest. He passed along the O'Laughlin letter to Roy Roberts of the Kansas City *Star*. "I wonder," White said to the *Star* publisher, "if it would be possible to get half a dozen meetings for this man Hirth in Kansas, say at Salina, Wichita, Topeka, Iola, Coffeyville, and Dodge or Great Bend. I'd like to know what you think of the proposal and what ideas you have about how to go at the arrangements."

Roberts, apparently because of Hirth's past record as an FDR supporter, was not biting quite so fast. Hirth "told us yesterday that he was not going to say anything until probably next Friday," Roberts reported back to White on March 13. "He did not indicate what his position was, but I rather gathered from Wallace, our man who talked with him, that it would be against the Court proposals. He said he was preparing a statement and would give it to us about next Friday or Saturday. After he has taken a position, then we could see about his making some speeches, but," Roberts insisted, "I would want to see what he says first."

The problem of whether to sign William Hirth for a few speeches against the Court plan before some farmers' groups now had already involved Senator Borah, a leading GOP opponent of the Court plan; O'Laughlin, a prominent Republican in Washington; William Allen White, the respected spokesman for the Middle West, as well as Roy Roberts, a prominent Republican newspaper publisher. It still had more to go. White next wrote to Alf Landon, the GOP Presidential nominee the previous year, saying:

About this man Hirth, Roy Roberts says not to bill him until we hear his speech. He is going to speak Friday. If he speaks his piece, as Shakespeare says, "trippingly on the tongue," and it sounds good, we will start him out in Emporia and I will write to a dozen of the newspaper fellows and ask them to pass him around. I will build up a little organization, possibly hire an extra stenographer for ten days or two weeks, and any help or blessing you can give to the cause will be properly appreciated.

The GOP concern about Hirth was unfounded. Although he had supported FDR in 1932 and 1936, Hirth announced he was unwilling "to blindly support anything he may do or propose, and if under the recent interpretation of my friend Farley this be treason to the Democratic Party, then I will cheerfully assume whatever ignominy may be involved." Anticipating the pleasure of a martyr's cloak, Hirth wrote Roosevelt, saying, "It is with a feeling of sadness that I realize that the latch-string will no longer hang outside the door for me, but this is the way of politics, and I will not complain." But FDR was a little too smart, one, to completely alienate a former supporter, and, two, to give Hirth a cause to complain. "My dear Hirth," he answered, "please do not get the idea that the latch-string is no longer hanging outside the door for you. I would like very much, one of these days a little later on, to have a good long talk with you." Also, however, FDR would not take a slap lying down. He added: "Frankly, my difficulty with some of the things you have said and written in the past couple of years is that they oppose and do not propose. You will remember T. R.'s quotation, 'We are both practical men.' I hope when you come East, you will give me some practical and concrete ideas."

The pains the opposition had taken in first checking out Hirth's opposition to the Court plan before scheduling him to speak indicates how thorough an organization was developed to oppose Roosevelt. It began almost immediately after Roosevelt announced his Court plan on February 5.

When Frank Gannett had first read the news accounts of FDR's Court plan, he brooded over it, trying to think of a means to stop FDR. Gannett's earlier support of FDR had faded because of the New Deal economic policies: too much money was going from the rich to the poor. When his attempt to swing the GOP nomination in 1936 to William Borah failed, Gannett then backed Landon against Roosevelt. In his unsuccessful attempt to push Borah into the Presidency, Gannett had been associated with a number of prominent Americans, wealthy and concerned persons. This became the nucleus of the National Committee to Uphold Constitutional Government, a "nonpartisan" organization devoted to defeating FDR's plan.

There is a technique for organizing a nonpartisan, "spontaneous" demonstration by the public against a proposed bill in Congress. The technique requires that the demonstration be anything but spontaneous and nonpartisan. Although the original money to finance the Gannett committee came not from the Republican party treasury, it did come from prominent Republicans who were opposed to Roosevelt and believed they could use the Court plan as a means of toppling him from his prestigious heights. The first thing the committee did was to send out ten thousand letters in a test mailing. A Los Angeles doctor received one of the letters, signed by Gannett. The letter read:

"There is no liberty if the power of judging be not separated from the legislative and executive powers."

That was said while adoption of our Constitution was under discussion.

Today this principle is attacked and in danger, although its vital truth is as self-evident now as then. Life tenure was assured to judges because the founders of this Government knew that to preserve government under law independence of the judiciary is indispensable.

The fight to protect our Supreme Court from subordination to the Executive can be won. It requires organization, national and local; immediate aggressive action and enough money to carry the cost of awakening public opinion. I have joined with others in organizing a national nonpartisan, nonpolitical committee to carry on this fight.

Will you sign and circulate the attached petition? Will you volunteer to help organize a nonpartisan local committee to cooperate with us in your own congressional district? The outcome in Congress will depend upon how well and quickly public opinion is mobilized in every congressional district and state. Will you protest to your senators and congressmen at once, sending me a copy?

Will you make a contribution to help carry the expenses of national organization?

Prompt mass action is essential. Please show this letter to friends and business associates. Enlist their cooperation with yours.

That form letter had not been sent to a doctor by accident. When organizing a campaign such as this one, it is not wise to waste time, energy, and money on people who are not expected to give support. Mailings by the Gannett committee were not sent to labor union members, nor to militant leaders of minority groups; neither to prominent spokesmen for urban groups nor to political liberals. Instead, the Gannett group sought out persons expected to be reasonably well off financially and conservative politically. The mailing list included 161,000 lawyers' names, 121,000 medical persons, about 140,000 ministers, and 70,000 businessmen. There were also 24,000 farmers on the list. These were farmers believed to be conservatives and against FDR. During the first month, the Gannett group sent out a half-million pieces of mail. Before the fight was over, a total of ten million mailings had been made. These included comments of prominent Americans against the plan, editorials, booklets; almost anything that denounced the FDR plan. The committee also ran advertisements in newspapers, calling to the readers: "What can you do about it? Bestir yourself. Talk to your neighbors, write to your senators, write to your congressman, write and sign petitions, help in every way you can this fight to save the Supreme Court from domination by President Roosevelt or any one who may become his successor, liberal or reactionary."

The existence of such an organization was of tremendous benefit to the members of Congress opposed to FDR. If they became concerned that their constituents were growing restless because of their opposition to Roosevelt, the Gannett committee could flood their state or Congressional district with a torrent of propaganda against the Court plan. Hopefully, this propaganda would shore up the member's position with his constituents.

The relationship between the Gannett committee and the members of Congress opposed to FDR is illustrated by a letter from Edward A. Rumely of the National Committee to Uphold Constitutional Government to a secretary in Senator Glass's office. The Senator had recently made a speech against the Court plan which had been printed in the *Congressional Record*. On April 1, 1937, Rumely wrote: "We understand the costs for a reprint of Senator Glass's speech to be sent out under the frank of Senator Byrd of Virginia are as follows: For the first 1,000—$68.97; 300,000 at $3.83—$1,149.00; $10.56 for new plates—$10.56; [totaling] $1,228.53. We hand you herewith a check for $1,228.53 in payment of 301,000 copies of the Carter Glass speech franked." The references to the "frank of Senator Byrd" meant that the right of a member of Congress to mail letters without paying any postage would be used to distribute the propaganda against the Court plan, that, in effect, through Jim Farley's Post Office Department the taxpayers were picking up the tab for the committee's mailing. It also was necessary for the committee to give the $1,228.53 to Glass's office and have the Senator's aides purchase the reprints of the speech from the *Congressional Record*. Nonmembers of

Congress cannot take advantage of the low printing rates available to members.

The letter continued with instructions on where the speeches in franked envelopes should be delivered, to firms in Maryland and in New York. "The 104,000 being sent to Cornelius Printing Company will be addressed to a list covering all Protestant clergymen and school superintendents in the United States. Those coming to New York will reach all Catholic clergy and all rabbis, also all delegates to the Democratic convention at Philadelphia and other special lists that we have. Senator [William H.] King [Democrat of Utah] intends to supply names for distribution in his state."

One time the Gannett committee sought to purchase some speech reprints directly but ran into some trouble, as this letter of complaint to the Government Printing Office indicates:

In recent order for reprints of the address of Carter Glass made March 29, 1937, we received a mailbag full of talks by James A. Farley. . . . In a previous order for talks of some other members of Congress, we received a mailbag full of copies of a talk by the President and Senator Robinson, in franked envelopes of Senator Robinson. . . . Will you check into this matter and see that we receive the copies of talks due us, or a rebate for any that have been lost because of misdirection to other channels?

It seemed that one could not even fight the federal bureaucracy without becoming that bureaucracy's victim.

The Gannett group, as well as other less-organized opponents, produced a large outpouring of mail against the plan. When a member of Congress determines the position he will take on a proposal, the count of his mail for and against the proposal is one of the factors he takes into consideration. If he is personally committed to a cause and a reasonably independent person, he will vote his own conscience—despite the mail count. This is because he feels that deciding how to vote is the responsibility his constituents placed upon him, and, also, because if he is wise enough to be committed and independent, he is wise enough to know that a large outpouring of mail represents a highly organized effort which has little meaning when the specific event is passed and the letter writers forget to what they had signed their names.

But many members grow nervous when the mail count becomes very high. Senator Royal S. Copeland of New York, a Democrat, early announced his opposition to the FDR plan, partly because of the mail he had received against it. On February 20, just two weeks after the Court plan had been announced, Copeland issued a statement describing "an independent judiciary as the sole protection of our people against political terrorism, religious bigotry, racial persecution and economic tyranny." Then he added: "I am confirmed in my belief by the 30,000 letters I have received from my constituents. Out of this huge total, only a few odd hundred approve the proposal." Another senator reported that he had received fifty thousand letters on the Court plan, all but three thousand against.

The pro-Roosevelt people scoffed at the mail counts. One day a Congressional office received twenty-seven letters against the Court plan. The letter writers were checked out. Eighteen were Republicans, expected to be against any major FDR plan; nine were Democrats. Of the twenty-seven, twenty-three were in the upper income brackets and, whether Democrat or Republican, were also expected to oppose FDR. The remaining four included three farmers and one plumber; even that was not a cause for concern because those last four were over fifty-five years of age and assumed to be conservative-oriented. Commented the congressman who had received those twenty-seven letters: "It was the coal miners below forty who sent me to Congress. When I begin to get twenty-seven letters a day from those fellows kicking about this 'outrage,' I'll begin to worry about Mr. Roosevelt's not knowing his politics." Maury Maverick, the Texas New Dealer who had rushed to have his name associated in the House of Representatives with the Roosevelt plan, cracked: "All this uproar in the mail bags means is that *The Literary Digest* voters are trying to conduct another election." This was a reference to a poll taken by the *Digest* magazine in 1936 demonstrating conclusively that Landon would beat Roosevelt. The poll had surveyed persons listed in telephone books, on professional rosters, and in other listings; it ignored the sad fact that most Americans in 1936 were too poor to have telephones or to be on any lists. The only wealth they possessed—which *The Literary Digest* also had ignored— was their vote.

Still the mail could be a potent factor for a member of Congress who was unsure how to vote and was searching for something to push him one way or the other. It could also influence those members who were easily swayed and more interested in voting what they thought their constituents wanted than what they believed was right.

The caliber of the letters varied on both sides. There were those who wrote that Roosevelt should be impeached and that the members of the Supreme Court should be even worse. There were some that were touching: "We thank you for your courageous stand," said one letter writer to Borah. One of the more thoughtful letters came to Senator George W. Norris of Nebraska. It was written by one of Norris' old supporters, C. A. Sorensen, and said:

To meet the situation created by judges who believe that Congress lacks power to regulate and control hours of labor, wages, crop production, generation and sale of electric energy, issuance of securities, and so on, I have long advocated, as you know, an amendment to the Federal Constitution. I still think that should be part of the longtime program.

But a crisis exists. The situation demands action *now,* as Roosevelt says. The apparent prosperity is only a mirage to millions of people. The little man is still being pushed around.

Therefore, I personally hope that you will see your way clear to support the President's program, amended to include your proposal that no law shall be declared unconstitutional except by a three-fourths majority of the members of the Court.

However, if you do not, I still will know that your vote will be for what you think for the best permanent interests of the country.

But the gentlemanly tone of the Sorensen letter was an exception. Most of the mail that poured into Capitol Hill revealed emotions and prejudices usually held in check. Groups against the Court plan collected signatures on petitions with headings like

"ONLY THEY DESERVE LIBERTY WHO ARE WILLING TO FIGHT FOR
IT." A popular piece of printed mail read: "Hands off the Supreme Court! Dear Sir: Believing that the proposal to revise and
weaken the United States Supreme Court would prepare the way
for dictatorship in our country, I earnestly urge you to use your
influence AGAINST the measure." Joe Robinson spoke out in the
Senate chamber against the mail barrage which, he said, "contained representations and suggestions which show a deliberate
and organized effort to mislead those who are charged with the
responsibility of determining the issues." He was referring specifically to a piece of printed mail being circulated by a magazine
known as *The Defender* and based in Wichita, Kansas. Entitled
"The Crisis Hour Is Here," the circular was addressed to "Dear
Christian Friend" and called the FDR plan "shocking" and "the
most ominous development toward the DICTATORSHIP ever to occur in the history of our country."

There were protest meetings across the nation. At one in New
York, a lawyer active in the Democratic party denounced the
Court plan as "the most transparent, tricky and immoral experiment that has ever emanated from the White House." A Roosevelt loyalist jumped to his feet and shouted in rebuttal: "I came
here as an observer and I believe the meeting has been conducted
fairly up to this point, but when the President is accused of an
immoral act I wish to rise in protest." Then the loyalist suggested
the attack on FDR had been prompted not by the speaker's chagrin at the Court plan but by his chagrin that he had not received
an appointment from the White House as a federal judge. The
audience of about six hundred broke into hisses and catcalls. A
fistfight was averted.

Appeals were sounded on the basis of religion, geography,
money, and race. The opponents used such arguments both for
and against the plan. In one radio speech, for example, Frank
Gannett appealed to Jews and to Negroes to stand against the
Roosevelt plan. "The other day," said Gannett in his radio speech,
"a barber was cutting my hair. He said to me: 'You know, Mr.
Gannett, I am deeply interested in preserving the Supreme Court.'

I asked him why. He said: 'I am a Jew, and therefore one of a minority. I realize that if it were not for the Supreme Court, I might be treated here as they treat the Jews in Germany!' " Gannett went on that "members of the colored race must feel the same, for the Supreme Court again and again has protected the rights of colored people. The Court stands as a defender of all classes, all creeds and all races."

On one occasion Sidney Hillman, the labor leader, came to Burton Wheeler and threatened him with the loss of labor's political support unless Wheeler went along with the Court plan. "If you don't go along with this," Wheeler recalled Hillman saying, "we're through." Wheeler answered by speaking of the days during World War I when a patriotic hysteria swept the country claiming persons with foreign-sounding names as its victims. Only the federal courts, Wheeler told Hillman, stood up before that hysteria. Then Wheeler continued, as he remembered it, by saying that the Supreme Court should not be tampered with because "there might be another hysteria sweeping the country. This time against your people." That last was a reference to Hillman's being Jewish.

Such appeals came at an appropriate time. Racial and religious oppression was growing. The campaign for the Presidency in 1928 by Al Smith was still well remembered with fear by many who shuddered at the hate it had unleashed because Smith was a Catholic. The violent anti-Semitism practiced in Germany had produced a favorable response in the United States. Perhaps the most popular orator in the country, even more popular than Franklin Roosevelt, was the anti-Semite, Father Charles Coughlin. Also, feeding on racial and religious discrimination, the Communists were becoming more active and greater in numbers, at least becoming loud enough to anger and frighten the businessman, who then transferred that anger to the religious and racial minorities. Still, because of the Supreme Court, saying that America is a haven for the oppressed was more than a cliché in the 1930s. The big cities were filled with persons who personally knew of the Cossack pogroms, of the knock at the door at night by the helmeted Fascist

policemen, of being caught between warring landlords. Freedom
from fear was a blessing they prized. If they did not fully understand American government, they sensed that it was the federal
judiciary that was blocking the dreaded "knock on the door" from
coming to America. The Supreme Court was a civil liberties court.
It threw out a state conviction of an Oregon man accused of being a Communist. His specific crime had been to help set up a
meeting of a Communist group. The meeting, said the Court, was
orderly and lawful, and then the Court criticized the state of Oregon for permitting such a conviction. In Georgia a Negro named
Angelo Herndon had been sentenced to a prison term of between
eighteen and twenty-four years for, in effect, being a Communist.
The Supreme Court overturned the conviction in April, 1937. (In
February, 1937, FDR was speaking with a group of youths at the
White House and asked them what they thought of his Court plan.
One youth answered: "Well, Mr. President, that depends on how
the Supreme Court decides in my case." The youth was Angelo
Herndon.) In another case, the state of Alabama had gone along
with a trumped-up rape case against nine Negroes and permitted
the nine to be sentenced to death. The Negroes' lives were spared
because of the federal courts. To even the most casual observer
of the American system it was apparent that if the Supreme Court
brought relief to people in such public disfavor, then the Court
was a bulwark on which all could depend. This sense, rather than
knowledge, that the federal courts were a barrier between the individual and the government beyond which the government must
not trespass made any attack on the Supreme Court a dangerous
one and ripe for the kind of propaganda that people like Gannett
were distributing.

The Gannett organization and the southerners in Congress with
which it worked to defeat the Court plan made a curious combination. While Gannett spoke of protecting the individual's civil
liberties—the right of free speech, of freedom from arbitrary imprisonment, and the like—against encroachment by government,
the southerners spoke of protecting the southern states against the
encroachment of individuals seeking civil rights. Senator Tom

Connally of Texas told his state legislature that although he was a personal friend of Roosevelt's, he had to oppose him on the Court plan. Said Connally:

You remember the history of that dark and dismal period after the War between the States—that cruel period that we refer to as the days of the Reconstruction. Let me remind you that the South had been disenfranchised; its Members had been expelled from Congress. Its fair fields had been ravaged by war; its slaves had been freed. The courageous soldier who had carried the banner of the Confederacy had been required to take test oaths, denied the right to hold office, denied the right to vote; and the South was stricken with suffering; and a rabid majority in the United States Congress, led by that southern hatred, enacted the most oppressive and the most rigorous laws which all the deviltries of passion and prejudice could devise for the regulation of the South. One of those laws was called the civil rights bill. What did that law provide? It provided that anybody in the South who denied to colored people the same facilities in hotels and in boarding houses, and in theaters, and trains, or in any other public assembly, should be subject to a penal offense, and either to a heavy fine or to imprisonment in the penitentiary. If you refused to place yourself upon social equality with the colored people of that time and that period, you became a felon and a lawbreaker. . . . Finally, they were able to get the case into the Supreme Court of the United States, and what did the Court do, though it was a Republican Court? It held that that act invaded the rights of the States in controlling their own internal affairs and in regulating their police power. . . . Thank God, we had a Supreme Court that said fearlessly: "Mr. Government, Mr. Congress, and Mr. President, you cannot invade the rights of the southern people; you cannot invade the rights of her private citizens; thus far can you go, and no farther."

Other southerners made similar appeals. When Carter Glass spoke over the radio against the Court plan, he first referred to Harold Ickes as one of the stalwarts behind FDR on the issue. Then Glass asked if the people of the South

know that [Ickes] recently reproached the South for providing separate public schools for the races; that he urged repeal of every statute and ordinance of segregation, that he practically committed the administration at Washington to a new force bill for the South, declaring that

not since Lincoln's day has it better been realized than now the necessity of laws to strictly enforce the three post-Civil War amendments
to the Constitution which kept the South in agony for years and re-
tarded its progress for well nigh half a century? This infuriated propa-
gandist [Ickes] for degrading the Supreme Court practically proposes
another tragic era of reconstruction for the South.

**Then, to make certain his listeners understood his point, Senator
Glass said:**

Should men of his mind have part in picking the six proposed judicial
sycophants very likely they would be glad to see reversed those decisions
of the Court that saved the civilization of the South and in spite of
the menace of passionate partisans, with their violent threats to "reorganize" the Court, prohibited the seizure and confiscation, without
pay, of the estates of private citizens. It was the Supreme Court that
validated the suffrage laws of the South which saved the section from
anarchy and ruin in a period the unspeakable outrages of which nearly
all the Nation recalls with shame.

These arguments did not represent any inconsistency on the
part of the Supreme Court. In 1937 it simply followed past practice; it protected the individual from the state, the state from the
federal government, and the rich from the poor.

This last practice, protecting the rich from the poor, remained
the primary issue about which the Court dispute revolved in these
early weeks of the duel despite the public references to civil liberties and civil rights. The federal government had so many resources
to distribute to the American people. FDR insisted that those resources be diverted to the people at the bottom of the economic
ladder. The main force against him consisted of those who objected to that revised distribution. The opposition still originated
with the business groups who believed they had the most to lose
by a more powerful Roosevelt in the White House, and by that
part of society with inherited wealth.

The Chamber of Commerce of the United States roused its
members against FDR's Court plan. Harper Sibley, the Chamber's
president, called upon "business men's organizations" to "provide
facilities for giving to their members, and all others who inquire,

accurate information as to the facts regarding allegations with respect to the Supreme Court and any of the Federal Courts." Sibley
promised that "the United States Chamber will aid its members
in supplying information, by responding promptly to all requests
sent to it." The American Bar Association joined in the opposition, devoting a full issue of its *Journal* to an attack against the
plan. "It looks like a propaganda magazine in opposition to the
President's plan," Homer Cummings complained. "After all," said
the Attorney General, "the Journal is not supposed to be a partisan publication giving only one side of a controversy." Local
chambers of commerce, trade groups, most newspapers, all the
powerful and influential organizations, came out strongly against
FDR. At a meeting February 20 of the Women's National Committee for Hands Off the Supreme Court, there were representatives of the National Society of New England Women, the
Daughters of the American Revolution, the Women's Practical
Law Association, and the New York City League of Business and
Professional Women. It almost came down to this: If one belonged
to a social, business, or professional organization, he was part of
the organized opposition.

William Allen White, in some private comments to newspaper
friends, explained the development that was taking place Majorities on election day are fine, said White, but

the day after election the middle class moves in and runs the show
through its various organizations of public expression, the newspapers,
the churches, the lodges, the clubs, the public corridors—from the
pullman's observation car on down to the filling station. The middle
class for one hundred fifty years has organized itself to rule by public
expression in these various outlets. The only way the proletariat makes
its will public is in the mob and riot which are soon suppressed and
generally remain echoes. Any President is powerless before middle
class opinion. And the sad ironic thing about the proletariat is that as
wages rise, the boys in the proletariat join the middle class and so,
until we have one long catastrophic depression which will materially
cut down the power of the middle class, no president can rely on mere
majorities to back him up in any serious fight.

Franklin Roosevelt was not aware of this analysis by White.

He probably would have agreed that the middle class, at least the upper middle class economically, was able to manipulate public opinion so that the wishes of the masses were drowned out. It was this manipulative ability of the upper middle class that FDR was fighting with his speeches, in his news conferences, and on the other public forums available to him.

Roosevelt also relied strongly for support on two groups which he had supported as President—the farmers and the unions. Their members had largely benefited under the New Deal, and Roosevelt considered it proper to expect some return. In this, however, he was to be disappointed.

Farmers were basically conservative and Republican. When Herbert Hoover was President, they did poorly, and so they supported a Democrat in 1932, although it was distasteful to them. They supported a Democrat again in 1936 because he promised more federal assistance to farmers specifically; their political and fiscal conservatism did not extend to farm policy. They were reluctant, however, to support FDR on the Court plan because it seemed to give him too much strength, more strength than the farmers needed him to have. But through their organizations they were willing to bargain with FDR—offer him support on his farm plan, through resolutions and urging their members to write members of Congress—if he would assure them of his continued support for various farm subsidies.

This situation came to a head at the end of February. Secretary of Agriculture Wallace wrote a memorandum to the White House reporting that several of the farm leaders wanted a meeting with the President. The memorandum said:

It is important that the President have in mind a reply to farm leaders bargaining for specific commitments in return for their support of judicial reform. Their tactics are to seek definite pledges of normal granary loan rates at parity, of levying processing taxes, of federal financing of needy cooperatives, and other legislative or administrative concessions. In response to such approaches, the President might say the government is seeking not for carte blanche to get any farm price or fix any wage rate that it wishes, but that it wants reasonable powers to function for the general welfare under a living Constitution sympathetically understood and administered. . . . Basically, the Supreme Court majority's insistence that agriculture is a purely local matter blocks all progress.

FDR evidently studied this memorandum carefully and understood its meaning: The farmers were demanding a trade from the Administration before giving their support on the Court plan. With a blue pencil he scrawled, "These people to come down to see me Monday." FDR was too careful a politician to affront leaders of powerful blocs by refusing to see them. Then he wrote with his blue pencil: "To serve the gen. welfare—No compromise in trade."

To every man comes a time to make a deal, to trade a little of what he thinks is right for what he considers to be the greater good, to compromise just a little with his principles and standards, to, in a popular phrase, "sell out." Such a moment had come to Franklin Roosevelt with the demand by the farmers for a trade. He turned it down.

Whatever farm support that came after that was perfunctory at best. A statement by M. W. Thatcher, chairman of the Wheat Conservation Conference, after a meeting at the White House is typical. "Farmers," said Thatcher, "as well as all other citizens, should properly assume that President Roosevelt—reelected by the greatest majority in history—is generally better informed relative to the affairs and needs of this nation than any other person. . . . We reaffirm our faith in his leadership and will give him our full support." The statement avoids endorsing the Court plan and, except for the vague "full support" phrase, does not call on farmers to back the President. They were not asked to write their congressmen, to work through their organizations, to do anything specific to help the President in his fight.

There did appear to be support from organized labor for FDR's plan. It reactivated its Nonpartisan League, an organization that had worked in 1936 to help FDR get reelected. "We have no fear of the outcome," said the League in a statement announcing it was supporting Roosevelt in the Court fight, "but the subject is of such far-reaching importance that we do not want to gamble."

William Green, president of the American Federation of Labor, announced his personal support also. Letters were sent to members of Congress telling them that the union leaders expected progressive liberal members of Congress—that is, members who would seek labor's support in their next campaign—to back the President. Still, there were problems with labor and within the labor organization that spelled trouble for FDR later.

One such trouble was burly and demanding John L. Lewis of the United Mine Workers. FDR's trouble with John L. Lewis was summed up in a two-hundred-year-old epigram which a newspaper columnist found and sent to Roosevelt. It read:

> To John I owed great obligation;
> But John unhappily thought fit
> To publish it to all the nation;
> Sure John and I are more than quit.

Lewis' union had given Roosevelt's 1936 campaign substantial assistance, financial as well as votes. After the election, Lewis had announced publicly that he expected to be paid in return, that he anticipated FDR and his Administration would back organized labor as the unions entered a troubled year in their relations with business. Obviously the New Deal was inclined to support labor unions in the fights they were having with big business, but Lewis seemed to wish to go a little further than that. His remarks indicated he wanted FDR to make the Democratic party into a Labor party. Roosevelt could not permit this to happen. He could visualize a gathering of liberal forces—he had geared his 1936 campaign to such a gathering—but such a gathering in Roosevelt's plans must include the labor leaders like Lewis as well as the wealthy businessmen like Joseph P. Kennedy, farmers and factory workers, city and rural dwellers. Only this way could the Roosevelt party be a national party. Only this way could FDR argue that he had a national mandate for his program. To make his party only an organization of the cities or only of the farmlands, only of the rich or only of the poor, only of the businessman or only of the union member, would make his party a local, a regional, a narrow-based organization. It would sever the United States into small groups, the East against the West, the North against the South, the rich against the poor. Such a proliferation would ultimately result in the death of the American political system. Because of this, FDR looked with great skepticism and concern on John L. Lewis' demands. In return, John L. Lewis in 1937 looked on Franklin Roosevelt with a growing distrust.

The difficulties that this situation as well as the situation with the farmers created for Franklin Roosevelt were not obvious at the beginning of the Court fight. They appeared later. The obvious difficulties were in Washington. They were with the Republicans, almost all the Republicans, and with a few Democrats, particularly Burton Wheeler.

When the Roosevelt plan was first announced February 5, the GOP was quick with the typical remarks that would be expected from the opposition party. "I most emphatically do not agree to packing the Supreme Court," thundered Arthur H. Vandenberg of Michigan. Said Senator Warren Austin of Vermont: "The message is, in my opinion, a most ostentatious request for power to pack the Federal Courts." The crucial question before the GOP, however, was not oratory but strategy. At a meeting between the party powers in the Senate—these were Vandenberg, William Borah, and Charles L. McNary of Oregon, the Republican leader—a decision was reached at McNary's urging to adopt a unique approach to battling FDR. The three decided that the GOP should go underground.

If opposition to FDR was believed by the public to be a Republican party position, then the great mass of the public that had voted against Republicans in 1936 would continue to be against the GOP—and for the Court plan. If the Republicans kept quiet, stayed out of the open fighting, and left the battling to the Democrats, this more than anything would convince the public that the Court duel was above partisanship. This approach was best summed up by Harold Ickes when he said: "The [GOP] strategy apparently is to let the Democrats tear each other to pieces and then for the Republicans to move in and enjoy the fruits of victory, if the President is defeated, without suffering any casualties themselves."

Writing to a businessman, William Allen White also made the point that Roosevelt's traditional enemies had to stay out of the dispute, at least as far as the public was concerned. "I hope," he said, "that the more evident representations of [Roosevelt's] economic opponents will not be too prominent in this political fight; by which I mean the Liberty League and the Du Ponts and the whole crowd. They are black beasts in the popular imagination and if they rally against the President, they are liable to make him friends instead of enemies."

So the prominent Republicans and the wealthy businessmen stayed pretty much out of the public dispute. They did supply money and assurance of negative votes in Congress, but generally they were not seen in the fight. There were a few exceptions, of course. Vandenberg could not resist the opportunity to get in a few swipes against FDR in a radio broadcast. In New York City, Senator Styles Bridges of New Hampshire denounced the plan. And one Republican, a freshman senator from Massachusetts named Henry Cabot Lodge, made one of the most convincing arguments against the plan in a radio address. "If we grant one man power to do a certain thing, we can be certain that another man who is far from good will one day use this same power," Lodge said. "We would, if we passed the present bill, establish a precedent which could be used to destroy this Republic." But largely the Republicans kept quiet. Even if it hurt some of them.

Before the Court plan had been announced, Alf Landon had agreed to address a Lincoln Day dinner of the National Republican Club in New York on February 9. He left Kansas, traveled by train for New York, and worked on his speech on the way. It was to be an attack on the Court plan. The party hierarchy understood that many Republicans wanted the chance to sound off against the Court plan. If Landon broke the GOP silence at a major occasion such as the dinner was expected to be, no Republican could be persuaded to keep quiet and the Court plan would become mired in open party politics. Landon had to be stopped.

There are several versions of what happened next. According to one account at the time, Representative Bertrand H. Snell, the House Republican leader, was dispatched to New York to dissuade Landon. "Unfortunately Landon got word of Snell's mission in advance and flew into the kind of temper any politician will fly into if you tell him that his utterances are likely to do anything but good," according to this account. It continued that two officials of the national party took over from Snell and succeeded in making their case with Landon.

According to a later version, Jouett Shouse, the head of the conservative Liberty League, called Roy Roberts, editor of the Kansas City *Star* and a friend of Landon's, to ask him to intercede. Roberts called Chicago, and when Landon arrived there to change trains, he was met by Colonel Robert R. McCormick, publisher of the Chicago *Tribune*, and "McCormick persuaded Landon to change his speech." This is Landon's version:

No one persuaded me not to make the speech. . . . As I remember, I left Topeka for New York a day or so after Mr. Roosevelt's Supreme Court proposal to make the Lincoln Day talk. . . . I reached New York the day before the dinner meeting. I had written a more or less rough draft which included an attack on Mr. Roosevelt's court plan. In Chicago and in New York, I had an opportunity to talk to some of the press and it was evident that it was best to let the Democrats carry the ball. By that time, I got some information from Washington on the Republican strategy which was, as I said, common knowledge and with which I agreed.

Landon did change his speech and deleted the attacks on the Court plan. He did not again threaten the GOP strategy. Herbert Hoover, however, was a constant threat. Almost chased out of office in 1932, Hoover wanted another opportunity to try for the Presidency. He wanted to redeem not only his personal self but also his philosophy and his approach to government. He had been making a few speeches which generally had been well received in Republican circles, and 1937 was the year to begin working toward the Republican Presidential nominating convention of 1940. He could place himself in the lead, he believed, if he could find an issue upon which to challenge Roosevelt. This had to be an issue which the people could appreciate and would be concerned by, and on which he could build a crusade. The Court plan was such an issue.

On February 20, a Saturday night, before the Union League Club in Chicago, Herbert Hoover became the first prominent Republican to deliver a major speech against the Roosevelt plan to enlarge the Court. "Mr. Roosevelt has sought many acts of Congress which lead to increase the personal power of the Executive. He has sought to more greatly centralize the government," Hoover said. Then came his nomination for the cry of the crusade: "Ladies and gentlemen, I offer you a watchword—Hands off the Supreme Court."

Hoover, however, had more than a speech. He had a plan. That same night he met with one of his close associates in the Drake Hotel at Chicago. The associate was a prominent Republican in Washington and at times acted as a Hoover agent in the nation's capital. He had taken his ailing wife to Arizona for her health but had left her to hurry and meet Hoover in Chicago at Hoover's request.

At the meeting Hoover outlined his proposal. Within a short time, he explained, Congress would approve the Hatton Sumners bill guaranteeing full retirement pay to Supreme Court justices. Hoover proposed that once that bill was law, Louis Brandeis, the dean of the liberal community, resign from the Court and then go on the radio and make a speech attacking Roosevelt and his Court plan. Such a tactic would, Hoover expected, alienate the liberal community from Roosevelt and, Hoover hoped, destroy the chances for success of the Court plan. Because talk is so cheap and plentiful in Washington, it would also be impossible for the tactic to become reality without Hoover's role as the mastermind becoming widely known.

Actually the suggestion that Brandeis resign was made on several occasions during the Court fight. Such suggestions were usually made in the context of Brandeis' sacrificing himself to protect the Court. One attorney wrote to the Justice: "It seems to me that a crowning act of your career would be your voluntary retirement along with the other of the oldest members, in the hope and with a reasonable expectation that thereby irreparable injury to the Court itself may be avoided." But these suggestions did not have the political overtones that Hoover's did.

Hoover, however, had difficulty with his proposal. His agent immediately returned to Washington and approached, not Brandeis, whom he did not know, but Justice McReynolds, whom he did know. It was an unfortunate choice. McReynolds told the agent he had no firm knowledge of Brandeis' attitude toward the Court plan but that he did believe that Brandeis opposed it. Then McReynolds explained that his relations with Brandeis were definitely not of a kind that would permit him to suggest to Brandeis that Brandeis retire and make the radio address that Hoover suggested. James McReynolds was a vicious anti-Semite who was very open in his hostility toward Jews. Brandeis was the first Jew to serve on the Supreme Court. In the twenty-one years the two men had served on the Court together they had not had a happy relationship. McReynolds suggested that the Hoover agent talk to the Chief Justice.

After first clearing it with a member of Hoover's staff, the agent then met with Hughes. The agent explained to the Chief Justice that Hoover was deeply concerned over the Roosevelt proposal and intended to do everything in his power to defeat it. The agent said that immediately after the plan had been announced Hoover called prominent Republicans and Democrats across the nation to urge them to organize against the Court plan. Hoover had gone on the radio the previous Saturday, the agent said, because the Administration had practically monopolized the radio but that Hoover's intention had been to speak not as a Republican but as a citizen and that the former Republican President regarded the matter as nonpartisan. The agent also assured the Chief Justice that Hoover wanted to cooperate with everyone involved in the opposition to the Court plan, particularly Senator Borah. Hoover visualized Borah's role as handling the debate in the Senate, the agent said, while Hoover organized the opposition outside Washington. The agent reported to Hughes that the nation's press was against the Court plan with the exception of a few newspapers in Philadelphia and New York and that the Senate count was thirty-seven senators "hostile" to the Court plan and twenty "doubtful." The agent said Hoover was convinced that the people of America would not permit the attack on the Court to succeed if they were made familiar with the real issues involved.

The Chief Justice listened attentively, and his eyes, the agent later reported to Hoover, filmed as the agent spoke of Hoover's devotion to the Supreme Court. It was then that Hoover's agent suggested that Brandeis retire and make a radio address against the Court plan. The Chief Justice responded that he could appreciate the significance of such an act but that he did not know whether Justice Brandeis was thinking in terms of retiring. Hughes recalled to the Hoover agent that there had been cases in the past when the Court, finding one of the justices sick or incapable of performing his duties, had suggested that the justice retire; but, Hughes quickly added, that situation did not exist on the current Court. Hughes said that Brandeis' health was better in 1937 than it had been when Hughes joined the Court as Chief Justice in 1930; he added that the same was true of every justice on the Court. Hughes described the suggestion that Brandeis retire as one of extreme delicacy and told the Hoover agent that he was unwilling to discuss it with Brandeis. If Brandeis was to initiate a discussion about the possibility of his retiring, the Chief Justice intimated, he might be willing to broach the matter of Brandeis' coupling his retirement with a radio attack on the Roosevelt plan, although he expressed the personal opinion that Louis Brandeis would not wish to make any such radio address. To illustrate the delicacy of the situation, the Chief Justice told the Hoover agent that what he suggested was comparable to talking with a man regarding the woman he proposed to marry.

The Hoover agent then said he was a personal acquaintance of Felix Frankfurter at Harvard. What would the Chief Justice think of the agent's writing to Frankfurter and suggesting that he urge Brandeis to retire? The Chief Justice responded that he himself would not be a party to any effort, directly or indirectly, to persuade Brandeis to retire, that the initiative for his retirement must come solely from Brandeis himself.

That ended Hoover's plan to persuade Brandeis to retire.

Hoover also was mistaken when he believed that the Republicans in Washington were interested in his intervention. To the nation he was the symbol of incompetence. To the party he was the symbol of defeat. The GOP in Washington figured Herbert Hoover was finished politically and would do more harm than good in the Court fight. This became apparent when the Hoover agent next visited William Borah.

Former President Hoover, the agent told Borah, is extremely anxious to cooperate with the Republicans in Congress and would be happy to supplement the Congressional efforts in whatever way he could. Borah responded to the Hoover agent by explaining the GOP strategy, stressing that only the Democrats could defeat the Court plan. That was why, Borah said, he and other GOP leaders were not speaking publicly about the Court plan and why Alf Landon had dropped the references to the Court plan from his New York speech. Borah also said that before Hoover had made his attack on the Roosevelt plan in his speech from Chicago Saturday night thirty-eight senators had lined up against FDR. After the speech, Borah continued, two of those thirty-eight had switched to supporting the President because they were Democrats and Hoover's speech had placed political overtones on the fight.

The Hoover agent then told Borah that Hoover had spoken out on the Court plan because up to that time the radio speeches had numbered fourteen supporting the plan but only one against, and that one negative speech had not been a forceful one. Borah said that he did not agree with those figures, that there had been more opposition than Hoover was aware of. Then the agent said that Hoover believed he had an obligation to speak out against the Court plan because, as a former President, no less as an American citizen, Hoover felt he had to make certain that the public understood he was against the plan. Borah answered that his own obligation was to promote the split within the Democratic ranks and that he wished Hoover would stay out of the fight entirely. Word of Hoover's activities would come back to the Democrats in Washington, Borah continued, and perhaps cause more Democrats to switch from opposition to support of Roosevelt.

Being squeezed out entirely was a tough blow to Herbert Hoover. He took it bitterly.

I have your letter about Borah. He obviously does not wish to cooperate in any form. His statement about the two Democrats is a typical Borah invention. The fact is, this issue will be won by an aroused public opinion and nothing else. The wobbly Democratic senators are awaiting this sound. They will respond to this alone and not to Mr. Borah's public or private arguments. Certainly he is contributing nothing to formulate such opinion. He could do so, but is as likely to duck it, just as he ducked the fight against the New Deal for the last four years. The response to that Chicago speech has already been greater than any public statement I have ever made. And that response reaches me from Democrats as well as Republicans. I do not believe at this time, however, that the proposal can be beaten—except by some rotten compromise. And when the Republicans go out to meet the 1938 elections they will be grateful that at least one Republican had the courage to speak and was not dominated by "hush hush" politicians in Washington.

Hoover's hopes of leading a crusade against the Court plan were rapidly fading. He made another attempt to place the mantle of the Republican Party on his shoulders in May of 1937 when he wrote to William Allen White in hopes that the influential midwesterner would be willing to support Hoover's drive for leadership of the GOP. Said Hoover:

It seems to me for a dozen reasons the Republican Party cannot be abandoned as a practical thing. It has to be revitalized and ought to be purged a lot. Today nobody knows what it does stand for. It is steadily and rapidly degenerating. Everywhere there is inquiry: What does it stand for? Yet no other party can be erected in time to furnish an alternative to the New Deal. If there be a strong and clean Republican Party then at least a bridge should be possible to connect two continents of righteousness.

It is certain that some time this whole American economic works is going to smash in a chaos from the artificial and crazy forces that have been put in motion. That means either the Fascist on horseback or a turn toward "Historic Liberalism." That turn will not come unless there is a party in the country with a banner up, with affirmative principles and a belief in its leadership. There is neither today.

Then Hoover came to the crux of his proposal.

So why not try to erect that banner? Why wait until party demoralization has split the sensible forces in the country into chaos as they were in Germany prior to Hitler? Thirty resolute men who will cooperate could do it. It will be disagreeable; it means saying some truths. But you and I haven't fifteen years more to go, so why not say it? I have need to talk with you. In the meantime, why do you not advertise that Colorado Springs speech [which Hoover had delivered] as a balloon to see what reaction you get?

The Hoover proposal that White send up a "balloon" was nothing more than a suggestion that White join in organizing a group to back Hoover in an attempt to regain leadership of the GOP. Perhaps it might have worked if Hoover had been able to lead the fight on the Court plan as he hoped. That would have made him a positive candidate, something more than a symbol of the GOP's drastic defeat in 1932. But he did not lead the fight on the Court plan, and the balloon did not go up. William Allen White in 1937 announced that he favored Mayor Fiorello LaGuardia of New York for the GOP Presidential nomination in 1940, saying: "When you have done laughing, remember how they laughed at Lincoln eighty years ago." Herbert Hoover was the first political casualty of the Court fight.

The whole Republican strategy of public silence, the strategy that forced Landon to change his New York speech and that worked against Hoover's attempts to use the Court plan as a personal vehicle, hinged on there being sufficient Democrats opposed to Roosevelt. There were. They came together one night at a dinner in the home of Senator Millard E. Tydings of Maryland shortly after the Court plan had been announced.

Most senators attending the dinner were southern conservatives, such as Harry Byrd of Virginia, Walter F. George of Georgia, Josiah W. Bailey of North Carolina. One man at the dinner, however, was not a southern conservative. He was a western liberal who had fought most of the southerners who now surrounded him. He was so liberal that in 1924 he had bolted the Democratic party to run as a Vice Presidential candidate with Robert LaFollette on the Progressive party ticket. This was Burton Wheeler.

The White House had quickly heard that Wheeler was deserting the President on the Court issue and had rushed emissaries to Capitol Hill to dissuade Wheeler from his course. First Charles Michelson, a publicity man for the Democratic National Committee and a Wheeler acquaintance, called Wheeler, asking to see him. Wheeler did not see him until after he had issued a statement attacking the Court plan. Burton Wheeler was making certain that the White House would not succeed in making him change his mind; he was going on record against the Court plan before talking to the White House. Michelson's message was that the President wanted Wheeler to come by for dinner. Wheeler's reply was that he had just announced his opposition to the Court plan and that he would eat elsewhere.

The next one to come down Pennsylvania Avenue from the White House to the Capitol was Tommy Corcoran. In the early New Deal years he and Wheeler had worked together on legislation and were old comrades. They had lunch at the Dodge Hotel, a graying building that served then as a Capitol hideaway. Corcoran pleaded with Wheeler to come over to the President's side. Corcoran said that FDR did not care if the traditional conservatives were against the plan, he had anticipated that, but he was concerned when a liberal such as Wheeler was so vociferous in his opposition. Corcoran then explained that if Wheeler refused to go along with FDR. the President would have to seek more support from the big city machines like New York's Tammany Hall. And, it followed logically, if FDR sought support from such organizations, he would have to listen to their advice when it came to naming the new justices. But if Wheeler supported FDR, then he would be the one who would have the President's ear when the Court appointees were named. It was this discussion which created the rumor that Wheeler could have named several of the new justices. Arthur Vandenberg said a few months later that "there probably never was a moment when Wheeler could not have dictated a compromise on five or four or three or two new justices—and I doubt not that he could have named them as well."

And so Burton Wheeler had come to the dinner at Millard Tydings' house to assume command of the forces against Roosevelt and to exhort his men to victory. When Harry Byrd expressed doubts about the chances of defeating FDR, Wheeler replied that most members of the Senate opposed FDR on the Court plan but were afraid to acknowledge that opposition because they were mercenaries, anxious for patronage and public works. Then Wheeler said, referring to the eighteen men massing against the President: "A small army that believes in principle can lick a larger mercenary army." Each member of their small group was given names of other senators to watch over, to cajole, bamboozle, threaten, seek to persuade, to take any action necessary to move a senator into the "against" column. Wheeler also talked tough. He would lead the opposition, but the others must obey his orders. They must recognize him as leader in fact as well as in name. The eighteen were willing to mass behind Wheeler. As long as he led the opposition, the fight was neither Republican versus Democrat nor conservative versus liberal. It was liberal against liberal.

Franklin Roosevelt had demonstrated he could win in duels with Republicans and with conservatives. But a duel with a liberal was another matter. The outcome could not be predicted.

Part Three

A Great Beast

7

THE DUEL in which Franklin Roosevelt entered had deep-rooted origins. When the American colonists and revolutionaries adopted the federal Constitution in March, 1789, the role of national governments was to protect the rich against the poor, the haves from the demands of the have-nots. Nations fixed taxes to soak the poor and bypass the rich. Laws were written to give the rich—the landlords, the squires, the feudal lords—whatever power they needed to thwart the will and independence of those who, because of poverty, were their subjects. Government was devoted to the preservation intact of a small clique of those of "noble" and wealthy birth. Government insured that their wealth could not be taken from them and that their status would not be weakened by a broadening of those with power. This far can you go, the government said to the poor, and no further. The American experiment attempted to break with this past. The colonialists began a revolution in what men construed to be the role of government, a revolution still not ended. But willing such a break is not the same as achieving such a break. And the achievement did not come easily. There were many attempts in the young United States to limit democracy. Voting was restricted to those of certain religious backgrounds or to those with property. The President was to be elected not by the people but by an elite group of citizens making up the electoral college and acting without regard to the popular will. Senators were chosen by devices other than the popular vote. Alexander Hamilton is said to have referred to the mass of people as "a great beast." Whether Hamilton made the remark is questioned, but the philosophy it represented was the philosophy of many Americans in the late 1700s and early 1800s.

Robert H. Jackson, an assistant attorney general during the 1937 Supreme Court fight, has written that "two kinds of power seem always in competition in our democracy; there is political power, which is the power of the voters, and there is economic power of property, which is the power of its owners." The voters did not have this political power at first. Gradually they achieved it. The electoral college lost its significance as an obstacle to the people's choice of a chief executive. More states adopted the popular vote as a means of selecting senators until finally a constitutional amendment made it universal in all the states. Religious and property restrictions to voting were abandoned.

As the mass of people, most of them of lower incomes, began to achieve power, the wealthy and propertied few sought a protector, a means of thwarting the will of the majority. Only the Supreme Court could fill this role. Unlike the President and the members of Congress, the justices on the Supreme Court are appointed rather than elected. Also they serve for life or as long as they themselves choose, not as long as the voters choose. If one economic class could control, or at least greatly influence, the selection of these judges, then that economic class controlled the nation.

This was particularly important after the Civil War, when the United States entered a great period of economic modernization and expansion. History establishes its own rules of conduct. And when the historians looked back at the decades at the close of the nineteenth century and at the opening of the twentieth, they generally agreed that the results of this modernization and expansion— the full use of American resources to make the United States into a great power—justified the actions, philosophy, and crimes of the economic monopolists.

But this economic group had too long a run unchecked and unrepentant. The stock market crash of 1929 among other things demonstrated that the men who controlled wealth in this era were also irresponsible. This same realization came to other nations at the same time, and they chose dictators to fight the privileged classes. In the United States, however, democracy remained a treasured possession and the American people decided to give it another opportunity. So they chose Franklin Roosevelt. New Deal historians argue whether the election of Roosevelt prevented a popular uprising, a revolution in fact, or whether it blocked a dictator from taking advantage of a nation turned so apathetic by poverty as no longer to care. Whichever theory is advanced, most agree that the economic revolution Roosevelt led by means of the legislative process substituted for a more violent kind. His revolution, while it did redistribute the nation's wealth, preserved the American system of government; another kind of revolution could have destroyed that system.

At first, because of the almost complete breakdown of the country's economic system, the wealthy supported Roosevelt. Once the system began to operate again, however, they opposed him. In a 1936 campaign speech, Roosevelt described the switch this way: "In the summer of 1933, a nice old gentleman wearing a silk hat fell off the end of a pier. He was unable to swim. A friend ran down the pier, dived overboard and pulled him out; but the silk hat floated off with the tide. After the old gentlemen had been revived, he was effusive in his thanks. He praised his friend for saving his life. Today, three years later, the old gentleman is berating his friend because the silk hat was lost."

This "nice old gentleman" relied on the Supreme Court to protect him from Roosevelt. The Court's job, as it had developed, had been to exempt business from any interference either by federal, state, or local government. In 1895, for example, the Court had ruled against the federal government, which was trying to break up a sugar trust that controlled almost all refining of sugar. Although the product, the sugar, crosses many state lines, the Court held that the trust was not involved in interstate commerce because the specific refining process did not require passage across a state line. The impact of that decision was to make the federal government helpless before the power of the trusts and the monopolies.

Ten years earlier the Court had knocked down an income tax

that had been imposed by the Congress on incomes over $4,000. The Court argued then that "the present assault on capital is but the beginning. It will be but the stepping-stone to others, larger and more sweeping." One justice, David J. Brewer, in 1893 warned the wealthy against "the black flag of anarchism, flaunting destruction of property . . . inviting a redistribution of property. . . . Here there is no monarch threatening to trespass upon the individual. The danger is from the multitude—the majority, with whom is the power." The Court continued as the friend of capital; for example, it struck down a state minimum wage law in 1923.

The wealthy and propertied class understood correctly that the mass of people was demanding a redistribution of wealth, but this class did not understand that a powerful tide of history made such a redistribution necessary. It would come either through peaceful means or through violence. Those with wealth believed they could stand, King Canute-like, before that tide and force back the trust-busting of Theodore Roosevelt and the "New Freedom" of Woodrow Wilson. Their instrument was the Supreme Court. When William Howard Taft left the White House after his 1912 defeat by the liberal Woodrow Wilson, he said to newsmen that above all other things, he was most proud of having named six of the nine members of the Supreme Court. "And I have said to them," Taft reportedly commented, "damn you, if any of you die, I'll disown you." The meaning of this remark is that the conservative, wealthy forces in the nation which had been represented in Washington by Taft now were relying on the Taft-appointed Court to look after their interests. It also meant that the justices on the Court were obligated, if at all possible, to stay on the Court while a liberal was President so that he would not have the opportunity to change the political philosophy of the Court.

The first appointment Wilson made to the Court was that of James McReynolds, who proved a conservative. The second was Louis Brandeis, who so shocked the business and banking communities in the United States that they launched a massive if unsuccessful campaign to have the Senate reject his nomination. Wilson probably would not have had the opportunity to make a third appointment to the Court, that of John Hessin Clarke, except that Justice Charles Evans Hughes resigned to accept the GOP Presidential nomination in 1916 to run against Wilson. During the four years of his second term, Woodrow Wilson did not make any appointments to the Court. The justices were holding on, hoping that a representative of the wealthy and propertied class would occupy the President's chair after the 1920 election and again make "correct" appointments.

William Howard Taft spelled this out very clearly in an article in the *Yale Law Review* in 1920. Taft wrote that Wilson "has made three appointments to the Supreme Court. He is understood to be greatly disappointed in the attitude of the first of these [McReynolds]. . . .The other two [Brandeis and Clarke] represent a new school of constitutional construction, which if allowed to prevail, will greatly impair our fundamental law." Taft continued: "Four of the incumbent justices are beyond the retiring age of seventy, and the next President will probably be called upon to appoint their successors." Now came the warning to the rich. "There is no greater domestic issue in this election," said Taft, "than the maintenance of the Supreme Court as the bulwark to enforce the guarantee that no man shall be deprived of his property without due process of law."

The next President after Wilson, Warren G. Harding, in three years named four members to the Supreme Court, including Taft himself as Chief Justice. And it was a Court well stacked for the conservatives.

In the Sunday, May 30, 1937, issue of *The New York Times Magazine* George Norris wrote of this situation. Norris, the senior senator from Nebraska, was an old liberal who chose to be known as an "Independent" rather than as either a Republican or Democrat. His comments came at the height of the Court fight. "Monopoly, special privilege, the interests of predatory selfishness," wrote Norris, "have lost their old commanding influence at the White House and Capitol. They are making their last stand in the Federal Courts. There, too often they have their way."

Because of this background and historic role of the Supreme

Court as the defender of the rich, Franklin Roosevelt was extremely suspicious of the Court. In 1932 Benjamin N. Cardozo of the Court of Appeals in New York State, the state's highest court, was named to the United States Supreme Court. Roosevelt, then governor of New York, made a remark to the effect that New York's Court of Appeals outranked the United States Supreme Court. He was referring to the quality of their members. Some newspapers immediately criticized the Roosevelt comment. FDR did not respond publicly to the criticism but wrote a note to Cardozo in which he said: "I was amused by the editorial call-down I received in one of the New York papers for daring to intimate that the Court of Appeals outranks the august body which you are about to join. I stick to my guns, although a few more appointments like yours will bring the balance even again."

During the 1932 Presidential campaign FDR did not hesitate to make clear his feelings toward the Court. He made a speech in which he spoke of the "Four Horsemen" of Republican leadership. These were "destruction, delay, deceit and despair." Then he went on to say: "After March 4, 1929, the Republican Party was in complete control of all branches of the federal government—the Executive, the Senate, the House of Representatives, and I might add for good measure, the Supreme Court as well." The reference to the Supreme Court was a last-minute addition, made personally by FDR. The morning after the speech was delivered, James Byrnes visited the Presidential candidate in his railroad car. Byrnes had helped prepare the speech and had been surprised by the reference to the Court. "I know what you are going to say before you say it," FDR quickly said, as Byrnes recalled it. "What I said last night about the judiciary is true," Roosevelt continued, "and whatever is in a man's heart is apt to come to his tongue— I shall not make any explanations or apology for it!"

This association of the Supreme Court with the GOP in 1932 should not have been completely surprising. Charles Evans Hughes, the Chief Justice, had been the GOP Presidential candidate only sixteen years earlier. Between his defeat then and his appointment as Chief Justice in 1930 he had been associated through his law practice with many of the wealthy businessmen who made up the backbone of the Republican party. During FDR's first term there were Republicans who considered Charles Evans Hughes's role as a Republican to be far from ended. During the "one hundred days" at the beginning of the New Deal, when Roosevelt legislative proposals were swamping Congress, one Republican "suggested to Bert Snell, the House minority leader, that Eastern Republican congressmen meet and plan a course of opposition to Administration measures. But Snell replied that he had consulted with party leaders Charles Evans Hughes and Charles D. Hilles, whose advice was to let things ride as they are, that the tide has not turned enough so that the leaders in the Republican party can afford to say much publicly relative to the President's program."

That justices of the Supreme Court indulged in partisan politics did not surprise Franklin Roosevelt. He assumed they were politicians. Part of this stems from the manner in which federal judges are selected. Senator Henrik Shipstead of Minnesota criticized this selection process when he said in 1937 that "I think there should be a change in the method of appointing judges. . . . Political influence and economic interests have had their finger in the appointment of Supreme Court justices. No reasonable man will deny that who knows the history of the Court."

There was a second reason why FDR was not surprised that Supreme Court justices engaged in politics. There was a belief in the United States, which FDR did not share, that the Constitution is a document of law. This is erroneous. There is very little "law" in the Constitution. It is a document of politics. It describes how men can join together politically to create laws. This is its main purpose; the Constitution places very little restriction on what laws these men can enact. And even those restrictions are vaguely worded so that they can be interpreted according to the pressures of the time.

Because he had this kind of understanding of the Constitution, FDR naturally assumed that the Supreme Court, one of its creations, as were the Presidency and the Congress, was also a political organization. That concept, sophisticated then, has become more accepted. Some years after the Court fight, one authority on the Supreme Court said that if the question is asked should not the Court "follow some certain body of rules called Constitutional Law the answer is that the Law as so conceived is a myth, it does not exist, and hence the Court, in order to function at all, must make law rather than simply follow it. Therefore, it must make what are bound to be, in a sense, political decisions."

Roosevelt came to Washington in 1933 hoping that "I can have at least in part the same type of delightful relations with the Supreme Court which I had with the Court of Appeals in Albany." He even made some efforts early in his first term to enter into a consulting arrangement with the Court. Occasionally an FDR aide chatted with a justice informally or consulted with a justice about a pending executive agency appointment. By tradition and common sense the Court declines to give advisory opinions on pending legislative proposals; a proposal pending can be far different from the proposal that is finally enacted. Also an attorney challenging a legislative act before the Court can present arguments that had not occurred to the justices. Because of this, the Court did not respond well to the FDR overtures, as feeble as they were. Members of the Court, however, when it pleased them, were not above giving an advisory opinion or two. Frances Perkins, Secretary of Labor in the New Deal, tells of having a chat with Justice Harlan Fiske Stone in 1934 when a Social Security system was still being developed. Miss Perkins expressed concern to the Justice that a system ever could become law because "your Court tells us what the Constitution permits." Miss Perkins recalls that Stone answered back in a whisper: "The taxing power of the Federal Government, my dear; the taxing power is sufficient for everything you want and need." The Social Security system was developed with financing by a special tax, as Stone suggested, rather than out of general funds.

In addition to his understanding of the Court as a political organization, FDR also believed it necessary for the three branches of government—the executive, the legislative, and the judiciary—to work together if government was going to succeed. He said to a friend in 1936 that "in certain fields there must be a guiding or a restraining hand of government because of the very nature of the specific field. The British power network of gridiron is a good example—production, transmission and distribution owned by many small operators, private and municipal, yet tied together with Government assistance and supervision. But, then, the Britishers do not everlastingly rush to the Supreme Court but instead sit round the table with the Government in good faith—and get results."

Each of the three branches of government can thwart the will of the other two. The Congress can refuse to pass a President's program, and a President can veto bills passed by Congress. A President can refuse to obey orders of the Supreme Court as Thomas Jefferson, Andrew Jackson, and Abraham Lincoln did. The Congress can except certain of its legislation from review by the Supreme Court as it did in one instance. And the federal courts, if they choose, can delay the implementation of a Presidential and Congressional program through injunctions and the declaration that the program is unconstitutional. The idea of such a delay is to prevent the program from moving from a proposal to an actuality until such time as a new and politically different administration comes into office and reverses that program. This is what the Supreme Court was doing in the 1930s. A favorite joke among newsmen at the time was: "All you need to do to scare the wits out of any administration leader is to creep up behind him and whisper, 'Injunction.' "

From 1790 until 1930 the Supreme Court had overruled only sixty acts of Congress, but once the New Deal came into power it stepped up the pace. In the four years of FDR's first term it declared twelve such acts void, including five in one year. To Administration people, the work of the Court caused genuine concern over whether the country could be governed. The "hot oil" case, one of the first New Deal laws declared void by the Supreme Court, quickly raised the problem. Congress gave power to the President to regulate the amount of oil one state could ship to another. The purpose was to limit production in order to keep the price level; in effect, to save the industry from destroying itself by overproduction. The industry had been unable to regulate itself, and the federal legislation was considered properly within Washington's constitutional power to regulate interstate commerce. The Court said, however, that Congress did not have the right to delegate to the President the detailed jurisdiction over the oil industry. The decision meant the legislative branch would have to administer such industries itself, something it was incapable of doing.

Even the Court, as much as it hated the New Deal, realized it could not oppose FDR completely. One issue did indeed involve whether the United States would continue as a nation. The issue concerned money. Paper currency is simply paper; it has no value in itself. It assumes a value when the governments that issue it promise to redeem the paper for a certain amount of a valuable commodity, such as gold or silver. In the wake of the 1929 depression many nations devalued their currency—said they would redeem their paper currency for less of whatever valuable commodity they used to back that paper. With Roosevelt in office, the United States did the same thing: reduced the amount of gold needed to back each paper dollar. This brought American currency more in line with foreign currency. The British pound, for example, then was worth approximately five American dollars. If the British devalued and the Americans did not, this would be the situation: If an American sold a product in England for ten pounds, he would have the paper equivalent of fifty dollars. But because the British had cut back on the amount of gold backing the pound, the American could only redeem those ten pounds for, perhaps, twenty-five dollars worth of gold. However, if a British merchant sold a product in the United States for fifty dollars, he could redeem those fifty dollars for fifty dollars in gold, then exchange that gold in England for twenty British pounds.

There was a catch to devaluing the American dollar, however. Many American contracts, mortgages, personal loans, and bonds had gold clauses specifying that payments be made in gold or its equivalent. A holder of a railroad bond, for example, said his bond promised that he would be paid $22.50 in gold. After the American dollar was devalued, the bondholder claimed he should receive $38.10 in paper money to have the equivalent of $22.50 in gold. That was actually the case argued before the Supreme Court. If the bondholder had won, then every debtor would have had to pay back almost twice as much in dollars as he had borrowed. To prevent this, Congress had passed a law declaring the gold clauses null and void. Congress acted within an old legal tradition that public laws preempt private contracts. A person, for example, cannot enter into a contract agreeing to make himself a slave even if he wishes to; federal law does not permit slavery. The gold clause case was important, perhaps the most important case to come before the Supreme Court in the 1930s. If the government lost and the gold clauses were upheld, Americans would be earning devalued money but paying debts with fully valued money. The economy simply could not take that blow. The Court understood this and, for that reason, grudgingly invalidated the gold clauses.

Still there were many fears that the decision would go the other way. In January, 1935, a month before the decision came down, Homer Cummings and Harold Ickes, as well as Roosevelt, talked about launching an attack on the Court if the Court did not find for the government. The day of the decision itself, February 18, 1935, was one of high nervousness on the part of Administration officials. Joseph P. Kennedy, then chairman of the Securities and Exchange Commission, arrived at his office at nine o'clock in the morning and quickly called a meeting of the commission to decide if the stock market should be ordered closed. The consensus of the commission was to wait and see how the Court acted. The meeting broke up then until noon.

Next Kennedy arranged to have an open telephone line from the marshal's office at the Supreme Court to his office and then another open line from his office to the White House so the decision could be flashed to FDR almost instantaneously. A few minutes before noon, when the Court was scheduled to begin its session that day, FDR's private secretary called Joe Kennedy "and in a very serious tone announced that since it was a very nice day the President had decided to take a nice, long automobile ride and would return sometime later in the afternoon or evening and was sure that everything would be well handled." When Kennedy realized the secretary was joking, he laughed. A few minutes later Kennedy heard from an aide at the Court building that there was no question but that the gold decision was coming down that day. "The marshal in charge of the Court," Kennedy reported he was informed, "had a little bun on and everything looked like it was getting started in the right direction."

The Court's decision was for the Administration. It killed the gold clauses in private contracts. In addition to being marked by a decidedly unfriendly tone toward the New Deal, the decision was also by a five-to-four vote. If one member of the Court had switched to a "nay" vote, the nation's economy would have been destroyed. The delicate balance in the Court was apparent to the Administration.

Three months later, in May, 1935, the balance did shift the other way. Congress had passed the Railroad Retirement Act, which had the effect of the government's establishing a compulsory pension system for railroad employees. By a five-to-four decision the Court ruled the act unconstitutional. To Cummings the split indicated "such a marked cleavage in the Supreme Court that it may be, and probably is, a forecast of what we may expect with reference to almost any form of social legislation the Congress may enact." Cummings told FDR, "This is a terrific handicap and brings up again, rather acutely, matters we have previously discussed, including a proposed Constitutional amendment." The talk within the Administration in 1935 about attacking the Court was not yet serious, however. The need to act had not yet overcome the reluctance to do battle with the Supreme Court.

There was another factor in that Railroad Retirement decision that turned out to be even more significant than the decision itself. In the majority decision striking down the act, the Court went beyond the specific law before it to say that Congress could not legislate in the area of compulsory pensions. This suggested that at a future time the Court would rule against any pension or social security program. It also did something more. Because a decision by the Supreme Court becomes a part of constitutional law and is binding on other judges and future generations, the Court traditionally speaks in the most narrow confines it can. It prefers, for example, to decide a case on a technical point of law rather than to hand down a decision that will become a constitutional edict. But with the railroad case the Court overcame its previous reluctance to attack the whole concept of government-regulated and compulsory pensions. Clearly the Court was saying that it was placing the New Deal under legal siege.

If there were any doubts that the conflict was underway they were resolved three weeks later on May 28, 1935—the day that became known to New Dealers as "Black Monday." The Court that day struck down three acts of the New Deal, including one decision that was construed as a personal affront to Roosevelt rather than an attack on his philosophy. In the 1920s the Supreme Court had upheld the right of a President to remove from office a person holding a Presidential appointment. With that as a precedent, FDR sought to remove a man named William Humphrey from the Federal Trade Commission. Humphrey appealed, and the case went to the Supreme Court. So sure was the Administration of victory that Stanley Reed, the new solicitor general, personally presented the government's case before the Court. This was in line with an old custom that a new solicitor general select an easy case as the first in which he represents the federal government so that he will begin his term as the government's trial lawyer with a victory. The Court, however, ruled against FDR. Some New Dealers claim this decision made Roosevelt more angry than any other decision. It certainly angered Stanley Reed.

The Court, on "Black Monday," also struck down a law designed to assist farmers in danger of having their farms foreclosed. And then it declared the National Recovery Administration unconstitutional. This was the NRA of the famous Blue Eagle. Under this law industries "voluntarily" formed codes of conduct and operation governing production, selling, and price setting. As with the "hot oil" cases, the purpose was to prevent one member of an industry from actions that could drive prices down or undercut a competitor. The NRA, with its members proudly flying their Blue Eagle flags, had been widely welcomed by American business at the beginning of the New Deal. But as business conditions improved, the larger concerns became disenchanted with the government regulations which seemed designed to help the small companies and the small stores.

Without the NRA to establish codes, FDR envisioned an economic anarchy. Two days after the decision, in an "off-the-record" session with newsmen, he spoke about this possibility, and his words revealed much about who he believed needed and should have government protection. He told the reporters:

Well, if I were going to write the story—I am afraid you are going to get something now, if I were going to write the story I would write it something like this: The spot news is not in Washington!

The newsmen looked up at him surprised. He continued:

Now, I know what a difficult spot that puts you in, all of you, because you are supposed to represent spot news. The real spot news in the present situation is what is happening as a result of the Supreme Court decision in every industry and in every community in the United States. That is the spot news. I have, for instance, a good many resolutions that have come in. Here is one, right in front of me, that came in to me ten minutes ago. It is from the Cotton Textile Industry Committee resolving that they recommend that the cotton textile industry make no change in the conduct of its business and urge the industry to accept this as a general policy. . . .

What are we going to do, let us say, in the cotton textile industry if some mill starts lengthening out its hours and cutting its minimum wages? That is putting it rather squarely up to the cotton textile industry and it all comes back to the same old thing. Ninety per cent of them, as I said a couple of years ago, want to play the game on the level. But what happens to their playing the game on the level if ten per cent of them go out and hit below the belt? You have a coal situation where everything has been going along pretty well for two years; you did not have any labor troubles and you won't have them if the present coal code provisions are carried on. What would you do as a miner, if your individual company, the individual company you are working for, went out and broke the present coal code procedure?

In other words, it all comes squarely back to spot news outside of Washington. What is going to happen and what is happening today? Are there any of the garment trade people in the city of New York who cut their wages from twelve dollars minimum to eight dollars today? That is where your spot news is. Are there any factories in New York or anywhere else this morning that said to the girls, "Instead of going home at five o'clock this afternoon, we have a lot of rush work on. You are going to stay until nine o'clock tonight." What are the girls going to do? Are they going to walk out at five o'clock and lose their jobs? That is where your spot news is for the next few days in this country. That is the way I would write the story.

Franklin Roosevelt believed that the majority of the people should have the right to use their government to protect themselves against the unscrupulous few. The decision of the Supreme Court knocking down the NRA upheld, as far as FDR was concerned, the unscrupulous few. Roosevelt said:

The issue is going to be whether we go one way or the other. Don't call it right or left; that is just first-year high school language, just about. It is not right or left—it is a question for national decision on a very important problem of government. We are the only nation in the world that has not solved that problem. We thought we were solving it, and now it has been thrown straight in our faces and we have been relegated to the horse-and-buggy definition of interstate commerce.

Roosevelt was convinced that federal legislation, the kind knocked down by the Supreme Court, was essential. The next month he said to a friend: "A very long experience convinces me of two things. First, if ninety per cent of an industry honestly works for social betterment and ten per cent pulls the other way, we get nowhere without some form of government enforcement. Secondly, if forty states go along with adequate legislation and eight do not—again we get nowhere!" The President realized then also that his program's future lay entirely in the hands of the Supreme Court.

Administration officials tried to make this clear, that the Supreme Court held all the trump cards. Also the officials suggested that the situation could not be permitted to continue in that manner: there must be a new deal. Homer Cummings, for example, told the Association of the Bar of the City of New York in December, 1935:

The absolute theory of one and only one rational construction of the Constitution renders impossible any proper understanding of the nature of our American constitutional method and of the functions of our Supreme Court. With us, the people have established a Constitution which is supreme over all the acts of government, legislative, executive, and judicial alike, because it is the highest expression of the popular will. Of necessity, it employs broad language which leaves a wide area for legitimate differences of opinion. Within this area of debate all voices must be heard.

The same day, Cummings told an assistant in the Justice Department that if the Court continued to knock down New Deal legislation "no doubt there will be strong pressure in many quarters for a Constitutional amendment." A few days later FDR discussed the matter with his cabinet, a discussion that made clear that, seven months after "Black Monday," a counterattack against the Court was seriously under consideration. At this session FDR talked about specific methods of fighting the Court. One was increasing its membership, the second was meeting each specific situation with a constitutional amendment, or, third, passing a single amendment that would somehow curtail the Court's power. Whether such a counterattack would be necessary depended on whether the Court continued to act against the New Deal.

The answer came less than two weeks later, when the Supreme Court struck down the Agriculture Adjustment Act. The AAA bolstered the farmers' income by regulating their products. The farmers were paid for reducing their crops or for other measures with money collected by a tax on the processing of farm products. The Court said AAA was "a scheme for purchasing with Federal funds submission to Federal regulation of a subject reserved to the states." The decision was a blow to the Administration, which interpreted the decision as destroying its chances to improve farm income. The farmers then were purchasing from and selling to industrial monopolies. The prices that the farmers paid for their raw goods as well as the prices they were paid for their final products were set administratively by a small group of businessmen without regard to laws of supply and demand. The farmers could not deal with this situation individually. If one farmer refused to sell his crops at below-cost prices, another would succumb to financial pressures and do so. Only the government, the New Dealers believed, could give the farmers the economic leverage they needed. If the government stood ready to purchase the farmers' crops at a fair price, the private purchasers had to meet that government price if they wanted to buy any farm goods; otherwise the farmers would sell everything to the government. That had been the purpose of the Agriculture Adjustment Act which the Supreme Court struck down in January, 1936.

That decision also made more public the split developing within the Supreme Court. The Court is made up of nine men who are no greater than men can be. When a man comes to the Court he brings with him the pride and the prejudice from his past, the philosophy and the ambition of his present, and the knowledge, perhaps the fear, that the future will remember him as part of its history. Once on the Court he is thrown into legal combat with eight other men, equally knowledgeable and equally determined. That there are splits and animosities within the Court is not surprising. And because the same members sit on the Court for many years these splits and animosities grow deeper and more vitriolic.

One bloc within the Supreme Court was made up of archconservatives. This consisted of James McReynolds, a member of the Court for twenty-two years in 1936; George Sutherland, who had been on the Court fourteen years; Pierce Butler, who came on the Court the year after Sutherland; and Willis Van Devanter, the senior member of the Court in tenure; he had joined it in 1911 and, in 1936, was serving his twenty-fifth year as an associate justice. They were called the "Four Horsemen," and they were united by many things, principally, however, their political conservatism, their consuming respect for wealth and property, and their distrust of the people.

A former Wall Street lawyer, McReynolds was the most churlish of the four. A book critical of the Supreme Court in the mid-1930s called him the Court's "greatest human tragedy." His tragedy was that he could not relate to—not really even associate with—other persons. When Hughes returned to the Court in 1930, McReynolds wrote him: "As you well know, you are returning to slavery." But the slavery for McReynolds was self-imposed. He was a victim of his prejudices. The Chief Justice, for example, had to divide the eight associate justices into two groups for dinner parties so that McReynolds did not meet socially the two Jews on the Court, Brandeis and Benjamin Cardozo. McReynolds' anti-Semitism was not an attitude of disdain but, instead, an open practice of contempt. But McReynolds did not save his discourtesies for Jews alone. At a Washington dinner once, where President Roosevelt was guest of honor, McReynolds broke protocol and exhibited great discourtesy to the institution of the Presidency by deliberately turning his back as Franklin Roosevelt left the room. A bachelor then in his mid-seventies, McReynolds had fashioned a successful career out of incompetence. As a young lawyer moving between Tennessee and Wall Street, McReynolds was passed along by his superiors, who wished to lose him to someone else. That, in fact, is how he became a Supreme Court justice. In 1914 Woodrow Wilson believed the worst mistake of his administration had been the naming of McReynolds as Attorney General. To get rid of him, Wilson appointed him to the Supreme Court.

Willis Van Devanter had his personal difficulties. He had an affliction described as "pen paralysis," which made it impossible for him to write decisions. This writing of decisions is the most time-consuming and arduous work the Court has. If one justice does not carry a reasonable share of the work load, then his work must be divided among the other eight. This is what happened to Van Devanter's work; the other eight justices did it. They were courteous about it and kind to Van Devanter. But he was not being fair to his fellow justices, and he refused to acknowledge his unfairness by resigning. The second oldest man on the Court, three years younger than Brandeis, Van Devanter had been a lawyer for the railroads. Through personal friends who also happened to be affiliated, formally or informally, with the wealthy interests that controlled the railroads, he was boosted up the judicial ladder until he reached the Supreme Court in 1911. In his years on the Court he was known as a consistent conservative.

Pierce Butler also was a former railroad lawyer, elevated to the Supreme Court because the powers that greatly influenced the Harding Administration in 1923 wanted a conservative, a "businessman's judge" on the Court. Like McReynolds, Butler was an anti-Semite—he joined with McReynolds in appealing to Herbert Hoover in 1932 not to "afflict the Court with another Jew" when Hoover was about to appoint Cardozo. But Butler kept his prejudices more private than McReynolds did. This was because Butler considered keeping the Court conservative more important than keeping it non-Jewish. He was the salesman for the Four Horsemen, the one always trying to convert other members to the conservatism of the Horsemen.

George Sutherland, the last of the Four Horsemen, was a westerner and a product of the old frontier, as were Van Devanter and Butler. A senator in the First World War period who impressed a colleague named Warren G. Harding, Sutherland assisted Harding's 1920 Presidential campaign (when Harding ran against the Democratic ticket of James M. Cox and Franklin D. Roosevelt). After Harding was elected, he paid off his political debt to Sutherland by appointing him to the Supreme Court. There Sutherland quickly became one of the apostles of economic conservatism. It was he who in 1923 wrote the opinion striking down a minimum wage law, saying the fact that "the employe needs to get a prescribed sum of money to insure her subsistence, health and morals" was an "extraneous circumstance."

Opposing these Four Horsemen was a tight bloc of three justices. Led by Louis Brandeis, it also included Cardozo and Harlan Fiske Stone. A tall, thin, slightly stooped man with unruly locks of gray hair falling over his forehead, Louis Brandeis ranks with Oliver Wendell Holmes as among America's greatest men of law in the first half of the twentieth century. In his "Brandeis briefs,"

Louis Brandeis engulfed his opposition with facts and statistics about the social problems involved in the case being argued. Many years later a Supreme Court scholar said of Louis Brandeis: "His emphasis on the factual, the pragmatic, was one of Justice Brandeis' great contributions. He related to reality rather than 'sacred principles.' The early Courts referred to previous decisions, rarely to nonlegal scholars and law review articles. It is now commonplace to refer to these sources. That is essentially a Brandeis technique." This attitude of Brandeis—that one should consider things as they exist when determining how things should be—stayed with him as a justice on the Supreme Court. He was not always with the New Deal, but he led in acknowledging that government must change as people change, if the government is to continue as the servant of the people.

Benjamin Cardozo was his ally. But where Louis Brandeis had been the crusader before joining the Court, actually the flamboyant lawyer, a kind of "great mouthpiece" for social welfare causes, Cardozo was a shy, withdrawn person who established his reputation as a legal scholar rather than as a Sir Galahad of the courtroom. His scholarship was such, however, that he was one of the most respected jurists in the nation when in 1932 Herbert Hoover needed to appoint a replacement to the Court for Oliver Wendell Holmes. The Cardozo appointment was controversial for several reasons. He was the second Jew on a Court which, until Brandeis' appointment, never had a Jew. Also, along with Chief Justice Hughes and Harlan Fiske Stone, Cardozo was a New Yorker and three men from a single state on the Court at one time was unique. Still, his reputation was such that his appointment went through without difficulty.

Harlan Fiske Stone, the third member of the liberal bloc, was an anomaly. A Republican who had served as Attorney General in Calvin Coolidge's cabinet, Stone had been a close friend of Herbert Hoover's. He was considered to be as safe a conservative as the Court could have. His background included a correct Wall Street firm in which he associated closely with the moguls of American finance in the early 1900s, the right brand of Republican politics, plus the deanship at Columbia University's law school. But Stone had strayed on occasion. When he was Attorney General he had turned the Justice Department's Bureau of Investigation over to a young lawyer named John Edgar Hoover with the directive that Hoover take the bureau out of politics and put it into honest police work. In the 1920s, when political liberals became the victims of red-baiting, Stone often had sided with the liberals. Once on the Court, he demonstrated firmly that liberalism was not limited to Democrats.

The remaining two justices were swing men. These were Charles Evans Hughes and Owen J. Roberts. Because Hughes had been so identified with the Republican party and conservatism during his career, his appointment as Chief Justice in 1930 produced a violent reaction from the Democrats. They were not strong enough then to block his appointment, however. And he did surprise them a little. When he realized how the New Deal was reacting to the tone of the Court's decisions, he had begun to move toward the liberal side. Apparently he envisioned his role as that of peacemaker, as preventing the Court from moving too far to the left or right.

Roberts, however, was a disappointment to the liberals. When he was appointed in 1930, the Democrats remembered him as the forceful and honest prosecutor of the Teapot Dome scandals, which had shaken the Republican party in the 1920s. They forgot that he was basically a Philadelphia Mainline lawyer and his interests lay largely with the wealthy. For his first few years on the Court he seemed uncertain of just what he wanted to do, of how he wanted to vote. This was most noticeable in 1936 prior to the Republican convention to name a Presidential candidate. There was much talk of various candidates, including the suggestion that Owen Roberts be drafted for the nomination by the party from the Court as Charles Evans Hughes had been drafted twenty years earlier. It was a suggestion encouraged by Roberts' friends and members of his family. It was during this time that his philosophy, as expressed in his Court opinions and votes, seesawed from the liberal to the conservative side. Finally, as the political suggestions grew louder, his philosophy became more in line with what was considered the philosophy of the Republican party. Roberts became the fifth horseman, riding with McReynolds, Van Devanter, Butler, and Sutherland, turning the conservative bloc into a majority.

Nearly two decades after Owen Roberts' brush with politics he himself commented on the hazards to those Supreme Court justices who were subjected to political pressure. In 1954 he said:

They have had in the back of their minds a possibility that they might get the nomination for President. Now, that is not a healthy situation because, however strong a man's mentality and character, if he has this ambition in his mind it may tinge or color what he does, and that is exactly what the Founding Fathers wanted to remove from the minds of the Supreme Court, to make them perfectly free knowing that there was no more in life for them than the work of the Court. I happen to have a personal knowledge of what that pressure is like, for twice ill-advised but enthusiastic friends of mine urged me to let my name go up as a candidate for President while I was on the Court. Of course, I turned a hard face on that thing. I never had the notion in my mind.

That a justice's philosophy eventually becomes a consuming passion with him should not be surprising. The men who sit on the Supreme Court of the United States sit in an insulated world above other men. Attorneys wishing to argue a case approach them only with their permission. The lawyers speak only as long as the justices permit. In the Supreme Court's conference room, a large room with American white oak paneling, there are nine chairs at the table in the center of the room in which the justices sit alone for their weekly conference. The doors, three inches thick, and the venetian blinds covering the full length of the three windows effectively shield the nine men from the clamor of the public. Here in the conference room they are free to decide cases without anything to interfere with their philosophical approach. The outside world cannot enter. The justices are protected from the alien thought, the disturbing suggestion, the upsetting picture, the anguished cry. The "Four Horsemen" demonstrated their separation from the real world in a dissent written in 1934. The state of Minnesota was providing relief for debtors, and the justices objected, saying:

The present exigency is nothing new. From the beginning of our existence as a nation, periods of depression, of industrial failure, of financial distress, of unpaid and unpayable indebtedness, have alternated with years of plenty. The vital lesson that expenditure beyond income begets poverty, that public or private extravagance, financed by promises to pay, either must end in complete or partial repudiation or the promises be fulfilled by self-denial and painful effort, though constantly taught by bitter experience, seems never to be learned.

Although the words are heavy with morality, they are empty of an awareness of what had happened to create the debt. The words ignore that the individual seeking relief had been not a profligate but a victim of a society and an economy that he could neither influence nor control. An important role of government is to construct a society and economy stimulating an individual's growth and development. When government ignores that role, as the Four Horsemen suggested it do, then it fails in its responsibility.

The drama of the philosophical struggle between the two blocs within the Supreme Court rarely was exposed to public view. The separate opinions masked the cleavage in dull legal terminology. But on occasion the dullness was ripped away. It happened in the Agriculture Adjustment Act decision. Prior to that case the Court had upheld the right of New York State to establish prices for the sale of milk. Justice McReynolds disagreed, saying price fixing by any level of government would destroy the *laissez-faire* system of economy that he believed businessmen practiced in America. In his dissenting opinion McReynolds said: "Plainly, I think, this Court must have regard to the wisdom of the enactment. At least, we must inquire concerning its purpose and decide whether the means proposed have reasonable relation to something within legislative power—whether the end is legitimate, and the means appropriate."

In all of the duel between the Supreme Court and Franklin Roosevelt there was perhaps no more arrogant statement than those words of James McReynolds. Not the Court but the people through their elected representatives determine the wisdom of legislation. The Court determines whether the legislation is constitutional, that is, whether it is consistent with the American political structure. That is the theory. In fact, as FDR well knew, the Court often judged legislation on whether the justices thought the acts wise. Years before the New Deal, a Supreme Court justice told a law school class: "I want to say to you young gentlemen that if we don't like an act of Congress, we don't have much trouble to find ground for declaring it unconstitutional." However, McReynolds' dissent in the New York case was an open flouting of the political system. It was a public declaration that the Court should be a superlegislature. The Court's role, as McReynolds seemed to interpret it, was to determine if legislation was good or bad and not only whether it fitted into the constitutional structure. Never before had a justice of the Supreme Court so openly called on the Court to usurp the role of the Congress and the President.

Other members of the Court were aware that McReynolds' approach to judging New Deal cases could lead, if his conservatism ever became the banner for a majority of the Court, to a dictatorship by five justices. And this seemed to be happening early in 1936 when the Court struck down the AAA. Associate Justice Harlan Fiske Stone believed it time to speak out against the trend toward judicial dictatorship. In a strongly worded dissent he first castigated the majority for producing a "tortured construction of the Constitution" to move against the AAA. Then, in an obvious reference to McReynolds' comments in the New York milk case, Stone continued that "the Courts are concerned only with the power to enact statutes, not with their wisdom. For the removal of unwise laws from the statute books appeal lies not to the courts but to the ballot. While unconstitutional exercise of power by the executive and legislative branches of the government is subject to judicial restraint, the only check upon our own exercise of power is our own self-restraint. . . . Courts are not the only agency of government that must be assumed to have capacity to govern."

Stone had stated the belief of the New Deal people better than they could state it themselves. "You spoke at a great moment and in a great way," said Cummings to the Justice, "congratulations!" Stone replied that "when one finds himself outvoted two to one he should be humble and perhaps skeptical of his own judgment. But I have a sincere faith that history and long time perspective will see the function of our court in a different light from that in which it is viewed at the moment." The Roosevelt Administration agreed with Stone; the New Dealers, however, were not willing to wait for the "long time perspective" to back them up.

"The objective of the Court's purpose," said Roosevelt of the AAA decision, "was to make reasonableness in passing legislation a matter to be settled not by the views of the elected Senate and House of Representatives and not by the views of an elected President but rather by the private, social philosophy of a majority of nine appointed members of the Supreme Court itself." The time plainly had come to begin moving against the Court.

A week after the AAA decision, in January, 1936, the President sent a memorandum to Homer Cummings asking for information about the McCardle case. The Constitution gives the Supreme Court appellate jurisdiction—a decision of a lower court can be appealed to the Supreme Court—"with such Exceptions, and under such Regulations as the Congress shall make." After the Civil War the Congress had passed a series of laws known as the Reconstruction Acts to bring the South into subservience. The laws were being challenged, and the challenge eventually would work its way to the Supreme Court. The Congress then invoked that constitutional phase "with such Exceptions" and forbade the Court to review the Reconstruction Acts; the Court obeyed that command. That was the McCardle case. It was the first and only time that the Congress limited the Supreme Court's right to hear cases on appeal.

Those close to FDR in early 1936 believed he actually hoped the Court would declare all New Deal legislation unconstitutional. After a Cabinet meeting with FDR, Ickes wrote: "It is plain to see, from what the President said today and has said on other occasions, that he is not at all averse to the Supreme Court declaring one New Deal statute after another unconstitutional. I think he believes that the Court will find itself pretty far out on a limb before it is through with it and that a real issue will be joined on which we can go to the country."

The problem was how to meet the threat posed by the Court, what specific action was necessary. At a luncheon with some sympathetic senators and Administration officials, FDR discussed the possibility of requiring the Court to give advisory opinions or of giving Congress the right by vote to overturn a Supreme Court decision. That same day, Cummings sent a letter to the President suggesting that it might still be possible "with all the ingenuity at our disposal [for us], to find a way to bring helpful national legislation within the explicit terms of [the Court's] decisions." If this could not be done, however, "we must frankly meet the issue of a Constitutional amendment." Cummings added that he did not believe that point had yet been reached. "The hand has not yet been played out," he said.

Taking on the Supreme Court was a major undertaking; everyone in the New Deal realized that and was reluctant to enter such a battle until it was demonstrated as an absolute necessity. The Court remained a revered and honored institution. In May of 1936 the Chief Justice, Charles Evans Hughes, demonstrated the public support for the Court when he appeared before a meeting of the American Law Institute. He began his speech with: "I am happy to report that the Supreme Court is still functioning." There was thunderous applause for that remark, lasting a full two minutes. One should be careful, it was clear, about fighting the Supreme Court.

Still, the Court continued to decide against the New Deal.

At the end of May, 1936, it ruled that the federal government could not establish a minimum wage. The next week, the last day of its 1935–36 session, the Court ruled that a state also could not establish a minimum wage. FDR summed up the situation for newsmen. "It seems to be fairly clear," he said, "as a result of this decision and former decisions, using this question of minimum wage as an example, that the 'no-man's land' where no government—state or federal—can function is being more clearly defined. A state cannot do it, and the federal government cannot do it."

FDR was not alone in comprehending that the Court's decisions meant that no level of government could act to protect the public welfare. At the same time FDR was making the above comments to newsmen, Supreme Court Justice Harlan Fiske Stone was writing:

> We finished the term of the Court yesterday, I think in many ways one of the most disastrous in its history. At any rate it seems to me that the Court had been needlessly narrow and obscurantic in its outlook. I suppose no intelligent person likes very well the way the New Deal does things, but that ought not to make us forget that ours is a nation which should have the powers ordinarily possessed by governments, and that the framers of the Constitution intended that it should have. Our latest exploit was a holding by a divided vote that there was no power in a state to regulate minimum wages for women. Since the Court last week said that this could not be done by the national government, as the matter was local, and now said that it cannot be done by local governments, even though it is local, we seem to have tied Uncle Sam up in a hard knot.

Then came the campaign and election of 1936 with the Republicans trying to force FDR to state his intentions about the Court and FDR parrying every such thrust. When the election was over and FDR had what he considered his mandate, he was ready to move. This was readily apparent to the White House circle and to Roosevelt's friends. At the first Cabinet meeting after the election, Ickes reported that "there was a good deal of discussion about the Supreme Court. I think that the President is getting ready to move in on that issue and I hope that he will do so." Several days later Roosevelt left Washington for a South American tour. "It will give me a chance to re-study the problem created for the nation by the Supreme Court," he said of his trip to a supporter, Joseph M. Patterson, publisher of the New York *Daily News*. "It is a mighty difficult one to solve but one way or another I think it must be faced. And it can be faced and solved without getting away from our underlying principles."

By the middle of December, 1936, several alternative plans were under consideration. One was to make retirement for the Supreme Court justices more attractive. (This was the Hatton Sumners legislation guaranteeing full retirement pay; it eventually did become law.) Another was raising the number of justices required to invalidate an act of Congress from the traditional five, a majority of the nine-man Court, to six or perhaps seven. Still another proposal was a permanent enlargement of the Supreme Court so that liberal appointments could be made. One White House aide, Ben Cohen, gave the President a memorandum suggesting an approach that would give Congress a veto over Supreme Court decisions. If the Court invalidated an act of Congress, the Congress would have the opportunity, after one election had passed, to vote on the act again. If it still favored the act, then the act would be law despite the Supreme Court's negative decision.

By this time, late in 1936, Roosevelt definitely had decided against the constitutional amendment approach. There were several reasons in addition to FDR's reluctance to run the gamut of corruptible state legislatures. An amendment could be of two kinds. One would be an amendment in general language either limiting the Court's authority, making it more difficult for justices to declare an act of Congress unconstitutional, or compelling the justices to retire at a certain age. Not everyone, however, could agree on a single approach; there was no consensus on which line such an amendment should follow. A second proposal was to pass specific amendments to deal with specific problems. One amendment could permit the federal government to establish a minimum wage; another, to regulate farm prices. But this was objectionable also because such an approach would make the Constitution too specific a document. Its great value in the past had been its lack of specifics, its reliance on generalities that men could interpret as they believed the times needed them to be interpreted.

And finally a proposal for a constitutional amendment must run a hazardous course. It requires an affirmative vote of two-thirds each of the House and the Senate as well as approval by three-fourths of the states. It was considered to be near-impossible to put any amendment through this course within a year or two. To spend more time than this meant the amendment would become law too late. And, of course, an amendment, once it was approved, was still subject to interpretation—by the Supreme Court.

So Roosevelt sought another way, and he relied on his Attorney General, the legal advisor to the President, to find it. This Attorney General, Homer Stillé Cummings, had a background similar to FDR's—good schools, wealth, a history of public service, and an involvement in partisan politics. Cummings had been a confidant of Woodrow Wilson's when Wilson was President, and Cummings and FDR often reminisced together about the Wilson days. As a lawyer Cummings had watched courts in operation for many years and did not have a high opinion of them. He realized they were political organizations. When he became Attorney General, for example, federal courts operated under the rules of the states in which they were located. This served no purpose except to increase employment among lawyers. A New Yorker being tried in a federal court in Montana would have to hire a Montana lawyer to defend him because he needed a lawyer who understood Montana's rules and procedures. Cummings persuaded Congress to adopt legislation establishing uniform rules and regulations for federal courts across the nation.

Cummings also understood that the American system of courts and justice was far from perfect. Thirteen years earlier, in 1924, a young man named Harold Israel was arrested in Connecticut and charged with the murder of a Catholic priest. Eyewitnesses identified Israel as the murderer. A ballistics expert said Israel's gun had killed the priest. And Israel confessed to the crime. It was an easy case for a prosecutor. Cummings was that prosecutor. Instead of prosecuting, however, he dared the opinion of his contemporaries in the legal field and the criticism of his community to assert that Israel was innocent. His successful defense of Israel, a defense in which he tore down the wall of evidence around the young man, became a classic story in the history of American law. It also raised a serious question. The demonstration of Israel's innocence was the result of an unusual effort by a unique man. How many Harold Israels were being unjustly treated in American courts because they did not have a Homer Cummings to defend them?

With this background Homer Cummings was eager for an attack on the Court. Such an assault was not out of keeping with American history. Presidents and other American officials had been struggling against the Supreme Court almost since its founding. In 1793 the Supreme Court invoked its specific constitutional right to try cases between a state and the citizens of another state. The legislature of Georgia, the state involved in the case, responded with a law making compliance with the Supreme Court's decision an offense punishable by hanging "without benefit of clergy." The Court's decision and its right to try cases between a state and the resident of another state were reversed by the Eleventh Amendment to the Constitution, a less bloody means of reversing the Court than hanging. With the exception of the Civil War, Americans continued to avoid physical violence when seeking to reverse a Supreme Court decision. But they tried almost everything else.

Thomas Jefferson, the nation's third President, called the federal judiciary "the subtle corps of sappers and miners constantly working underground to undermine the foundations of our confederated fabric." As President, Jefferson refused to fill judicial vacancies, constantly warred with the Supreme Court, and had one federal judge impeached. During the Presidential term of Andrew Jackson, the Supreme Court with John Marshall as its Chief Justice handed down a decision that Jackson did not like. Jackson is reported to have replied: "Well, John Marshall has made his decision. Now let him enforce it." Although there is some doubt whether Andrew Jackson ever said those specific words, it is certain he agreed with their philosophy. "The opinion of the judges has no more authority over Congress than the opinion of Congress has over the judges," Jackson once said in a written message, adding: "And on that point the President is independent of both." What Jackson, Jefferson before him, and Franklin Roosevelt a century later were doing was denying that the Supreme Court did indeed have wide authority to review and declare acts of Congress unconstitutional. This question of judicial review is one of the great philosophical questions of American politics. How it is answered depends upon where the man making the answer sits. The Jackson statement denying this power of judicial review had actually been written for "Old Hickory" by his Secretary of the Treasury, a man named Roger Taney. Taney himself later became Chief Justice of the United States and in the Dred Scott decision upheld the Supreme Court's right of judicial review, the very right he had denied twenty years earlier when he was part of the executive branch.

In Abraham Lincoln's first inaugural address he acknowledged "the position assumed by some that constitutional questions are to be decided by the Supreme Court. . . . [but] at the same time, the candid citizen must confess that if the policy of the Government upon vital questions affecting the whole people is to be irrevocably fixed by decisions of the Supreme Court, the instant they are made in ordinary litigation between parties in personal actions, the people will have ceased to be their own rulers, having to that extent practically resigned their Government into the hands of that eminent tribunal." As President, Lincoln refused to obey writs of habeas corpus issued by the federal courts. Following a policy announced by Thomas Jefferson when he had been President, Lincoln conceded the right of the federal courts to issue an order to the President but denied that a President was obligated to obey the Court order.

A popular device in the war against the Supreme Court during the nation's history was to change the size of the Court. John Adams, as his Presidency came to an end, had Congress pass a law to reduce the size of the court from six to five members, to take effect when the next vacancy occurred, so that Thomas Jefferson, his successor, would not have an opportunity to fill a vacancy. When Jefferson was President he was able to make appointments by having the Court restored to six justices and then raised to seven. In 1837 the Court was increased to nine. In 1863, to pre-

vent the Court from blocking Lincoln's war policies, the Court was
increased to ten, to, in effect, pack the Court in Lincoln's favor.
In 1866, when there were two vacancies on the Court, the Congress
reduced the Court's membership from ten to eight so that President Andrew Johnson might not be able to fill the two empty seats.
In 1869 the eight-man Court had one vacancy. It also called unconstitutional the Legal Tender Act, by which the Union had financed the Civil War. Congress increased the Court's size to nine,
giving President Ulysses S. Grant two appointments, the one vacancy and the new judgeship. As soon as his two appointees took
their seats on the Court, the Court voted again on the Legal
Tender Act and approved it. Court packing had won out.

When James McReynolds as Attorney General in 1914 suggested
that the federal judiciary be enlarged on a temporary basis by the
appointment of a co-justice for every justice over seventy, he was
on ground made somewhat firm by a historical practice of juggling
with the size of the Supreme Court. This apparently is what made
the device so intriguing when Cummings came across it in late
December, 1936, and sold it to FDR as the device with which the
Court could be humbled.

One advantage of the plan was that it would give FDR immediate appointments to the Supreme Court. He was angered because he had gone through an entire first term without being able
to make even one such appointment. Frances Perkins recalls FDR's
saying to her at the beginning of 1935: "You know, I have been
in office for two years and haven't had an appointment for the
Supreme Court. That is most unusual, I am told. What the Court
needs is one Roosevelt appointment. Then we might get a good
decision out of them." As Roosevelt entered his fifth year as
President, still with no appointments, Homer Cummings raised
the same issue:

The judges themselves exercise great control over the personnel of
the various courts since they may withhold their retirement until a
President to their liking occupies the White House. The courts may
thus "pack" themselves. . . . Every previous President from the
beginning of the Republic who has served a full four-year term has

appointed from one to five justices of the Supreme Court. Even Harding, in his short incumbency, appointed four. But now, for the first time, a President has served a full term without making a single appointment to the Supreme Court. It is a matter well worth pondering.

One New Dealer later described in this manner the situation of aged justices' holding onto their berths: "The Court seemed to have declared the mortality table unconstitutional."

Roosevelt did have a strong case for being angry at the Court for the packing in reverse. Even one of the justices, Owen J. Roberts, conceded this some years later. In 1948 Roberts, sixty-two years old during the Court fight and the youngest man then on the Court, endorsed a constitutional amendment requiring justices to retire at age seventy-five. He referred then back to the 1937 fight when "the superannuated old gentlemen hung on there long after their usefulness had ceased." Compulsory retirement also, he said, "tends to provide for each administration an opportunity to add new personnel to the Court, which, I think, is a good thing. I think it is a bad thing for an administration to run as long as President Roosevelt's did without a single opportunity to name a justice to the Court."

After the Court-packing approach had been decided upon, several weeks were required to prepare the message that would be sent to Congress, particularly with the inaugural and its speeches and festivities consuming time in January. The material was basically ready at the end of the month. In a meeting January 30 the question came up of when the message on judicial reform should go to the Congress. The President was having his traditional dinner for the Supreme Court justices the night of February 2 and obviously the message could not go up before then; it would make the dinner a too embarrassing situation. The Solicitor General, Stanley Reed, was scheduled to argue some government cases before the Court on Monday, February 8, and Roosevelt wanted the message public before then. Cutting the time span almost down the middle, the date of Friday, February 5, 1937, was chosen.

The judiciary dinner was on a Tuesday night. Within three days FDR would be sending to Congress his message challenging the

Supreme Court to a duel. But this night he chatted with the members of the Court as if they were his closest friends. He was seen particularly to be enjoying himself immensely with the Chief Justice and with Justice Van Devanter, one of the conservatives at whom Roosevelt would be aiming his most devastating weapons. This dinner was an important social occasion in Washington, and it was well attended. Of the nine Supreme Court justices, for example, only Brandeis, who avoided social engagements, and Stone, who was ill, were not present. Other guests included the widow of President Woodrow Wilson, Henry Ashurst of the Senate Judiciary Committee, and Senator William Borah. On the Senate floor the previous day Senator Borah had angrily charged that the President might be considering making an attack on the Supreme Court. Tonight, of course, he and the President were friendly.

Those who knew Roosevelt thought he looked extremely relaxed that night. And well he should. For more than two years he had been plagued by the Supreme Court, aware that he was moving on a collision course with another branch of the federal government. But now the indecision, the doubts, had come to an end. A choice had been made. His friends and enemies would know about it a few minutes after noon Friday, February 5. The time then would be for action.

8

FRANKLIN ROOSEVELT was not the only government official in the mid-1930s who believed that something should be done about the Supreme Court. In January of 1936 a United States senator disembarked from the ship the *President Adams* at Jersey City, New Jersey, and was besieged by newsmen. What did the senator think about the Supreme Court? "There has been a great deal of talk about the sanctity of the Constitution," replied the senator. "But I suggest that constitutions are made for men, not men for constitutions." And the senator demanded: "On what does the Supreme Court base [its] claim to power?" Some months later that same senator was again asked about the Supreme Court, and he responded that both the federal and state courts "could stand some cleaning." The Senator was Burton K. Wheeler. The same Burton Wheeler who would lead the fight to defend the Court against the attacks of Franklin Roosevelt.

Another member of the Senate concerned about the Supreme Court in 1936 was Senator Joseph O'Mahoney of Wyoming. A Democrat, O'Mahoney was in debt to the Administration because he had used the appointive position of assistant postmaster general in the New Deal as a springboard to the Senate. Like most New Dealers, he did not like the Court. In January of 1936 he told the President that "a bold and dramatic stroke that would probably appeal to the nation would be to defy the Supreme Court by urging upon Congress a law to deprive the Supreme Court of the authority to declare any statute unconstitutional save by unanimous vote." But when the Court plan was sent to the Senate by Roosevelt, Joe O'Mahoney described it as obnoxious, undemocratic, and an insult to the Senate.

Representative Emanuel Celler of Brooklyn, a prominent Administration supporter on the House Judiciary Committee, said in January of 1937 that "the Supreme Court must be made to follow the election returns. . . . If the Court again sends back our measures there will be but one course to follow—and Congress will follow it—pack the Court." After the Roosevelt plan was sent to Capitol Hill, however, Celler announced: "I disagree with the President's plan for six young additional judges to replace those eligible for retirement. I sympathize with the President's objective, but disagree with his method of obtaining it."

Senator George Norris of Nebraska, the liberal Independent, argued in January of 1936 that "it takes twelve men to find a man guilty of murder. I don't see why it should not take a unanimous court to find a law unconstitutional." Referring to the practice in which a majority of one on the Court—a five-to-four vote—was sufficient to overturn a law, Norris declared that five men, a court majority, can exercise a veto on the government. He then said: "No court should be allowed to set aside a law passed by Congress and signed by the President on the votes of five men." Later in 1936 a group of liberals called on Norris to chair a convention to be held in 1937 on measures to counter the Supreme Court. These liberals included George Soule, an editor of *The New Republic;* Henry T. Hunt, legal adviser to Secretary of Interior Ickes; Morris L. Ernst, a New York City attorney; and W. Jett Lauck, an economist with the United Mine Workers who was understood to be acting for John L. Lewis. Even Burton Wheeler joined in urging Norris to chair such a convention, saying: "You are the only one who can unite all forces upon a single plan." Norris responded to their pleas and agreed to head the conference. When the Roosevelt plan was announced, however, the influential Norris was not among its supporters.

Even William Borah, the lion of the Republican opponents to FDR's Court plan, had expressed his dissatisfaction with the Supreme Court. Early in 1936 he had explained that he too was troubled by five-to-four decisions but said he did not know what to do about them. Years earlier, he acknowledged, he had introduced a bill requiring a vote of seven-to-two by the Court to overturn an act of Congress. But, he explained, he had introduced the bill to spark discussion of the problem rather than because he favored that specific remedy.

Another influential Republican member of the Senate was Hiram Johnson of California. In 1912 he had run for Vice President on the Progressive party ticket as Theodore Roosevelt's running mate. There he had made acquaintance with a number of young liberals, both Republican and Democratic, including Harold Ickes. As part of the Progressive party's platform in 1912 Johnson had supported the principle of judicial recall, overturning a Supreme Court decision by a vote of the public. But now in 1937, when he was a quarter of a century older, he too was crying hands off the Court.

One day during the Court fight Harold Ickes was up on Capitol Hill testifying at a hearing. He met his old friend Hiram Johnson after not having seen him for a year. "In the interval he has become an old man," thought Ickes. "He looks it and he has the voice of an old man. All the resonance and timbre in his voice—and he had a wonderful speaking voice—are gone." Johnson conceded to his old friend from a bygone day that his health was failing. He didn't spend too much time in the Senate chamber, he confessed. He must spend the time resting. Ickes studied the old man and decided there was not much fight left in him, perhaps not even a radio speech. Hiram Johnson, the veteran of many a Senate battle, the friend and foe of many a President, made clear how he would use his strength, if he could muster it. The former advocate of judicial recall would be against the Roosevelt Court plan, he insisted, absolutely against.

What had happened to these liberals? To these Congressional critics of the Supreme Court? Why did they not mass behind the FDR plan or join with him in seeking a compromise? Together with the President they could have solved all their difficulties with the Supreme Court. Why did they not go along with him when their criticisms of the Court seemed so similar?

If the Court were to be attacked and attacked successfully, it would lose power; that must be the purpose of the attack. Who should gain the power the Supreme Court lost? The answer to this question revealed why so many members of Congress who were angry with the Court were not angry enough to side with Roosevelt. Under the Roosevelt plan, the power lost by the Court would be picked up by the Presidency. Success for FDR would mean that the President had triumphed, and a Court swollen with FDR appointees probably would not dare challenge him. In contrast, Congress wanted the power lost by the Court to rest with Congress. This could be done under the terms of the Burton Wheeler proposal for a Constitutional amendment. This would give Congress a veto over Supreme Court decisions It was Wheeler's proposal on which Ben Cohen had based his memorandum in December of 1936 suggesting that FDR endorse such a plan. This proposal would have meant that the Supreme Court, when formulating its decisions, would have to consider whether Congress would or would not veto that decision. Congress would have become the boss of the Supreme Court.

Of the two plans, Wheeler's and Roosevelt's, Wheeler's undoubtedly was the more dangerous to the American system of government. If the principle of a Congressional veto over Supreme Court decisions were written into the Constitution, it could not be revoked except with great difficulty. The loss of the Court's power would be nearly as permanent as anything can be in the American system of government. The strength of the Court—the freedom to ignore the public's clamor—would be lost as Congress, a body particularly responsive to public clamor, assumed authority over the Court. If the Roosevelt plan passed, however, the Supreme Court would have the opportunity to regain its independence at a later time. The Roosevelt plan would give FDR a rush of appointments. But once those appointments had been made and the new justices had assumed their seats on the high bench, there would be no way the President could touch them. And the history of judicial appointments is filled with the names of justices who changed their philosophy after being appointed to the Court. At least two members on the Court in 1937 surprised their original backers with their switch to conservatism. These two were McReynolds, who had been part of Woodrow Wilson's "New Freedom," and Roberts, who had been cheered by Democrats when he joined the Court. There were others in the past, like Roger Taney, who visualized their role in government from a different point of view once they donned the robes of a justice of the Supreme Court of the United States.

If Roosevelt won, the members of the Court would have felt a hesitancy, perhaps even a fear, to buck the New Deal. That fear might have lasted for years, influencing members of the Court to endorse Presidential programs. This, of course, was exactly what FDR wanted. Gradually, however, the Court could have regained its independence simply by asserting it. The Court had been humbled before by Presidents and by Congresses but always had managed to regain its position as a coequal branch of government, even if the process took decades. At least under the Roosevelt plan the Court would have that opportunity. It would not under Burton Wheeler's proposal.

There were other reasons why some members of the Senate were cool toward Roosevelt's plan. Back in 1912 a young New York Democratic politician was influential in having New York State Democrats switch their support from Champ Clark of Missouri to Woodrow Wilson for the party's Presidential nomination, insuring that Wilson became the President. In 1937 that young New York Democrat was President of the United States while Champ Clark's son, Bennett Clark, was Democratic senator from Missouri. The Clarks never had forgotten FDR's role at that convention twenty-five years earlier. This memory helped persuade Bennett Clark to withhold his support of FDR on the Court plan.

Tom Connally of Texas had also been expected to line up behind Roosevelt. He had supported the New Deal, and he and his state had benefited handsomely by the largesse of the Roosevelt Administration. But Tom Connally was basically a conservative. He found much in the New Deal to support; specifically, the stranglehold the eastern bankers had on Texas was broken and federal funds were pouring into the state for irrigation and reclamation purposes. But now that this was taken care of, Tom Connally could see no reason for supporting programs that would be helping people in places far from Texas. In addition, the more prominent Texas politicians—Vice President Garner, Hatton Sumners, Sam Rayburn among others—were distinctly cool toward the Court plan. So Connally played it safe and went against FDR on the Court plan.

There was another reason, unknown to Roosevelt, why the Senate in 1937 was not going to be as good a spot to wage his Court fight as he anticipated. Once there had been a time when to be a senator was to possess the highest honor. The Senate of the United States was the world's greatest deliberative body. In its chambers members imagined they could hear the echoes of Daniel Webster, Henry Clay, John Calhoun. Even in 1937 there

were members of the Senate whose names already had been firmly
placed in American history books—William Borah and George
Norris, Burton Wheeler and Hiram Johnson. These men were
giants of American politics. They were giants for several reasons.
In Washington, far from their constituencies, rarely bothered by
news media watching their every act, they enjoyed a freedom to
think, speak, and act in the Senate as their conscience dictated.
They were free to be as big men as they wish to be. This
was particularly important in the 1920s, when there was no other
agency of government trying to develop a philosophy of politics
for the twentieth century except the Senate. There was no one else
in government suggesting ideas, waging arguments, fighting for
causes. The United States Senate was a creative forum, a powerful
branch of the federal government.

Then came Franklin Roosevelt. The genius of government immediately shifted. No longer was it the ninety-six men in the Senate;
it was the one man in the White House. He and his aides produced
the ideas, transformed them into proposals, wrote them as bills,
sent them up to the Capitol, and expected the Congress to pass
them quickly. And Congress obliged at first. During the first one
hundred days of the New Deal, Roosevelt sent a banking bill up
to the Capitol. The House approved it by acclamation after only
forty minutes of debate. The Senate spent longer on the bill, a
total of three hours. No one in Congress could really have understood what was in that legislation. "If I had been in favor of the
bill," said Borah in explaining his vote against the banking legislation, "I would not have voted for it under such circumstances.
I decline to be an intellectual slave, even when I am being lashed
in the direction in which I want to go."

But the lashes came harder and harder from the White House.
FDR besieged Congress with drafts of proposed bills. He greatly
enlarged the office of the Presidency—through the device of having
aides like Tommy Corcoran on the payroll of federal agencies
while actually working for the President. With this increased staff
he was able to write the laws, prepare the debates, guide the
Congressional hearings, watch more closely over Congressional

patronage. Franklin Roosevelt made clear that the initiative and the creativity had passed to him. One Republican grumbled that Franklin Roosevelt has left "Congress with no more legislative power than Gandhi has clothing." By 1937 the Congress was jealous of Franklin Roosevelt.

Another cause of the difficulty was the young men surrounding FDR, giving him their intelligence, their loyalty, and their personal devotion. Tommy Corcoran and Ben Cohen were the most famous. These two were a team for the New Deal on Capitol Hill. It was said that Corcoran had the charm while Cohen had the brains. That was a generalization that included some truth. "Tommy the Cork" was a charmer. A handsome Irishman with an engaging personality, he had a wealth of stories and songs and made himself an asset at any dinner party or gathering of political figures. There he picked up all the gossip, made himself a reservoir of valuable information. A brash young man, he did not hesitate to lecture, sometimes dictate, to the senators and representatives. He was, in effect, the Administration's salesman. Ben Cohen, however, was a shy, introspective person of great brilliance but with little of the exuberance of Tommy Corcoran. But Cohen actually did much of the drafting of the New Deal legislation in the 1930s.

In 1934 a magazine writer spent some time with Corcoran and Cohen and some of their friends, then reported: "Here, for the first time in peacetime Washington, youth is offering to government its tireless vigor, its expert yet unprejudiced mentality. and its unconquerable idealism. . . . Perhaps it is our own long awaited youth movement, a movement not of marching legs and upraised palms, but of active brains and hearts." Perhaps it was all this. But it was also something else. It was a collection of young people who believed their opponent was not necessarily the Republican but, instead, the politician no matter what his political loyalty. These young men considered themselves idealists, the vanguard of a new political movement. Political power was to be snatched away from the "old guard." In the 1930s this old guard was made up of senators and representatives who once had been young and idealistic themselves. It was not that they had become cynical in their old age, nor that they had "sold out." They had simply become suspicious. They had seen too many young men charge into Washington with ideals, only to move out slowly years later under the weight of the wealth they had accumulated in Washington, as many of the New Dealers would do. They had listened to too many ideas for proposals that just could not be denied, that just were too necessary to be ignored, only to realize years later that no one remembered what any of them were about. They had spent too many years in government to forget that operating a nation like the United States requires compromise and slowness as well as dedication and speed. They also believed they knew something about writing legislation, a point the Administration did not wish to concede.

At the beginning of the New Deal, when the nation was in desperate straits economically, the members of Congress were willing to forget their suspicions temporarily. But as conditions improved, they remembered them. Those who disliked Roosevelt most and prized their own independence highly were among the first to speak out. When Carter Glass of Virginia announced his opposition to the Court bill, he vowed to oppose it with all the strength available to him. Then he added, "But I don't imagine for a minute that it'll do any good. Why, if the President asked Congress to commit suicide tomorrow they'd do it."

The members of the Senate did not like being dictated to. They did not like the young men like Tommy Corcoran and Ben Cohen who scurried around from one Capitol Hill office to another, writing bills, ordering members of Congress to fall into line. They did not like to hear James Farley say things like this at the height of the Court fight: "Before I close, I just want to call something to your attention regarding the Supreme Court issue. We have let the Senate talk all they want to. Then the House will take up the matter, and there they will talk until they are tired. After they are all talked out we will call the roll. You will find we have plenty of votes to put over the President's program." Those words were too much a shout of confidence by Farley. "We will call the roll" he had said, and on Capitol Hill it sounded as if he were dictating the vote, announcing that the members had better vote his way or they would be in trouble.

By the time 1937 came there were many members of the Senate who believed the bossing of Congress by the White House had gone on long enough. Franklin Roosevelt was too liberal for many of them and too demanding in his assumption of power. He had to be stopped. An issue was needed, one that would command wide public support, where the fight would not seem to be over Franklin Roosevelt but over something else. But the fight also had to be one in which the Congress would have the opportunity to demonstrate its regained status.

When on February 5, 1937, Franklin Roosevelt announced his plan to enlarge the Supreme Court by appointing co-justices for each of the Supreme Court justices over seventy years of age, he provided such an issue.

Everything then was background for the fight in the Senate. The letter writing, the speeches, the propaganda—all had been aimed at bringing pressure to bear on one side or the other when the Senate actually began its consideration of the bill.

The night of March 9, 1937, Henry Ashurst, the chairman of the Senate Judiciary Committee, was toastmaster at a dinner honoring Manuel Quezon, president of the Philippine Commonwealth, held at the Mayflower Hotel in Washington. He arrived home at midnight and went immediately to bed. He rose early the next morning, March 10, and took a Turkish bath. He then proceeded to the Senate Caucus Room—"a large room in the Senate Office Building with marble-tiered walls and damnable acoustics." In an anteroom off the Caucus Room he met the seventeen other members of the Judiciary Committee. They lined up in order of political party and seniority, which is how they would sit at the big table at one end of the hearing room. Waiting for them in the Caucus Room were five hundred spectators, one hundred reporters, and a great number of Administration officials. At precisely ten thirty, led by Ashurst, who was dressed in striped trousers and a morning coat, the committee members marched into the Caucus Room.

This was the beginning of the Judiciary Committee hearings on

the Roosevelt bill to enlarge the Supreme Court—S.1392 as it
was known officially. These hearings would not be the climax.
That would come weeks later in the Senate chamber itself. But
the hearings would be hand-to-hand combat, and they would
draw blood.

Henry Ashurst rapped on the table before him with his gavel.
"The committee," he said, "will be in order. It is obvious that there
is a quorum present."

Part Four

The Baby Is Born

9

THE SENATE JUDICIARY Committee's hearings on Franklin Roosevelt's plan to reorganize the judicial branch of the government were of little value to the Administration. No new friends were made. No brilliant arguments were voiced or could be voiced like thunderbolts unleashed to sway the multitudes on behalf of the President's program; the most significant thunderbolt available to the New Dealers was Franklin Roosevelt himself, and he had struck in his March 4 Victory Dinner address and his Fireside Chat five days later. The White House understood this and wanted to bring the hearings to an end as quickly as possible. Tommy Corcoran, after the hearings had progressed for a short period, blandly suggested that both sides call it quits after each used up an additional week for witnesses. Burton Wheeler and his allies turned down the offer. Then Corcoran and some other White House aides suggested that the Administration finish its witnesses after a total of only two weeks of testimony. The theory was that the opposition would respond with a similar gesture and the hearings would come to an end. This was an incorrect guess. The opposition chortled and spent a total of four weeks bringing almost seventy witnesses before the Judiciary Committee to drown out the Administration's arguments.

Burton Wheeler and his associates could not lose by long hearings. First, the hearings provided ammunition for their cause. Homer Cummings, the Attorney General, was the first witness before the committee. When he finished reading his five-thousand-word statement the morning of March 10, he looked up at the members of the committee, grabbed at the armhole of his vest with his thumb, leaned back in his chair, smiled, and said: "If there are any questions, gentlemen, I shall try to answer them." Although the grueling cross-examination by the Republicans and conservative Democrats did not materialize as expected, the senators were able to elicit some damaging remarks from Cummings. William Borah, for example, began his questioning in a rather casual fashion.

"General," he said, "I just want to ask you one question."

Cummings replied innocently, "Yes, Senator Borah."

Borah then asked: "Suppose after the six additional members of the Supreme Court are appointed, the Court should divide seven to eight, this entire plan would fall, would it not?"

Cummings answered: "It would depend upon which side the seven were on and upon which side the eight were on."

A few minutes later, Joseph O'Mahoney, one of the Democrats on the committee but an opponent of the Court plan, followed up that point, pressing Cummings to concede that the Court structured as FDR wanted it could still split eight-to-seven against FDR. Cummings acknowledged, "That might happen. I said it might happen . . . if the liberals should turn out to be conservatives, but I would not expect any such result."

The questioning by Borah and O'Mahoney had produced from Homer Cummings the concession that the purpose of the plan was to stack the Supreme Court with Roosevelt puppets. The next day when Robert Jackson, an assistant attorney general, appeared, the opponents of FDR continued the same line of attack "We do not ask judges to commit themselves to us," Jackson insisted. "I am willing to take the adverse decision of an open-minded judge at any time. I have taken many of them." But then, a few minutes later, he conceded: "Yes, I think it is fair to say that it is absolutely true that [whether FDR's plan works] will depend on the men appointed." As if in defense of himself, he told the committee hearing: "If the Constitution is what the judges say it is, then we should have something to say about who the judges are "

The value of such statements was not that they revealed anything new about the Administration's intentions. Rather, such statements spelled out these intentions for the world to read. And a senator seeking some means to justify to his constituents his opposition to the Court plan could use those words as a demonstration of FDR's hope of dominating the Court. The longer the hearings lasted, the greater the case built up against the Administration's plan.

But there was a second reason, a much more important one, why the Roosevelt opponents wanted long hearings. Wheeler and the others were, in reality, conducting a filibuster against the Court plan. Traditionally, filibusters consist of long-winded speeches on the Senate floor to delay votes. Actually a filibuster can be any delaying technique, and there are many of them other than speech making. A delay of action is an important strategic move. The Roosevelt opponents knew this and had always considered the filibuster as one dueling device to fall back on. Two days before the Senate hearings opened, for example, a prominent Republican said that "unless there is a change of attitude caused by the tremendous propaganda of the Administration, there are enough senators pledged to speak against the President's proposal to prevent a vote upon it." During a filibuster, whether it be by lengthy committee hearings, by the laborious and time-consuming writing of a committee report, or by obstructionist tactics on the Senate floor, several things can happen. In the case of the Court bill, the legislation could have been withdrawn. Although this was not likely, some members of the Senate hoped that FDR, at least, would agree to a compromise. Another possibility was that the situation creating the need for the Court bill might change. Unknown outside the marbled walls of the Supreme Court building, exactly that had happened. But this remained a secret until it was too late, until the momentum of the Supreme Court conflict had become so great that the dispute became not the symbol of a cause but a cause itself. The duel between Franklin Roosevelt and the Supreme Court already was unleashing so much bitterness, so much concern about the future of the Presidency and of the Democratic party that it became itself an uncontrollable thing with a *raison d'être* of its own.

Another purpose of a filibuster is to persuade members of the Senate to oppose the controversial legislation just for the sake of getting rid of it so that the Senate can go on to other things. The Judiciary Committee appeared to be divided eight-to-eight on the President's bill with two undecided. FDR believed that in the Senate itself he had about forty votes behind him, perhaps thirty votes against him, with the votes to produce the magical majority of forty-nine somewhere among twenty uncommitted senators. If any of those uncommitted senators could be persuaded to turn against the Court plan because it seemed to be blocking everything else, the filibustering technique would be moving toward success. At the committee hearing level, the success of the filibuster depended upon Henry Ashurst's being amenable to the delaying tactic. He was. Permitting the filibuster was his contribution to the arsenal being used against FDR. But he could not admit it publicly without having the Democrats on the committee loyal to FDR rebel against him. "I could win easily in June," Ashurst blithely told the press as the month of March neared an end and the hearings were in their third week. He continued that he could win "more easily in July, quite easily in August, and by September it would be no fight at all." He assured the newsmen: "Time is my invincible ally because, when the people understand it, there will be a tremendous feeling throughout the country that the reform is needed. A man would have to have a leaky brain-pan to hurry when time is his ally. This bill is wholesome, a good reform. I am not afraid to have the searchlights played on it for weeks. I court searchlights."

Just the opposite was happening. Rather than being the ally of the Court bill's successful passage, time was the enemy. Time permitted the opponents to gain strength, extend their propaganda, augment their forces. The White House understood this, and relations between the FDR aides and Ashurst became icy. Several times one of the bright young New Dealers came to see Ashurst or called him by telephone to ask, sometimes even to command, that the hearings be speeded up. But the senator from Arizona calmly replied that the White House must understand the difficulty in persuading senators to àgree or that shutting off the opposition was bad strategy, smacking too much of dictatorship.

"The Nine Old Men." The Supreme Court as it was constituted when Franklin Roosevelt announced his bill to "pack" the Court. From left to right, the Justices are, standing: Owen J. Roberts, Pierce Butler, Harlan Fiske Stone, Benjamin N. Cardozo; sitting: Louis D. Brandeis, Willis Van Devanter, Chief Justice Charles Evans Hughes, James C. McReynolds, George Sutherland. This formal portrait shows the Supreme Court as its members and its defenders like to think it is—dignified, stately, respectable, trustworthy. *Photo by Harris and Ewing, Washington, D.C.*

This cartoon by Leo Hirshfeld, which carries a dedication to President Roosevelt and which was drawn at the height of the Court duel in 1937, represents another opinion of the Supreme Court, one much less flattering. *Franklin D. Roosevelt Library*

Franklin Roosevelt with his Cabinet in 1937. Clockwise from the President: Secretary of the Treasury Henry Morgenthau, Jr., Attorney General Homer S. Cummings; Secretary of the Navy Claude Swanson, Secretary of Agriculture Henry A. Wallace, Secretary of Labor Frances Perkins, Vice President John Nance Garner, Secretary of Commerce Daniel C. Roper, Secretary of Interior Harold Ickes, Postmaster General James A. Farley, Secretary of War Harry H. Woodring, and Secretary of State Cordell Hull. *Photo by Harris & Ewing, Washington, D.C.*

A Congressional triumvirate. From left to right: Senator James F. Byrnes, Democrat of South Carolina; Vice President Garner; and Senate Majority Leader Joseph T. Robinson. This picture was taken in 1935 when the conservatives of the Democratic party, represented here by Byrnes and Garner, stayed with FDR and the New Deal. In the Court duel they split with him. Robinson, however, remained the loyal party lieutenant in the Senate. *Acme Photo*

Acme Photo

This picture and the four pictures following indicate the magnetism of Franklin Roosevelt's personality. It was this quality—interpreted as concern about people, at a time when most persons thought no one cared—that so significantly built up public support.

Library of Congress

Acme Photo

Homer S. Cummings. Cummings, the Attorney General in the President's Cabinet, devised the specific plan used by FDR in trying to pack the Court.

Hatton W. Sumners. As chairman of the House Judiciary Committee, Sumners could play an important role in pushing the Court bill through the House. But Sumners declined to support the bill, meaning that the Senate would have to act first. *Library of Congress*

Senator Henry Fountain Ashurst, right, Democrat of Arizona, was chairman of the Senate Judiciary Committee. He publicly supported the FDR bill but actually worked to insure its defeat by use of delaying tactics. In this picture, Ashurst is welcoming Robert H. Jackson, assistant attorney general, to the committee hearings. *Underwood & Underwood*

ABOVE LEFT: Joe Robinson, the Senate Majority Leader, was a loyal party workhorse. He fought for FDR's Court plan even though he opposed it personally. The fight claimed his life. However, it should be noted that he hoped to win a seat on the Supreme Court as a result of his support. *Library of Congress*

ABOVE RIGHT: At a Democratic Victory Dinner on March 4, 1937, FDR dropped the pretense that he wanted to enlarge the Court only because its members were unable to handle the work of the Court. Instead, he appealed for support of his plan on a strictly philosophical basis. Here he is shown at the dinner chatting with Jim Farley, his Postmaster General, the Democratic Party's national chairman, and FDR's chief political lieutenant. *Wide World Photos*

BELOW: This picture of Vice President Garner and President Roosevelt was taken in May, 1937, before the split between the two men became too great to be healed. Garner, who became angry in 1937 because FDR was not retrenching on his New Deal program, eventually worked within the Administration to help defeat the program. *Franklin D. Roosevelt Library*

FDR had a great rapport with the press. Often he spoke with them informally and off the record. Many of his hopes and ambitions were outlined in these discusisons. Here he is holding an informal news conference at Warm Springs, Georgia, in March of 1937. *Acme Photo*

When FDR realized that he was losing much support in Congress, he organized a mammoth three-day party at the Jefferson Island Club. He tried winning back the members of Congress with good humor and fellowship. Here he is with Senator Alben Barkley of Kentucky, and Farley. *Acme Photo*

When Joe Robinson lay in state at the Capitol in Washington, President and Mrs. Roosevelt visited the Capitol to pay their respects. FDR did not go to the Robinson funeral in Arkansas. *Franklin D. Roosevelt Library*

After Robinson's death, the job of Senate leader of the Democrats was open and soon became a struggle between the Presidential forces who backed Alben Barkley and the conservative Democrats who backed Senator Pat Harrison of Mississippi. Although the fight for the position was a desperate and a hard one, it was all smiles for the photographers. This picture was taken shortly before the vote and shows, from left to right: Harrison, Garner, Barkley, and Senator Key Pittman of Nevada. *Franklin D. Roosevelt Library*

THE ILLEGAL ACT.

PRESIDENT ROOSEVELT. "I'M SORRY, BUT THE SUPREME COURT SAYS I MUST CHUCK YOU BACK AGAIN."

The Supreme Court did not permit a lot of the New Deal legislation, declaring it unconstitutional. *Franklin D. Roosevelt Library*

Looks Like the Boys Would Have to Find a New Wailing Wall!

Throughout Roosevelt's entire term of office the business community was bitterly opposed to the New Deal and the President himself. *Franklin D. Roosevelt Library.*

This cartoon appeared a month before the President introduced his Court Bill, and depicts the gulf between Roosevelt and the Supreme Court. *Franklin D. Roosevelt Library*

Reaction to Roosevelt's attempt to control the Court was usually critical. *Library of Congress*

Further examples of the public reaction to the President's attempt to alter the Supreme Court. *Franklin D. Roosevelt Library*

The Supreme Court itself took very strong objection to Roosevelt's attempt to alter its membership. *Library of Congress*

The Court itself was split, Charles Evans Hughes trying to hold together the liberal Stone and the conservative McReynolds. *Library of Congress*

Precedent for the President

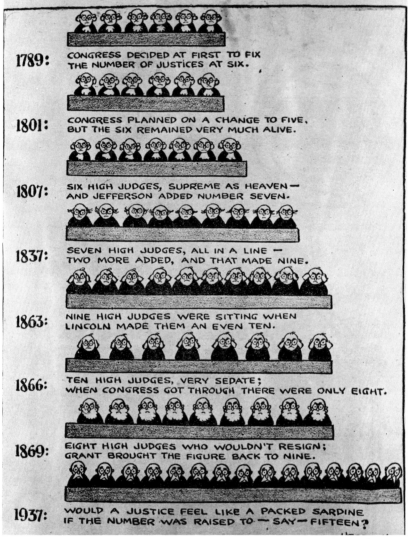

1789: CONGRESS DECIDED AT FIRST TO FIX
THE NUMBER OF JUSTICES AT SIX.

1801: CONGRESS PLANNED ON A CHANGE TO FIVE,
BUT THE SIX REMAINED VERY MUCH ALIVE.

1807: SIX HIGH JUDGES, SUPREME AS HEAVEN —
AND JEFFERSON ADDED NUMBER SEVEN.

1837: SEVEN HIGH JUDGES, ALL IN A LINE —
TWO MORE ADDED, AND THAT MADE NINE.

1863: NINE HIGH JUDGES WERE SITTING WHEN
LINCOLN MADE THEM AN EVEN TEN.

1866: TEN HIGH JUDGES, VERY SEDATE;
WHEN CONGRESS GOT THROUGH THERE WERE ONLY EIGHT.

1869: EIGHT HIGH JUDGES WHO WOULDN'T RESIGN;
GRANT BROUGHT THE FIGURE BACK TO NINE.

1937: WOULD A JUSTICE FEEL LIKE A PACKED SARDINE
IF THE NUMBER WAS RAISED TO — SAY — FIFTEEN?

An early example of one of Herblock's cartoons. The number of Justices on
the Supreme Court had varied considerably since the Founding Fathers.
Franklin D. Roosevelt Library

The split between the President and Congress grew wider as opposition to the Court Bill increased. *Franklin D. Roosevelt Library. Library of Congress*

The defeat of the Court Bill in the Senate was the first serious blow Roosevelt had received from Congress. *Franklin D. Roosevelt Library*

The issue became a bit touchy at times. Once, Senator Edward R. Burke of Nebraska, a Democrat but an opponent of FDR's on the Court issue, expressed some concern within the Judiciary Committee about obtaining witnesses to speak against the plan. Senator Neely of West Virginia turned to Burke. "May I ask," Neely said acidly, "whether the opposition feels that it needs assistance in the matter of producing witnesses? Does not the able Senator [Burke] believe that the Liberty League or the Republican National Committee will render such assistance?" This kind of remark between Democrats only served to widen the chasm now separating the party members who supported FDR and those who opposed him.

The Supreme Court justices believed they should not comment on the proposal because it was in the nature of a personal attack on them and they did not wish to engage in anything that would demean the Court. Still, the opponents of FDR feared the country might believe that the Court was divided on the issue, with some justices opposing and others of the nine Court members supporting the President. Charles Evans Hughes tells what happened next:

As the opponents of the bill were about to present their case [before the Senate committee], Senators Wheeler, King [the ranking Democrat on the committee] and Austin [representing the Republicans on the committee] called upon me—I think it was on Thursday, March 18th, 1937—and asked me to appear before the Committee. I was entirely willing to do this for the purpose of giving the facts as to the work of the Court. Even in appearing for such a purpose, however, I thought it inadvisable, in view of the delicacy of the situation, that I should appear alone. It seemed to me that at least one other member of the Court should accompany me—preferably Justice Brandeis— because of his standing as a Democrat and his reputation as a liberal judge. I so informed the [senators]. But when I consulted Justice Brandeis I found that he was strongly opposed to my appearing—or to any justice appearing—before the Committee. I stated the desire of the Committee to have the facts as to the state of the work of the Court and suggested that I might, in response to a request, write a letter for that purpose. With that suggestion Justice Brandeis fully agreed. I found that Justice Van Devanter took the same view. Accordingly, I telephoned to Senator King and to Senator Wheeler on the morning of Friday, March 19, 1937, that I had found that there was

a very strong feeling that the Court should not come into the controversy in any way, and that it was better that I should not appear; but
that if the Committee desired particular information on any matters
relating to the actual work of the Court, I should be glad to answer
in writing giving the facts.

Burton Wheeler did not grasp the full significance of Hughes's
offer to "answer in writing," or perhaps Hughes did not make the
offer as deliberately as he remembered doing. Instead Wheeler believed he had received a blunt refusal of his hopes eliciting from
the justices a public reaction to the Court bill. However, he was
in for a surprise. He and Mrs. Wheeler were old friends of Justice
and Mrs. Brandeis. And that Saturday Mrs. Brandeis drove across
the Potomac River to Alexandria to see Burton Wheeler's new
grandchild. After chatting a few minutes with Wheeler's daughter,
Mrs. Elizabeth Colman, Mrs. Brandeis said: "You tell your father
I'm for him." As soon as the Justice's wife had left, Mrs. Colman
called her father and gave him the message. Burton Wheeler understood its significance immediately. "I'm going to call up Brandeis," he announced. "He may throw me out, but I'm going to try
it." Brandeis, however, did not throw him out. Instead, he met with
Wheeler in his private study. Burton Wheeler then explained to
Brandeis that what he wanted was a statement, signed by Hughes
as Chief Justice and a Republican and by Brandeis as a liberal, defending the Supreme Court against the FDR attack. Wheeler explained that the people were inclined to accept statements from the
President and the Attorney General attacking the Court rather than
accept statements by senators like Burton Wheeler defending the
Court. But, Wheeler added, he was certain that a statement agreed
to by both Hughes and Brandeis could convince people that the
Court should be left untouched.

Brandeis explained that he had advised Hughes not to appear
personally before the committee because he believed the entire
process and procedure would be demeaning to the Court. Then
Brandeis told Wheeler: "You call the Chief Justice. He'll give
you a letter." Wheeler, however, was reluctant to call Hughes.
Burton Wheeler had been one of those most vociferous in opposi-

tion to the appointment of Charles Evans Hughes as Chief Justice seven years earlier. When he had approached Hughes about appearing before the Judiciary Committee, it was as part of a formal group, along with senators King and Austin, making the request. To make such a request as an individual in a private fashion worried Wheeler. Brandeis, however, would not permit Wheeler to leave without taking advantage of the opportunity available to him. "I'll call him up," the Justice said. He led Wheeler to the telephone and held him there as he dialed the Chief Justice's telephone number.

Hughes was cordial. He invited Wheeler to come to his house. When Wheeler arrived it was approximately five thirty in the afternoon. The next day was Sunday, and the following day, Monday, March 22, was the day set for opposition witnesses to appear before the Judiciary Committee. Wheeler was to be the first of the opposition witnesses. He explained to Hughes that he needed the letter from the justices, if it was to come, by that morning. Such a letter would have impact, and Wheeler wanted that impact to come at the beginning of the opposition's presentation. He also wanted the drama of the moment of presenting the letter to be his. The two men, Hughes and Wheeler, agreed that the letter should be geared to the same level as the President's original message. It would discuss only whether the Court was behind in its work and whether it needed younger men sitting on it, as FDR had insisted. Although the President himself had abandoned this argument in his March 4 speech, Hughes did not feel he could speak publicly about the politics of the situation. To do so would destroy forever the Court's public posture of being above politics.

Charles Evans Hughes had the letter ready the next day, Sunday. Associate Justices Willis Van Devanter and Louis Brandeis read it over, agreed with its contents, and signed it with him. Hughes did not ask any of the other justices to read or sign the letter. He did not even inform any of the other six about the letter, although they all lived within a few minutes of his house on R Street in northwest Washington and could have gathered at his residence quickly if he had requested them to. This was a factor that was to trouble

Charles Evans Hughes for many years to come. When Wheeler came over that afternoon to pick up the letter, Hughes handed it to him and in the manner of a conspirator said: "The baby is born." The two men talked for a few minutes, Hughes saying that Franklin Roosevelt never had properly understood the independent role of the Supreme Court in the federal government. Hughes also blamed much of the trouble for the current difficulties on Homer Cummings, saying: "We not only had to be the justices, but also do the work of the attorneys. Laws have been poorly drafted. Briefs poorly written and arguments poorly presented." As Wheeler left with the letter, the Chief Justice expressed the hope that the Senator would see that the letter received wide publicity. Burton Wheeler assured him that it would.

When the hearing began at ten thirty Monday morning, the Caucus Room in the Senate Office Building was packed. For almost two weeks Administration witnesses had praised the FDR plan, to the growing boredom of the committee and the press. Now the opposition was beginning. This meant not only arguments against the plan but hints of the strategy to be used in the Congressional struggle. For this reason some of the excitement that usually envelops the opening of Congressional hearings on controversial subjects had returned to this session of the Judiciary Committee. As soon as Henry Ashurst caught sight of the smug look on Burton Wheeler's face and the smile on Mrs. Wheeler's, he knew there was cause for excitement. "I don't know what he's going to spring," Ashurst said to a fellow Democrat about Wheeler, "but it'll blow us out of the water," Ashurst, a man with a sense of humor, decided to play up to Wheeler, to build up to the moment when whatever Wheeler was going to spring would be sprung for all to see, "Senators," the Arizonan began, "we are signally honored this morning. We have before us one of the most, if not the most distinguished member of the United States Senate, Senator Burton K. Wheeler of Montana." Even in a body such as the Senate, where members were given to exaggerated praise of each other, that introduction was a bit heavy.

Wheeler began his testimony by expressing his "reluctance" to appear in opposition to the President. He then said his appearance should not be construed as meaning he has "any unfriendly feeling" toward FDR. He described his long record of supporting Franklin Roosevelt. This was a very calculated ploy. Emphasizing his past support for FDR served to underline Wheeler's present opposition, to make it more significant. "And so I was shocked and surprised when I picked up the paper one day when I was in New York, not visiting the economic royalists"—and he smiled here—"but visiting with the people who were investigating the economic royalists—the railroads of this country—and read the President's message to Congress" about the Court bill. Wheeler continued slowly, in an almost rambling fashion, but building up the suspense. By now almost everyone in the room was certain that Wheeler, in Ashurst's phrase, was going to "blow" things out of the water. As he sat in the witness chair before the semicircle of committee members he seemed a bit too sure of himself to be empty-handed. He was saying:

It was only after the Attorney General of the United States came before this committee, as I understood from the newspapers without reading his testimony, and repeated the charges that he had previously made that I went to the only source in this country that could know exactly what the facts were and that better than anyone else, to see if it was possible to refute the reflection that had been made upon the Court and upon the integrity of those individuals who constitute the Court.

Burton Wheeler paused for a moment and looked about the room, a signal to his fellow senators, to the newsmen, and to the spectators that he was about to let go with his surprise. For the first time since the hearings had begun March 10, the giant Caucus Room was still. The reporters at the press tables stopped their low-voiced joking. The buzz of chattering among the spectators ended. The senators leaned forward slightly, waiting in silence. "And I have here now," said Burton Wheeler when his audience was as he wished it, "a letter by the Chief Justice of the Supreme Court, Mr. Charles Evans Hughes, dated March 21, 1937, written by him and approved by Mr. Justice Brandeis and Mr. Justice Van Devanter. Let us see what these gentlemen say about it."

"My Dear Senator Wheeler" began the letter that Burton Wheeler read. For seven pages the letter defended the Court against the charge that it was unable to do its work. "The Supreme Court is fully abreast of its work," the letter insisted. ". . . There is no congestion of cases upon our calendar. . . . We have been able for several terms to adjourn after disposing of all cases which are ready to be heard." To back up that assertion, the Hughes letter then produced a statistical table, showing the number of cases ready for the Court at the beginning of each session since 1930 and how they had been disposed of when the session ended months later. There had been congestion in the Supreme Court prior to 1925, the letter conceded, but this had ended when Congress in that year passed a law giving the Supreme Court the right to determine which cases it will hear and which it will refuse to hear. Actually the argument made by FDR was not that the Court could not handle all the cases it chose to hear but that, instead, it only chose the number of cases it could hear without inconvenience or strain to itself. Roosevelt insisted that eighty to ninety per cent of the cases going to the Supreme Court were rejected without hearing by the Court. Hughes did not speak directly to this point except to say that hearing a case "is not a matter of favor, but of sound judicial discretion."

Toward the end of the letter, Hughes wrote: "An increase in the number of justices of the Supreme Court, apart from any question of policy, which I do not discuss, would not promote the efficiency of the Court." To the contrary, said Hughes, "There would be more judges to hear, more judges to confer, more judges to discuss, more judges to be convinced and to decide." That was as close as Charles Evans Hughes came to publicly attacking the Roosevelt plan. Everyone understood, however, that the purpose of the letter was not only to defend the Court against an already abandoned charge but to refute the whole approach of the Roosevelt attack.

Was Hughes alone in this response, or did the other justices agree with him? This was a crucial question. The last paragraph Wheeler read went this way: "On account of the shortness of time I have not been able to consult with the members of the Court generally with respect to the foregoing statement, but I am confident that it is in accord with the views of the justices. I should say, however, that I have been able to consult with Mr. Justice Van Devanter and Mr. Justice Brandeis, and I am at liberty to say that the statement is approved by them."

That last paragraph with its careful phrasing led to the general impression that the Court endorsed the letter unanimously, that the liberal justices as well as the conservatives were opposed to Roosevelt on the Court plan. Turner Catledge wrote in *The New York Times* that "the author said [the letter] was approved specifically by Associate Justices Van Devanter and Brandeis and, perhaps, by all the justices." A Republican wrote to Herbert Hoover that the letter "was made the more pointed because it expressed the unanimous view of the Court." Wheeler also contributed to the general impression that the Court was unanimously behind the letter. Later that week, he said: "It should be borne in mind that, although the members of the Supreme Court may have differed on a great many things, they are unanimous with reference to the letter of the Chief Justice; at least that is my understanding of the matter." It was this widespread impression of unanimity on the part of members of the Court that did so much to give the Hughes letter its force.

The extent of the letter's impact was significant. Wheeler's claim is that after the letter had been read, Vice President Garner telephoned FDR at Warm Springs, where the President was vacationing, and said: "We're licked." Robert Jackson later said the Hughes letter was the most significant factor in the defeat of the Court plan. The letter obviously was successful in persuading many members of the legal profession, not previously convinced, that the Roosevelt plan was faulty. It also influenced many other citizens who accepted the letter in good faith to oppose FDR's plan. As one participant in the Court fight on FDR's side said years later: "The Hughes letter strengthened the doubts and fears of a great number of people, confirmed their feeling that the plan was a phony and that the real reasons had not been given." Hughes himself later said: "This letter appears to have had a devastating effect by destroying the specious contention as to the need of additional justices to expedite the work of the Court. It had the effect of focusing attention on the real purpose of the bill."

A day or so after the letter had been read and had received its considerable share of publicity, Hughes met with all the Supreme Court justices. He told them the situation, saying he had not had the time to meet with them before giving the letter to Wheeler and "I hope that they all approved my action. Several justices at once spoke up, saying that they did, and the others seemed to me to acquiesce. No justice, either then or later, expressed to me a contrary view, nor throughout the period when the bill was before the Senate did I hear that any of the justices were in any way dissatisfied with my action."

Several of the justices were, in fact, very dissatisfied with Hughes's action. But no good could be accomplished by fighting with him about it in the confines of the Court's conference room after the letter had been made public. Nor could a public dispute do any good. It would only increase the disrepute of the Court in the public's eye. So none of the justices spoke out in defiance of Hughes's action at that time. A year later, however, Harlan Fiske Stone, who most resented the Chief Justice's action, did tell a newsman that the letter had not been approved by all the justices. Stone said the letter could have been shown to the other justices in advance and should have been, and that a dispute within the Court was prevented only because Stone and the others dissatisfied with Hughes's action preferred to avoid a fight. Stone continued to voice his displeasure at Hughes's action. In 1939, for example, he told Felix Frankfurter, by then also an associate justice of the Supreme Court, that he had not been aware of the letter until he saw the stories about it in the newspapers and that he as well as Justice Cardozo were not in favor of it. "There was no reason of which I am aware," Stone continued to Frankfurter, "why all the members of the Court should not have been consulted in connection with the preparation of a document which purported to state 'the views of the Justices,' or for expressing the views of Justices who for any reason could not be consulted. Although the Court was then in recess, all its members were in the city. They could have been brought together for a conference on an hour's telephone notice, or less. Throughout the recess Justices Sutherland, Cardozo, and myself were in our homes, which are within five minutes' walk of the residence of the Chief Justice."

Hughes's authorized biographer, Merlo J. Pusey, has written: "Considering the delicacy of the issue, Hughes' action with the approval of only two of his eight colleagues was certainly a tactical error." That "error" has since haunted Hughes's place in history. In retrospect it appears that an error was the least it was. If Hughes had sought permission of all the justices, he would not have received it. Whatever Stone's attitude toward the politics of the act, he also disagreed with some of the contents of the letter, specifically one section of the Hughes letter which said that a fifteen-man Court could not divide into two bodies and split up pending cases before it. This had been one of the minor suggestions made in FDR's original message. Stone believed, as did Cardozo, that such a statement amounted to the Supreme Court's giving an advisory opinion, a practice the Court did not traditionally engage in. "I simply cannot believe that you," said an astounded Felix Frankfurter to Stone, "for instance, would have concurred in giving the advisory opinion that Article III precludes the possibility of sitting in divisions."

Stone replied: "You are right. I did not see the C.J.'s letter, or know of it until I read it in the papers. I certainly would not have joined in that part of it which undertakes to suggest what is and what is not constitutional."

If objections of this kind had been made to Hughes before he turned the letter over to Wheeler, Hughes would have had either to cut from the letter sections that he wished retained or else to acknowledge publicly that the Court was divided on the letter. His argument that he did not have sufficient time to consult with other members of the Court is not an effective one. By his own admission he had agreed by phone on Friday morning to present a letter and had both Friday and Saturday, two full days, to work on it before giving it to Burton Wheeler. Also, in his Saturday conversation with Burton Wheeler, Hughes had offered to have the letter ready Monday morning. By telephoning Wheeler Sunday afternoon to say the letter was then ready, Hughes voluntarily cut the time available to him. The approach the Chief Justice did choose, writing a letter and then showing it only to the two justices he knew would approve it, was the only approach that could present a reasonably strong letter while giving the appearance of support from a unanimous Court.

Harold Ickes summed up the situation in this manner:

It was good tactics. This episode proves again the mistake of going to court with a weak case. I refer, of course, to the fact that the President's special message on the question of judicial reform was almost entirely based on the proposition that we needed more federal judges because, on account of old age and decrepitude, we haven't enough able-bodied judges to keep up with the work of the courts. We abandoned this ground some time ago but, shrewdly, Hughes chose to fight his skirmish where we were the weakest. . . . Although the letter carefully negatived any suggestion that the Court was discussing the broad, general policy involved, the whole thing has the appearance of a unanimous Supreme Court opposing the President's proposal.

As for Franklin Roosevelt, he was angry at the letter, angry at being outfoxed, at being embarrassed; and also he was angered by Hughes's assertion in the letter that the Court was up on its work, that its calendar was clear. FDR acknowledged the Court calendar was clear, but this did not impress him. He figured he knew how it was kept so up to date—the Court simply refused to hear cases—and he told this story to illustrate his point:

When I was a practicing lawyer in New York in 1907, I used to have occasional police court clients, people who had been disorderly at two o'clock in the morning in Times Square, and they generally would be taken by the police to the old Jefferson Market Court. There was an old fellow down there, an old Tammany magistrate, who was a law to himself—there was no supervision over magistrates in those days—and he had a rule that, by God, he was going to close his court at one P.M. every day. Well, if I had a Harvard friend to defend on a Tuesday morning, that was all right. There would be only twenty cases before the old judge and he had from ten to one to dispose of his twenty cases. My client would get heard; he would get heard and he would get a fair deal from the court. But, if my client happened to have been picked up on a Saturday night cr a Sunday night and had to appear in Monday morning court before the same old judge, there would be 220 cases. But he had his rule about one P.M. and he would run those 220 cases through his court without hearing the defendant. It was ten dollars or ten days. And they were all tried. His calendar was not crowded on Mondays any more than it was on Tuesdays. He was always up with his work.

As for Harlan Fiske Stone, the Charles Evans Hughes letter was only another item in a long list of grievances Stone felt against the Chief Justice. Within a few weeks these grievances would reach their climax.

Hughes did not again speak directly on the Court plan. But he continued his opposition by indirection. When an acquaintance wrote him criticizing the plan, Hughes answered back that although he could not comment on the Court plan, "I warmly appreciate the personal interest which prompted you to write." On another occasion, appearing before the American Law Institute, Hughes spoke of the success of democracy depending upon the triumph of reason over tyranny. "Between these society must choose," he said. "If society chooses the processes of reason, it must maintain the institutions which embody those processes." His meaning was clear, and the members of the Law Institute applauded him for a full minute. On several other occasions also he spoke in a similar vein so that his supporters would continue to understand that his opposition to the President's plan was not flagging; also, to continue rallying his supporters to his cause.

Other members of the Court reacted differently.

Benjamin Cardozo did not speak publicly of the President's plan, but he did announce his feelings to his friends and relatives. "Off the record and not for transmission," he said to one, "I am with you altogether in opposition and amazement. . . . These are exciting days for aged judges." Then he cracked: "I must try to prove my judicial quality by not writing all I feel." One day in March, while chatting with a young friend, Cardozo watched with amusement as the friend did a somersault in Cardozo's apartment to demonstrate his youthfulness. The justice commented that "it might be helpful if you would come down and teach some of my colleagues to do that in their judicial decisions." Cardozo, as the conversation that day continued, also said his basic complaint against the President's proposal was that fifteen men on the Court were too many. He added that he sometimes thought nine were too many.

Some other justices, however, were more public in their comments, particularly James McReynolds. In March he was a guest speaker at a Phi Delta Theta fraternity dinner. McReynolds later claimed that his remarks were intended only for his fellow dinner guests and that he did not believe they would be made public. That a man with McReynolds' experience in Washington believed he could make a significant statement about a controversial subject before a large gathering and not have that statement eventually work its way into the press is difficult to believe. A couple of months later an Administration official, James Farley, also claimed surprise when some "off-the-record" comments of his about the Court plan were published. Such claims of offended privacy may be acceptable from Washington newcomers, not from old professionals like McReynolds and Farley.

In his comments before the fraternity dinner, McReynolds did not mention the FDR plan specifically but made clear that was the object of his remarks. "The evidence of good sportsmanship is that a man who has had a chance to present a fair case to a fair tribunal must be a good sport and accept the outcome. . . . I should like to be optimistic. I should like to tell you that the situation is rosy. I can't." His speech was repeatedly interrupted by applause. With his usual flair for the clumsy act, McReynolds also referred in the course of his comments to Negroes as "darkies." Administration officials quickly grasped hold of the incident and used it whenever they could throughout the remainder of the Court fight to persuade Negroes to back FDR or to help influence liberals friendly to the Negroes' cause. McReynolds' conservative friends tried to dismiss the incident, saying the Justice's use of the word "darkies" was not intended as a slight of Negroes but that "for a southerner that was a natural description to give to the Negro." The explanation served only to persuade more Negroes to support FDR.

McReynolds also did not hesitate to do a little work behind the scenes. Shortly after the Roosevelt plan had been announced, McReynolds met with an associate of Herbert Hoover's. This was when Hoover still hoped to be an active force in the fight against FDR. To the Hoover associate, McReynolds mentioned the name of an attorney in San Francisco and suggested that Hoover might wish to get in touch with him. The San Francisco lawyer, McReynolds said, was an authority on such things as personal liberty, the Bill of Rights, and several decisions of the Supreme Court written by McReynolds and "of the utmost importance to the Catholic Church." The San Francisco lawyer, McReynolds assured the Hoover associate, had been referring to these cases in letters he had addressed to Catholic members of the Senate, asking them to oppose FDR's plan.

What the Court was rumored to do was talked about almost as much as what it did do. A popular story, for example, was that the Supreme Court members would resign en masse and then issue a joint statement criticizing the Court plan. In talk reminiscent of Herbert Hoover's old plan, Louis Brandeis was often reported to be on the verge of giving up his seat on the Court in a protest of the FDR action. The White House frequently heard these rumors and shrugged them off. They were not true. Most often the members of the Court kept quiet about the Court plan, both in the privacy of their own circle of friends and before the public. Henry Ashurst recalled attending a dinner with a number of the justices in late February "and there was not even a remote reference to the judiciary reorganization bill." The one exception to this, the one member of the Court who worked more to defeat the FDR plan than even Charles Evans Hughes did, although with less results, the one justice who saw the Court plan as a device to fulfill personal desires, was Harlan Fiske Stone.

In 1930 Harlan Fiske Stone was an associate justice of the Supreme Court and William Howard Taft was Chief Justice. Taft died and the President then, Herbert Hoover, was faced with the problem of selecting a new Chief Justice. According to a story popular in Washington in the 1930s, Hoover called in one of his confidants, a State Department official named Joseph P. Cotton, and explained his problem. This problem was that Hoover wanted to elevate Stone from the position of associate justice to the position of Chief Justice, but—and the "but" was a big one—Hoover believed that Charles Evans Hughes wanted to be asked to become Chief Justice. Hughes had campaigned for Hoover, the President explained to Joe Cotton, and had support throughout the nation. Cotton told the President not to be concerned. Go ahead and make the offer, he advised Hoover, adding that it was impossible that Charles Evans Hughes would accept. Hughes was almost seventy years old, had held numerous important government positions, and was, in effect, at the end of his career, not ready to take on such an arduous task as being Chief Justice. Hughes might want the honor of being asked, but he did not want the job itself, insisted Cotton. An added point, Cotton said, was that Hughes's son was Solicitor General, the man who argued the government's cases before the Supreme Court. If Hughes accepted the position of Chief Justice, his son would have to resign as Solicitor General, and Evans Hughes would not nip his son's career like that. So armed, Hoover called Charles Evans Hughes and asked him to become Chief Justice of the United States. Hughes quickly accepted.

That was one version of how Hughes became Chief Justice. Hughes himself recorded another version:

From the time of my resignation as Associate Justice in 1916, I had no desire to return to the Bench. I should certainly have refused an offer of an Associate Justiceship, and I did not for a moment contemplate being chosen as Chief Justice. I was greatly surprised when this was proposed near the end of January 1930. At President Hoover's request, I came to Washington on the night of Thursday, January 30th, and I saw the President at the White House early the next morning. It appeared that Chief Justice Taft was failing rapidly; there was no hope of his recovery, and the fear was entertained that unless he resigned at once he might lapse into a mental condition which would make it impossible for him to resign and in which he might continue for an indefinite period. The President wished to be ready for the contingency of the Chief Justice's resignation and proposed my appointment. I demurred, referring to my age—I should be 68 in the following April—and my desire not to assume further and heavy responsibilities. After some discussion in which the President strongly urged me to accept, I finally told him that I would, making the qualification that I did not wish my nomination to evoke any contest over confirmation.

The first version, that Charles Evans Hughes was a usurper in the Chief Justice's chair, which rightfully belonged to Harlan Fiske Stone, haunted Hughes for years. He would not acknowledge this specter, of course. To one correspondent who asked him about it, he replied: "I appreciate your personal interest. Of course I do not pay any attention to such gossip." Still, Hughes was greatly disturbed when the story was reprinted as fact in the 1936 book *The Nine Old Men,* by Drew Pearson and Robert S. Allen. Hughes was greatly appreciative when Hoover provided him with a formal denial "so that you might file it away in your memoirs, although I think it is hardly necessary." Hoover told Hughes that "I am not capable of expressing my indignation at that book and its authors." Then Hoover launched into a personal attack against Pearson and Allen.

Hughes was not the only one concerned by the story. Harlan Fiske Stone obviously was also. He found Charles Evans Hughes an irritating person for several reasons, not the least of which was that Hughes might have been sitting where Stone believed he should be. Another was that in the philosophical clashes that the justices engaged in when they wrote their decisions, Hughes was a slippery, evasive person—or so Harlan Fiske Stone believed. In the private discussions behind the thick walls of the Court's Conference Room, each justice can speak as he wishes and each has one vote. In that respect, the Chief Justice and the eight associate justices are equal. But in one area the Chief Justice has considerably more equality than the other justices have. He can assign much of the writing of opinions. It works this way: If the Court divides on a case, say in a five-to-four vote and the Chief Justice is with the five-man majority, he can determine which of those five men, himself or one of the four associate justices, will write the majority opinion. The senior justice among the four-man minority determines who will write the minority opinion. If the Chief Justice is with the minority, he can determine who will write the minority opinion. Each justice can add his views in separate opinions, but it is the majority and minority opinions that generally form the legal philosophy by which the Court is known and which influence lawyers, legal scholars, and politicians. It is also a neat way the justices have of demolishing each other's philosophy. What irritated Stone was that Hughes "has never given me a chance to tear him to pieces." According to Stone, Hughes often would take the conservative side during the discussion in the conferences but then either would vote with the liberals if they had a majority without him or, if he stayed with the conservatives, not write the decision. This meant the liberals could not have any tangible printed arguments of Hughes's to puncture and demolish. This is what Stone ached to do, puncture and demolish Charles Evans Hughes in the only manner available to him—by attacking his legal philosophy. But Hughes was not giving him the chance.

Stone's interpretation of Hughes's role in the conference was not universal. Some years later—Hughes had since died—Owen Roberts spoke of him in conference with words of respect and admiration:

His presentation of the facts of a case was full and impartial. His summary of the legal questions arising out of the facts was equally complete, dealing with the opposing contentions so as to make them stand out clearly. When this had been done he would usually look up with a quizzical smile and say, "Now I will state where I come out," and would then outline what he thought the decision of the Court should be. Again in many cases his treatment was so complete that little if anything, further could be added by any of the justices. In close and difficult cases, where there were opposing views, the discussion would go around the table from the senior to the junior, each stating his views and the reason for his concurrence or his difference with those outlined by the Chief. After the Chief Justice had finished his statement of the case and others took up the discussion, I have never known him to interrupt or to get into an argument with the justice who was speaking. He would wait until the discussion had closed and then briefly and succinctly call attention to the matters developed in the discussion as to which he agreed or disagreed.

Obviously, then, the opinion of Charles Evans Hughes in conference depended partly on personal predilections.

Still, Stone was not alone in suspecting Hughes's tendency to be found, publicly at least, in the liberals' corner and also to avoid giving people like Stone an opportunity to attack him. During the Court fight one Republican wrote to Herbert Hoover that Hughes was concerned, first, by what history's verdict of him would be if the Court were changed while he was Chief Justice and, second, by his desire for popular favor. The Republican continued that Hughes's desire for popular favor apparently began after his defeat for the Presidency in 1916. Now, on the Court, he seemed to believe that being tagged a "liberal" was the way to woo the public, particularly with the example of Louis Brandeis—known as the greatest liberal of them all and highly esteemed by the public. This version of how and why Hughes developed his philosophy in the manner that he did agrees somewhat with a description of Hughes made some years later by Owen Roberts. "I am sure that it was his inveterate habit not to undertake any work without a careful and rational analysis of what was involved," Roberts said in 1948. "Once he had made that analysis and had satisfied himself of the course he should pursue, he laid aside all further questions as to the program and plunged into it according to his own blueprint." Charles Evans Hughes, so Stone believed, had carefully plotted out how to influence history's verdict of himself and then worked zealously to achieve that influence.

Harlan Fiske Stone decided to thwart Charles Evans Hughes's plotting.

Although Hughes was a former governor and Presidential candidate and was expected to have the most political inclinations, he was actually second in that respect to Stone. No one intrigued more behind the scenes than did the former Attorney General. Early in March, for example, Representative Emanuel Celler made a radio speech in which he said the Roosevelt plan was unnecessary because two justices of the Supreme Court planned to retire within six months to one year. His source, Celler told his radio audience, was "a distinguished jurist of highest authority—he shall be nameless." Celler, a graduate of the Columbia University Law School, had a close association with Stone, who was a former dean of that school. Stone was the "distinguished jurist" who had told Celler about the possible double retirement. In so doing, Stone gave what was only a rumor the appearance of a fact; he had no real knowledge that any of the justices did plan to retire as he told Celler he did. Stone also did something few justices of the Supreme Court ever did: in private conversations with non-Court members he discussed the possibility that future decisions by the Court would move toward a New Deal liberalism and negate the need for FDR's plan. This hinting of what went on in the Court's Conference Room was a violation of tradition and may have been unique among members of the Court. Stone's intention was to undercut the President's proposal by suggesting that the need for it would not exist in the near future.

At the same time, Stone played a double game. As he spoke to his acquaintances of his anxiety about the President's proposal— "I have no hesitation in saying, for your own personal information, that I think the present proposal is too high a price to pay for the correction of some decisions of the Court"—and worked against it in other ways, he also did not hesitate to be a source of information for FDR on the inside workings of the Supreme Court. He frequently spoke to newsmen and other Washington figures, knowing that they would carry his message back to the White House, either to the President directly or to Presidential aides like Tommy Corcoran. One of Stone's assistants at this period later described the justice as indiscreet.

Stone's chief emissary to the White House was Irving Brant, a reporter. Stone used him to carry to FDR Stone's message of a compromise on the Court fight. This compromise also would have eliminated Charles Evans Hughes from the Supreme Court. That was its purpose.

After talking with Stone, and at Stone's suggestion, Brant wrote a lengthy memorandum to the President. Dated April 7, 1937, the memorandum begins by describing its contents as "some thoughts on the Supreme Court situation, representing in part my own conclusions, and in part information given me by members of the Court. In some instances the origin is self-evident; in other cases deductions as to origin would be misleading, but I think it best not to separate them." Brant then reported that "all members of the Court are opposed to having fifteen members because it would destroy intimacy of contact and interchange of thought in conference. The liberals believe nine is preferable if all are able and willing to do their share of opinion-writing. Eleven would make opinion-writing easier but would injure the work of the Court in conference. I think the preference for nine is definite." Brant then argued that the liberalization of the Court should not appear to be forced, otherwise it would not have widespread support. He continued then that an increase to twelve members would be better than an increase to fifteen, and "I should regard it as a grave error in tactics to let the number fifteen appear in any way in the final plan, because it has become a symbol of all the fears conjured up by the opposition both among your enemies and your friends."

Then Brant discussed Charles Evans Hughes. "If there are no voluntary retirements and the court is enlarged," he said, "there will still remain an important inside problem, centering in Chief Justice Hughes." Brant next claimed to "have found a key to [Hughes's] seeming contradictions" guided "by a brief remark made to me." This "brief remark" had come from Stone. Then Brant proceeded to explain Hughes's techniques of assigning opinion writing and of voting so that he appeared to be a liberal and how Hughes did not permit the liberal members of the Court to attack him.

Further inquiry shows that when Hughes essays to speak for the dissenting minority, there is usually a separate dissent by Brandeis, Stone, and Cardozo. That is because Hughes is too stubborn to accommodate himself in the slightest degree even to those who are in agreement with his position. To sum up, the Chief Justice is a reactionary on economic questions—with some concessions to public opinion, a liberal where

civil liberties are concerned, and is at all times governed by stubbornness and foxiness, these traits centering in a desire to win a reputation
for liberal leadership while playing a reactionary game.

So far Brant had told FDR little more than the President already
knew about Hughes, but this had been just the warmup. "Suppose
the court is enlarged and you get a consistent liberal majority,"
continued Brant. "Hughes, as Chief Justice, will be able to join
the majority and write the opinions in key cases. He will be able
to validate acts of Congress in terms so narrow and grudging that
the opinions will bar the way to some actions while opening the
way to others. You might have a broader concurring opinion joined
in by the majority of the Court, and therefore representing the
views of the Court, but it would be discounted in the popular mind
by the precedence given to the Chief Justice's opinion. As long as
Hughes heads the court," emphasized Brant, "he is likely to be
more harmful in agreement with a liberal court majority than in
dissent from it." At that point Brant suggested that Roosevelt, in
addition to his present Court fight, seek a constitutional amendment
requiring Supreme Court justices to step down from the bench at
age seventy-five. In 1937 Charles Evans Hughes would pass his
seventy-fifth birthday and Harlan Fiske Stone would become sixty-
four.

The White House at this time was so opposed to the idea of a
constitutional amendment that Brant's proposal for one requiring
the justices to retire at seventy-five was not given much attention.
Stone's opportunity to become Chief Justice did not come until
1941, when Charles Evans Hughes chose to retire; then Stone was
able to fulfill his ambition.

The same day that Brant was writing his memorandum to the
President expressing Stone's views, Stone was writing: "Roosevelt
is giving the Court a lively time, but for the most part I am sitting
pretty. I have said nothing which I have to unsay, and nothing
which has drawn serious criticism from either camp in the fight."
And the next day Stone said: "I go my way, doing the day's task,
and render unto Caesar the things that are Caesar's, by letting the
political arm of the government decide whether they want six new

judges or are content with nine." Seldom, however, had one who claimed to "render unto Caesar" hidden more behind his own skirts than did Harlan Fiske Stone.

Stone's machinations have so much of an air of intrigue about them because he knew that the problem that had caused Franklin Roosevelt to attempt to pack the Court was even then disappearing, that the problem of a conservative majority on the Court had begun to fade actually weeks before FDR had called his Cabinet members and Congressional leaders together to announce his proposal that morning of February 5. Even as the Congressional hearings droned on and as the advocates of both sides collected what strength they could find, the process had begun that would turn FDR's duel with the Supreme Court into a conflict of vague, eerie, and sometimes awesome shadows. In time these shadows would part to reveal the true antagonists, antagonists whose conflict would sear the pages of American history for decades.

10

IN 1923 THE SUPREME COURT had ruled that the Congress could not establish a minimum wage in the District of Columbia, the nation's one federal city. In June of 1936 in another case involving a similar issue, the Court ruled that the state of New York could not establish a minimum wage for women working within its borders. Associate Justice Owen J. Roberts joined with the four conservative members of the Court to bar New York's minimum wage law in this 1936 decision. On March 29, 1937, less than ten months later, Roberts voted with the liberal bloc—Hughes, Stone, Brandeis, and Cardozo—to uphold another state minimum wage law. A young New Deal lawyer named Abe Fortas characterized Roberts' change as "the switch in time that serves nine." This Roberts switch on minimum wage which gave the New Deal philosophy a majority on the Court was the start of the "Roosevelt Court." No move by the Court or by any member of the Court did more to hurt FDR's plan than this. "Many who had felt obliged to support the plan 'to save the Constitution from the Court and the Court from itself,' " said one New Dealer, "had done so with sadness in their hearts. As soon as the Court began to show contrition and to do penance for its sins, sentiment grew for forgiveness."

The Administration naturally believed the shift in the Court's philosophy was a riposte to Roosevelt's original thrust on February 5. "Utterly baseless," replied Charles Evans Hughes to such suggestions, insisting: "The Court acted with complete independence." And Owen Roberts, the man who did the original switching, told Felix Frankfurter almost ten years later that "no action taken by the President in the interim had any causal relation to my action."

In the spring of 1936 when the Court was ruling five-to-four against New York State's right to establish minimum wages, Franklin Roosevelt was under a great deal of public criticism for his liberal policies and the Court was being stoutly defended for blocking his plans. This criticism of the President and the defense of the Court were so loud that persons believed they were more widespread than they actually were. This was also the time when there was talk that Owen Roberts would be pulled from the Court by the Republican party to become its Presidential candidate. It is against this background that Roberts joined with the conservatives to strike down a state's authority to establish a minimum wage. Roberts did not concede that this situation influenced his vote. When the New York case was first brought up in conference, the question was whether the Court should consider it. Roberts claimed that "when my turn came to speak I said I saw no reason to grant the writ [agree to hear the case] unless the Court was prepared to re-examine and overrule the Adkins case." This was the 1923 decision barring a minimum wage in the District of Columbia. "To this remark," according to Roberts, "there was no response around the table." Since four justices had already agreed to hear the case before Roberts spoke, there was no need for comment and the writ was granted (four justices are enough to determine if the Court will hear a case). During the arguments by the attorneys before the Court, the claim was made that it was not necessary to overrule the 1923 decision. "The argument seemed to me to be disingenuous and born of timidity," Roberts said later. "I could find nothing in the record to substantiate the alleged distinction. At conference, I so stated, and stated further that I was taking the state of New York at its word," and voted against the state's minimum wage law.

During the months that followed, several things happened. Alf Landon became the GOP's standard bearer, not Roberts. It became obvious that the 1936 Presidential campaign was partly a public trial of the Supreme Court and that if FDR won, he might make some move against the Court. It was also becoming obvious that FDR would win and win with a big majority. Against that background the Court met in conference on October 10, 1936, to determine again whether it should grant a writ to another state minimum wage case. In the briefs filed in this case, the 1923 decision was being questioned. The Court, if it upheld the right of a state to establish a minimum wage, would have to reverse its 1923 decision as well as the decision handed down the previous June barring New York from setting minimum wages. The Supreme Court often has reversed itself, but rarely has it done so in the course of a few months. Usually years are required to build up a body of legal commentary that can demonstrate to the Court members the error of the previous decision. It was for this reason that the October, 1936, conference was expected to reject the proposal that the Court hear another minimum wage case. The expectation did not prove true. Roberts voted to grant a writ. His reason, he later said, was because the 1923 decision was being challenged, but he was not certain that he mentioned that reason in the conference. There was a considerable amount of surprise among his fellow justices, and one nudged another, saying: "What is the matter with Roberts?"

The case was argued in December, 1936, and the justices voted on it in conference December 19, after FDR's smashing victory in the November elections. "I voted for affirmance," said Roberts— four words that signaled a mighty switch in the Supreme Court. At the time, however, there were only eight members of the Court. Harlan Fiske Stone, a few weeks earlier, had been stricken with a severe attack of dysentery and was required to be away from the Court, recuperating for several months. A final vote on the case could not be taken until he returned. Stone came back to the Court in January. The Chief Justice went to Stone's office and brought him up to date on what had been happening in the Court during his illness. When Hughes spoke of Roberts' changing his attitude toward minimum wage laws, Stone could not believe it. As Hughes explained Roberts' reason—that this second minimum wage case had challenged the 1923 decision while the New York case did not—he conceded the reasoning was difficult to accept. The case was brought up again in conference on February 6, the day after FDR had announced his Court plan. As expected, Stone joined with Hughes, Brandeis, and Cardozo—and Roberts—to uphold a state's right to establish a minimum wage and, by reversing the 1923 decision, also to uphold the right of Congress to establish a minimum wage. The decision writing was assigned, and the case was announced on March 29. Technically, it is true that the switch was made before Roosevelt's specific plan was announced. However, it was made after the strength of FDR with the people had been amply demonstrated at the expense of the Republican party and of the Supreme Court members whose cause the GOP had made its own. Some years later Roberts, speaking somewhat spontaneously, again referring to this period in 1936 and 1937, acknowledged that he had been "fully conscious" of "the tremendous strain and threat to the existing Court."

At the same time that Owen Roberts appeared to be caught in the political crosscurrents of 1936, however, it is true that he was caught in the philosophical crosscurrents also. Because of his background as a lawyer for business and as a Philadelphia Mainliner, it was natural for Roberts to move toward the conservatives when he joined the Court. He became a friend, some even thought a protégé, of James McReynolds. With FDR's blunt introduction of a completely new economics with his New Deal, the world of business and of McReynolds and Roberts responded sharply in opposition. But with Roberts this opposition always was troublesome. His whole background directed him to be against FDR and the New Deal approach to government, but his intellectual viewpoint was not quite so rigid. One student of the Supreme Court has written that Roberts "was anxious to learn . . . and conscientious to weigh and consider. I have it on first-rate authority that at the time of [one case] he paced the floor of his Washington home until the early hours of morning until he finally decided how he should vote."

Whether Owen Roberts, the big, square-jawed man, was a political opportunist whose conversion to liberalism was forced by a correct reading of the political winds, or whether his conversion reflected a change in his own philosophy is a question without a positive answer. Perhaps even Roberts, like most men if asked to explain their real motives, could not have answered it.

As a Monday in 1935 had become known as "Black Monday" because of the adverse decisions handed down by the Court that day, the Monday of March 29, 1937, became known as "White Monday" to the New Dealers. The Court building was packed with Easter visitors to the capital, milling about the halls, lining up in hopes of entering the already crowded Chamber where the nine justices in their dark robes sat before crimson velvet curtains. Outside, the day was bright and clear. Inside, there was an aura of excitement. Most of the wives of the justices also were present, as were a number of senators. As it often does in Washington, the "word" that something of significance was to take place this day in the Court building had passed through the offices of the nation's capital.

Chief Justice Hughes read the majority opinion upholding the minimum wage. In this decision Hughes explained that the Court was doing in March, 1937, what it had refused to do in June of 1936 because in June of 1936 it had not been asked to overrule its earlier 1923 decision. To one New Dealer, Robert Jackson, sitting at the government's table, "this doctrine that the Court would apply bad constitutional law to a case unless the lawyers asked it specifically to correct itself was a bit of face-saving for the Court." Jackson enjoyed himself immensely; he recorded later that "the spectacle of the Court that day frankly and completely reversing itself and striking down its opinion but a few months old was a moment never to be forgotten."

The minority decision, speaking out against the government's right to establish a minimum wage, was read by Justice Sutherland. Fourteen years earlier he had been in the majority when he declared that the Congress did not have the right to establish a minimum wage for the District of Columbia. Then he and his philosophy had been in the ascendancy; the nineteenth century, the past George Sutherland had admired and was placed on the Court to represent, still held sway. Now he was in the minority. Sutherland must sit quietly while the Chief Justice intoned the words that reversed Sutherland and his philosophy, the words that proclaimed the Supreme Court was joining with the Presidency and the Congress in supporting the New Deal philosophy, in welcoming the twentieth century. When it was Sutherland's turn to read his dissent, he began slowly in a curiously muffled voice. As he continued to read, however, his voice grew stronger, the words more distinct. Sutherland knew more perhaps than others did that he was sounding a dying cry. The myth of *laissez-faire,* the legend that the American businessman was a rugged individual—it was all coming to an end. The promise of America, that government would become a tool for the mass of people rather than for the select few with wealth and property, was reaching its fulfillment. No longer would the Supreme Court be the bulwark of that property class; it was assuming a new role. Sutherland understood the change and tried to block it, charging in his dissent: "If the Constitution, intelligently and reasonably construed in the light of these principles, stands in the way of desirable legislation, the blame must rest upon that instrument, and not upon the court for enforcing it according to its terms. The remedy in that situation— and the only true remedy—is to amend the Constitution."

George Sutherland had a look about him of the nineteenth century. His neatly trimmed beard belonged to that era, as did the pince-nez that squeezed his nose. His gray hair was parted near the center of his head, his collar was high, and his look was stern. What he was now insisting in that chamber was that his interpretation of the Constitution, forged against the high-collared past he both loved and resembled, must prevail. The only exception he would allow was by constitutional amendment, the most arduous course open to the people. He could not concede and bluntly refused to acknowledge that he could be in error in the slightest bit, that the light he wanted to keep burning brightly was indeed the light of failure.

No one could be certain, until other decisions came down in later weeks, whether the switch was a one-shot thing or whether it really did represent a historic shift in the Court's approach— whether in fact the Court had defeated Franklin Roosevelt by surrendering to him. Whichever, it was obvious that the decision upholding the minimum wage would make it more difficult to push FDR's Court plan through the Senate.

"I would like to refer to the fact that the Supreme Court," said Joe Robinson, interrupting the discussion on the Senate floor that afternoon, "has reversed itself in the Adkins case and probably in the New York wage case." Burton Wheeler could not resist the temptation to throw out: "I am sure the Senator from Arkansas is delighted because they did it." Robinson snapped back: "Certainly, I am delighted." Actually, the attitude among the FDR supporters in the Senate was one of gloom because their enemy had faded away before them. Wheeler found the situation enjoyable. When one senator announced a day or so later that "I, for one, am very glad the Court ruled as it did," Wheeler replied sarcastically: "May I offer my congratulations for being the first senator in favor of the plan I have heard express that sentiment."

Harlan Fiske Stone did not believe that the single decision would dampen the enthusiasm for Court reform. A couple of days after the decision he commented privately that what impact it would have on the President's bill "remains to be seen." He then spoke of what would become the new Administration argument. "I am fearful, though," he said, "that the dissent of the four so-called conservatives, expounding their views of a rigid and changeless Constitution, apparently to be applied always in the same way, no matter how much the subject matter to which it is applied may change, will stimulate the criticism of the Court and give emphasis to the demand that it be reformed." Harold Ickes had a somewhat different reaction. "It seems to me that, on the whole, the effect will be to weaken the prestige of the Court in public estimation," he said, "because when it was under fire, the Court ran to cover. For my part, I would have had more respect for the Court if it had gone down fighting and snarling after the manner of Justice McReynolds. Hughes and Roberts," Ickes added, "ought to realize that the mob is always ready to tear and rend at any sign of weakness."

As far as the Administration was concerned, the Court had switched only because of Presidential pressure. The White House officials believed this even more strongly when, two weeks later, the Court upheld the Wagner Labor Act—a New Deal measure that the labor unions called their Magna Charta and which was anathema to industry. In upholding the Wagner Act, the Court, in effect, was overruling some of its previous decisions in part. "Certainly it cannot be seriously denied that there was some causal connection between the announcement of the President's program and the decision of the Court on the Wagner Act," was the official Administration position. And Jim Farley quoted the line by humorist Finley Peter Dunne that "no matter whether th' Constitution follows th' flag or not, th' Supreme Court follows th' illiction returns."

The concern remained, however, that the conversion was only short-lived and that the Court would revert to a conservative stance once the impetus for reform had been lost. Homer Cummings charged that "the enlightened judgment which has given us these recent decisions by the narrowest of margins may be eclipsed tomorrow by a return to abstract theories and mistaken assumptions. . . . We find ourselves now in a moment of light. Our problem is to keep that light burning." Cummings was warning the nation to guard against the possibility of the Court's switching back to its conservative stance. He was suggesting that the Court might have surrendered not the war, as some were saying, but only a single battle so that it could then come back to claim a final victory. This then became the new public posture of the Administration, as Stone had predicted: that a one-man majority on a nine-man court was not adequate. "It is not a wholesome situation when an administration, under a mandate to carry out a progressive program," said Cummings, "must face a court of nine, with four votes lost to it in advance." He added, "The margin is too narrow and the risk is too great." Only the appointment of liberals to the Court, the Administration insisted, could assure the permanency of the Court's switch.

FDR, chatting with some newspaper friends, had his own way of describing the situation of his program, being now dependent on the sufferance and "aye" vote of Owen Roberts. Referring to the decisions that had seemed to place certain areas, such as that of minimum wages, in a no-man's land where neither the federal nor the state governments could act, he said, "We have all been worrying about the future of the country as long as the 'No Man's Land' continued to exist. Well, in the last two days the 'No Man's Land' has been eliminated but see what we have in place of it: We are now in 'Roberts' land.' " He then continued that the question to be answered before he made any decisions about dropping his Court plan was whether the reversal by the Court was a temporary or permanent one. "Where do we go from here?" he asked. "Have we any assurance?"

Still, he was having himself a great time. The day the Court upheld the Wagner Act happened to be Speaker Bankhead's birthday. FDR telephoned the Speaker to congratulate him, then added: "It's been a pretty good day for all of us." The morning after the Wagner Act decision he saw a copy of the New York *Herald Tribune*, an opposition newspaper, which praised the upholding of the Wagner Act in an editorial titled "A Great Decision." FDR could not leave that alone. He had Steve Early, his press secre-

tary, do a little research. FDR's memory was correct. Early found
an editorial the *Herald Tribune* had carried two years earlier titled
"Thumbs Down on the Wagner Act," describing what horrible
conditions would develop if the Wagner Act was ever declared
constitutional. "I have been chortling all morning," said a beam-
ing FDR, ". . . and I haven't read *The Washington Post* and I
haven't got *The Chicago Tribune* yet. Or *The Boston Herald*. Today is a very, very happy day."

On Capitol Hill, however, old Joe Robinson had different problems. The Court's reversal cost him votes. He knew it. His job
was to convince the White House of it.

After the Wagner Act decision was handed down, Robinson
had a session with a White House aide. The Senate Majority
Leader carefully went over the Court's decision, point by point,
interpreting it liberally. Then he announced that the White House
had won almost everything it wanted and should not be greedy.
"The thing to do," he said to the White House aide, "is to settle
this thing right now. This bill's raising hell in the Senate. Now
it's going to be worse than ever, but if the President wants to compromise I can get him a couple of extra justices tomorrow. What
he ought to do is say he's won, which he has, agree to compromise
to make the thing sure, and wind the whole business up."

Perhaps winding up "the whole business" at that point would
have been a good idea. Henry Ashurst's delaying tactics were succeeding. The Judiciary Committee hearings were dragging on,
producing only more witnesses and pages of newspaper columns
against the FDR plan. Members of Congress were growing nervous; they wanted to get on with other business. FDR apparently
was getting the decisions he wanted from a compliant Court. There
was much to recommend Robinson's proposal to claim victory and
then accept a suitable compromise. This, however, Franklin Roosevelt believed he could not do. The Court fight obviously had become more than a means of settling a dispute between the executive
branch of the government and the judiciary. The duel now was
openly a struggle between liberalism and conservatism. When senators Harry Byrd and Carter Glass of Virginia made common

cause with William Borah on the Court fight, they found they had more in common than mere opposition to FDR's plan to enlarge the Court. Basically their political philosophies were similar. The party names they went under were not significant. Harry Byrd's allegiance to the Democratic party was to the Democratic party of Virginia; he had no loyalty toward the national Democratic party. This was not unusual for the time. When the modern Democratic party had begun to develop more than one hundred years earlier under Andrew Jackson, it was a "national" party only in the respect that it had members in each state. These state organizations were loosely linked by the understanding that only by joining together could they receive what they wanted, whether it be a canal for the West, slavery or, later, the subjugation of the Negro for the South, or a high tariff for the Northeast. But when Franklin Roosevelt attempted to forge a national purpose onto the party, the segments making up the party rebelled. Democrats like Harry Byrd realized they were much more closely aligned philosophically with the conservatism of the midwestern Republicans than with the political philosophy enunciated by the man in the White House who called himself a Democrat. This movement toward a coalition of southern Democrats and midwestern Republicans had been in the works since FDR's first one hundred days as President when he inundated Congress with his liberal proposals and succeeded in having most of them approved. But it had taken a long time to develop; the political habits of generations are difficult to overcome in a few years. It was very difficult for the southern Democrats, most of them with memories of the Civil War or of the Reconstruction Era, to approach a Republican about working with him or to respond to a Republican if he made the initial overture. But the aversion to the Roosevelt program by conservatives of both parties had been drawing those conservatives together, forcing them to the point where they would have to join if they wanted to give FDR any effective opposition. In the House, a young Republican from the Midwest, Charles A. Halleck of Indiana, was casting sheepish eyes at Howard W. Smith of Virginia, one of the leading Democrats from the South. Even as the Court fight began they were edging around each other, doing a dance of political Romeos and Juliets.

The Court plan completed the coalition process between the conservative Democrats from the South and the conservative Republicans from the Midwest. Although the coalition was led by a Democratic liberal, Burton Wheeler, he was only a front man to disguise the fact that the duel was between liberals and conservatives. Even Wheeler acknowledged that, if in words less cruel to himself. If there had not been a Court plan, then another issue would have brought the two groups of conservatives together; if not in 1937, then perhaps in 1938 or 1939. The movement toward coalition was obvious. It required only a sharp push, such as the Court plan, to close the gap.

Roosevelt always had believed he could deal with the conservatives in his own party. He had done it successfully in the political campaign of 1932 and had demonstrated in 1936 that he could do as he wished with the electorate even as Carter Glass sat on the sidelines declining to cheer FDR on. But the joining of those few Democrats with the midwestern Republicans created a more powerful opposition. If it was allowed to succeed, it would forge a coalition growing stronger with each success and challenging liberalism for years and years. The struggle over the Supreme Court had become a symbol, a symbol of the struggle for the direction of government—toward conservatism or toward liberalism. At the time not everyone understood this. But the politicians—the good ones with the intuitive sense to spot tomorrow's trends before others do—did.

Compromising in the Court dispute—even worse, of course, would be losing it—meant sacrificing to the conservatives of the future the gains of the New Deal and the liberal directions it had begun in American politics. Franklin Roosevelt could not relent in his determination to have complete victory.

He still believed he could win because he had the people behind him. This, as far as he was concerned, was his great strength. When a person wants to believe something, it is easy to respond to the evidence that supports such a belief. For this reason, Franklin Roosevelt began to put too much emphasis on some incidents that were of little significance rather than the straws in the wind he believed they were. Early in April, for example, a federal judge, not on the Supreme Court, wrote FDR, endorsing the enlargement of the Court, saying: "I believe every experienced judge who knows the facts would say the same thing if uninfluenced by personal or political considerations. I further believe that if the matter was submitted to the country at large and every citizen could vote upon it, your original bill would be heartily endorsed by a large majority." The judge added he wished he were a member of the United States Senate so he could vote for FDR's plan. But this was an endorsement from a man who happened to be an old Woodrow Wilson liberal, not a real harbinger of judicial and public reaction.

In March, Harold Ickes had gone down to North Carolina to make a speech in favor of the Court plan. He then told Roosevelt, "There isn't any doubt that North Carolina is behind you with great enthusiasm. The people there are not only for you, they are for your plan to reform the federal judiciary. I had a fine meeting Friday night and a most enthusiastic one." Ickes told the President that people from every part of the state had shown up, and he added: "I have never had such a response from any meeting to which I have made a speech." The haggard Ickes was worn out by people who shook his hand and assured him they were for the Roosevelt plan. They were, those that Ickes saw. But he had permitted his enthusiasm to run over his judgment. Such gatherings usually turn out supporters rather than opponents. Particularly was this true when the people were so closely tied to and dependent upon the New Deal. The real question was not whether the crowds that turned out for a New Deal figure were exuberant in their praise of the President but whether this exuberance was widespread enough and forceful enough to be a political factor, whether, in fact, it could influence reluctant members of Congress to vote for the Court plan.

Tommy Corcoran, on whom FDR relied as an extra pair of eyes and ears on Capitol Hill, believed that it could. A few days after

Ickes' appearance in North Carolina, Corcoran and Ben Cohen joined the Interior Secretary for dinner. In his usual expansive mood, Corcoran predicted that only twenty-two senators would oppose FDR on the final vote. He acknowledged that more than that number had announced either publicly or privately their opposition to the plan. Corcoran was confident, however, that some of those opponents would eventually retreat to the Presidential bosom. Only a few senators, particularly Wheeler, had gone too far in their opposition to be able to retreat when the time came. Corcoran based this estimate of great Roosevelt support, so Ickes said, on the assertion that "the country is beginning to be heard from."

The "country" would be heard from most emphatically almost three weeks later, on April 10, 1937, when a Texan who aspired to political success bet his future on the Court plan while campaigning for a seat in Congress and rolled a winner with his first throw of the dice. Texas was believed strongly against the President's plan. The state was traditionally conservative. This tradition would continue to influence the state's political posture for some decades. Once the New Deal succeeded in breaking the economic hold that eastern bankers had on Texas, the Texan politicians lost interest in the New Deal. In February the Texas state legislature became one of the first local governmental units to go on record in opposition to the President's plan. When the White House found out that a resolution condemning the Court plan was moving through the Texas legislature, Steve Early immediately telephoned Vice President Garner, asking his help to stop it. Garner put Early in touch with Democratic politicians in Austin, where the legislature was meeting. Garner also said that he, working by telephone from Washington, was trying to block the protest against FDR himself. The last-minute try was doomed to failure. Garner was against the Court plan, as were Hatton Sumners and Sam Rayburn, as well as Texas two Democratic senators, Tom Connally and Morris Sheppard. Almost unanimously, the legislature adopted the resolution condemning the Roosevelt plan. Condemnation of a Presidential action by a state legislature was a unique move, a factor making the Texas action that much more serious.

True, late in the month of February Harold Ickes had gone down to Texas to a joint meeting of the state senate and house and defended the Court plan in the midst of a speech about a number of other things. "I could hear a gasp go up as I disclosed my purpose to discuss this issue," he recalled. His remarks, he thought, were rather well received. Certainly the legislators were friendly to him. Well they should have been. Whatever Ickes said about the Court plan, he still was the head of the government agency that was pouring federal funds into the state of Texas for the dams, irrigation projects, and roads that were transforming the state economically. He was the "hand-out" man, and nobody in Texas was going to offend the man who dispensed the government's financial largesse. So, despite this reception accorded to Ickes, Texas still was a good place to be against the Court plan if one wanted to have a political future. At least that was the popular conception when a young man, looking somewhat like a beanpole, filed as a candidate for the vacant seat in the Tenth Congressional District. The man's name was Lyndon Baines Johnson.

Lyndon Johnson was a political switch-hitter who kept his eye always on the main chance. He had first come to Washington as an administrative assistant to a conservative Texas congressman. Then Franklin Roosevelt came to the nation's capital with his New Deal, and the shift obviously was from conservatism to liberalism. Johnson was part of this shift, eventually leaving the conservative congressman to become head of the National Youth Administration in Texas, a New Deal program. His personal hope, born out of the poverty he had known as a youth, was to succeed as himself rather than as some other person's assistant or as head of an agency following someone else's policy. For Johnson this meant developing his own political power; the way his life was developing, politics appeared the only avenue open to him leading to success.

His opportunity came when the congressman for the Tenth District in Texas died and a special election was called. Johnson was in a race for the seat with seven other candidates, most of them better known than he and with more funds for a campaign than he had. But Johnson was smarter than the other candidates. Although all eight were nominally Democrats, the other seven based their campaign on opposition to Franklin Roosevelt and the Court plan. One of the other candidates, Polk Shelton, a former county district attorney, sounded their call with his cry of "no yes-man judges." Johnson realized that these seven were dividing the anti-FDR vote among themselves. His strategy was to gather the pro-FDR vote to himself. So Lyndon Johnson campaigned on a platform of supporting Franklin Roosevelt, including Roosevelt's plan to enlarge the Supreme Court. Soon the entire nation was watching the election contest in that previously little-known Texas Congressional District. If Johnson won, so went the word among the political professionals in Washington, his victory would have an appreciable influence on the attitude of the southern members of Congress. It would be a sign that the unknown quantity referred to as "the people" were behind FDR.

Johnson's strategy was correct. There were enough pro-Roosevelt voters in the District who, when gathered behind a single candidate, were strong enough to elect him. Johnson had followed the technique of divide and conquer. But he had not had to divide his opponents. They did it themselves.

The election was Saturday, April 10, 1937, and Johnson won. *The New York Times* carried a front-page story the next day about the victory of "youthful Lyndon B. Johnson, who shouted his advocacy of President Roosevelt's court reorganization all over the Texas Tenth District." Johnson, according to the story, said he considered his victory "a vote of confidence" in the President and his program. So did Franklin Roosevelt. The *Times*'s story assured the Johnson victory would be well known across the country, and Roosevelt frequently spoke of it in the following weeks. Many years later one of Franklin Roosevelt's close aides at this period reminisced about this Johnson victory. "When Lyndon Johnson won by taking all the pro-Roosevelt votes, FDR relied on this as a show of public opinion in his own behalf—perhaps more than he should have. But," continued the aide, "the key to politics is optimism."

The Johnson victory never had the expected impact among politicians. Two days after the vote, a delegation of Texans appeared before the Senate Judiciary Committee to present a petition with ten thousand signatures against the Court bill. The senators asked the delegation about Johnson's victory, and the Texans' spokesman answered that the election should not be construed as a victory for the Court plan. "The campaign turned on personalities," said L. L. James of Tyler, Texas, "not issues." Later that week another group of Texans, led by Mayor Thomas Miller of Austin, appeared before the committee to insist that, to the contrary, the sole issue in the election had been the Court plan. Miller argued that Johnson had been a relatively unknown person when he entered the campaign and won only because he had promised to support President Roosevelt's program "with the Court issue as the first item on his program."

And so the Johnson election, billed in advance as a great indicator of public sentiment, degenerated into a squabble over its significance. The Administration and its supporters continued to proclaim its symbolism. When Johnson was sworn in as a member of Congress on May 13, Maury Maverick, the Texan who had formally sponsored FDR's Court plan in the House, came to the well of the House, where Johnson stood. "Mr. Speaker," said Maverick, "I ask unanimous consent to address the House for one-half minute." Then said Maverick: "The gentleman just sworn in, Mr. Lyndon Johnson, supported the President's judiciary plan and was overwhelmingly elected." The Democratic members of the House joined in the applause.

Franklin Roosevelt appreciated Lyndon Johnson's accomplishment and admired the young Texan. FDR had planned a fishing trip in the Gulf of Mexico and on his way back traveled through Texas. He made a special point of meeting Lyndon Johnson, in full view of photographers. They posed for one picture shaking hands and another when photographers asked them to pose again. FDR later signed those photographs for Lyndon Johnson, saying on the first, "To Lyndon B. Johnson from his friend," and on the second, "For Lyndon with another handshake." These photographs and the Presidential benevolence they obviously represented were a big boost for the young congressman, both in Texas and nationally, the first of such assists he received from the man in the White House to recompense him for his seeming to demonstrate that the public endorsed the Court plan.

Coming back to Washington, Franklin Roosevelt carried that message with him: the public was for him. The Congressional leaders came to the White House, their faces glum and their predictions bleak. But FDR would have none of their despair and defeatism. He presented them with a list of "must" legislation which, he commanded, was to be passed. Prominent on the list was the Court plan, the full plan, not any compromises such as Joe Robinson was angling for. Speaker Bankhead and Sam Rayburn agreed FDR had his "fighting" clothes on, but they found the situation more amusing than worrisome. The problem was the Court plan, but that was Joe Robinson's problem, not theirs. And it was a very unhappy Senate Democratic leader who emerged from the President's office to tell newsmen that as far as the Court plan was concerned "the battle will go on." Pressed by the newsmen, the worried Robinson conceded the vote would be close, but he insisted that the plan had a "fair prospect" of passage. Robinson was being the good soldier. His leader told him he wanted something done; he would try to do it. That was the Senate Majority Leader's position then—more than a flunky, but not much more.

The same day he met with the Congressional leaders, FDR also had a session with his Cabinet. Again he was his exuberant, forceful, domineering self. He began the Cabinet session by describing his train trip through Texas, saying he had talked with a number of local politicians and was convinced the public backed his plan. Those members of Congress who did not support him, he said, probably would be defeated by their constituents. FDR told his Cabinet members that the thing to do to sell the plan was to "hit them hard," mow down the opposition. The people, he said, like a battle. Harold Ickes thought he had never seen FDR "so full of fight." Jim Farley caught the spirit too. His main personal prejudice was against Joe O'Mahoney, who had come to the Senate from Farley's Post Office Department and with the blessing of the New Deal but then had backed out on supporting the Court plan. Farley announced then to the Cabinet members that O'Mahoney would have difficulty obtaining Administration favors in the future. There also were a dozen or so other senators listed as doubtful. Farley suggested FDR meet with each of them separately and "put the screws" on them.

But the belief that "the people" backed him and that the members of Congress would respond to their command only obscured for Roosevelt that his plan was in deep trouble on Capitol Hill. The trouble was not only caused by the reluctance of the cautious members of Congress to go along with such a daring program as attacking the Supreme Court, not only by the members' desire to strike back at FDR, not only by the new strength of the conservative coalition; it was also caused by the incompetence of the FDR forces. The Court fight should have been the crowning victory of the White House if, as was thought at the time, the White House was the boss of the government. Actually, the White House was the "boss" of very little. What had been FDR's genius in his first term was not the bossing of anyone but the assuming of leadership of a nationwide desire for change. He guided that desire into generally constructive areas, at times promoted it, pushed it a little. He succeeded because the Congress, the tool for this change, understood the nation wanted the change and was willing to accede to it. The Court plan was a new challenge for FDR, however. Particularly after the Roberts switch, there was no nationwide desire for altering the Court, and, as a result, no great desire in Congress either. FDR's job now must be to impose his will on a reluctant Congress. This he had not done before on a major issue.

After the first few weeks it was apparent that no one was really sure which way the Congress would go on the Court plan. At the end of February, for example, one knowledgeable Republican senator made this private assessment: "I think the Roosevelt program in its present form is blocked. I feel quite certain we have enough votes to upset him. . . . The protests reaching Washington from all sections of the country have been overwhelming. We have seen nothing like it in many years." A couple of Saturdays later, however, a group of Democratic senators supporting FDR gathered together to discuss prospects for the Court bill. "It was encouraging to me," said one of those senators, speaking privately also, "to find that the unanimous opinion of all present was that we should reject any suggestions of compromise and stand fast by the original proposal. . . . Every senator present indicated supreme confidence in the ultimate outcome. They regarded the suggestions of compromise from the opponents as an indication of their sense of weakness."

By the end of April the outcome still was doubtful. Harold Ickes had some indirect lines to the Republican National Committee and learned that the GOP could rely on only thirty-seven votes in the Senate against FDR; forty-nine was a majority. When he reported this to the President, FDR said that figure was about right for the opposition. His problem was, the President continued, that he could count only forty-two sure votes himself. This meant the outcome would be decided by the seventeen uncommitted senators. By this time also, however, it was clear the Roosevelt forces were relying on faulty information and vain hopes. Included among those seventeen "uncommitted" votes, for example, were senators Gerald Nye of North Dakota, the Republican who made one of the first radio speeches against the Court plan in February, and Henrik Shipstead, the Farmer-Labor party man from Minnesota who had already made known his opposition to the plan to his Senate colleagues and would shortly announce it publicly. But White House aides—Tommy Corcoran and some of the others— insisted that such senators as Nye, Shipstead, and a few of those known to be against the plan were in fact undecided and could be persuaded to support FDR eventually. This was a gross miscalculation by young men who did not understand the Senate or the senators. It was a miscalculation made by men who believed that only they were men of principle and that their opponents were grubby politicians who could be easily manipulated. It was one of many such miscalculations in the Court fight.

Another miscalculation was made by FDR himself when he assumed that Henry Fountain Ashurst could or would block his Judiciary Committee from forming a public position against the President's plan. A chairman of a Congressional committee has a great deal of power but not nearly so much power as a Congressional outsider believes he has. A committee chairman can delay or harass legislation. But he can only block or substantially alter legislative proposals when a majority of the committee agrees with him. A chairman has some leverage to exert on his committee members, some deals to offer in exchange for votes, but not too much, and very little on major issues which have the political spotlight turned on them. When the Judiciary Committee hearings finally ended on April 23, it was obvious, even if not publicly stated, that a majority of the committee opposed FDR's plan and would write a report criticizing it. Against this background, Roosevelt summoned Ashurst to the White House. Ashurst told the story of that session:

Eff Dee leaves tomorrow for a two-weeks' fishing cruise in the Gulf of Mexico. At the White House today the mercury of his manners toward me registered zero as he suggested that his bill for judicial reorganization be reported from the Senate Committee on the Judiciary in the Senate *without recommendation* and he handed me a memorandum containing some data he desired should be used in such proposed Report. He requested me to show the memorandum to Senator Robinson, Democratic Majority Leader, which I did during the afternoon and upon exploring the situation, Senator Robinson and I ascertained that to report the bill without recommendation was not feasible.

I was not surprised this evening when a "Friendly Voice," nameless here, came over the telephone warning me that Eff Dee believes that I have killed his judicial reorganization bill by Fabian Tactics and by delay and postponement in that although he submitted his plan to the Senate on February Fifth, last, I did not commence the hearings before my Committee until March Tenth and then strung the testimony out.

Beyond doubt my refusal to pass his judicial reorganization bill through the Senate has alienated him from me and has also damaged my prospects for re-election to the Senate in 1940 as a majority of my constituents are intensely pro-Roosevelt and, similar to other constituencies suffering from an economic depression, are torridly radical and favor this bill.

Ashurst was making his comments in the privacy of his diary, a document that would continue to remain private. His acknowledgment there that he was indeed refusing to cooperate with Roosevelt on the Court bill and that he was endangering himself politically was not a play for sympathy votes, only a play for the understanding of later students of his career.

Publicly, Ashurst continued to speak like an FDR man—a tactic that made his secret opposition all the more effective. When the committee ended its public hearings on Friday, April 23, and announced that its closed-door sessions would begin on Monday for the drafting of a report, Ashurst scoffed at the prospect of a negative report. "An unfavorable report would in no sense be a fatal blow," he insisted to newsmen. "Everybody knew from the start that the committee was not for the bill." He then insisted that the nation was anxious for the Congress to pass the Court plan over the wishes of the Judiciary Committee. Ashurst's statement was ludicrous. It often happens that committee members from the President's party oppose him in the privacy of a closed-door committee session. It happened many times before the Court plan; it has happened many times since. Usually, however, the opposition is not a wild shout of defiance at the party leader but a quiet, although still effective, move. Committee members can simply decline to report legislation out of their committees. This makes their point without their having to go on public record against their President. Another device often used in the privacy of committee sessions is to change the bill completely or to compromise it in some fashion. With the Court bill, for example, if FDR refused to compromise, there was nothing to stop the committee from forcing the issue by reporting out a new bill, one that embodied a compromise, rather than FDR's original proposal. It could even report the bill "without recommendation," as FDR wanted. But Ashurst was announcing that his committee, controlled by the President's own party, would not do any of these things. Instead it would choose the path of most insolence to the President. As much as Ashurst tried to shrug this off, it was a fact that stunned Washington. And a stunned Washington would become a shocked Washington when the actual words of the committee's report became public.

On Wednesday, April 28, three members of the Judiciary Committee who had not formally announced their position on the Court plan publicly stated they were against it. These three were Pat McCarran of Nevada, Carl A. Hatch of New Mexico, and Joseph O'Mahoney of Wyoming—all Democrats. Actually their opposition had either been known, as in O'Mahoney's case, or was anticipated. But their public statements meant that the Administration forces could not hide that the committee was divided ten-to-eight against the Roosevelt plan. In his usual melifluous manner, Ashurst simply dismissed the breakdown, now known to the public, as incidental. He announced grandly that the Senate would vote on the bill in the middle of July and that passage was expected. "The plan has passed from the stage of ridicule to the stage of argument. From the stage of argument it will pass to the stage of enactment," he said. Then there was the first public hint by Ashurst that the outcome might go the other way. "I am going to get a clean victory," he said, "or a clean defeat."

Mixed in with FDR's difficulties in Congress over his Court plan was a gathering of other troubles. He was dividing with the conservatives in the Democratic party, including Vice President Garner, over labor and budget differences. The unions' newest tactic, and one gaining them a great deal of success in 1937, was the sit-down strike. The union members just sat at their places of work when quitting time came, refusing to move. At first it seemed like a joke, but it wasn't. The union members proceeded to take over the factories where they worked, preventing production. Management could not persuade them to leave voluntarily. If management attempted to force them out, then management would be placing its own valuable factories in danger of physical damage. From labor's viewpoint the tactic was a brilliant maneuver. It's biggest success came early in 1937 when General Motors, after six weeks of having its plants "occupied" by a dirty, bearded, hungry, and jubilant army of United Auto Workers, gave in to the UAW. A few weeks later the United States Steel Company met union demands without a fight; it would not risk trouble. Plainly, to the businessmen and the political conservatives, the sit-down strike had to be stopped. They appealed to their friends in Washington. As a result, Vice President Garner managed to arrange a discussion on the situation at the White House. It was not a happy gathering. The conservatives believed the strikes were lawless. Also, they believed the strikes had the President's tacit approval. At this session the President did nothing to disabuse them of that notion. Garner's next move was to have Jimmy Byrnes, the Democratic senator from South Carolina, introduce a Congressional resolution condemning the strikes. This was thwarted, however, when Labor Secretary Perkins announced she supported them. FDR did not make a comment on her announcement, a sign that was interpreted by the public to mean he favored her position of supporting the sit-down strikes.

The conservatives, led by Garner, were angered again when during the spring of 1937 they became involved with Roosevelt in an argument about the federal budget. Garner naturally was pressing FDR to reduce expenditures. The President's usual response to this was to make some vague comment about doing just that—next year. Again there was a White House discussion, this one on the budget. Roosevelt had proposed a relief expenditure figure of $1.5 billion. The Congressional leaders, led by Garner and Jimmy Byrnes, argued that the relief bill should be cut by several hundred million dollars. It was an angry session, with Franklin Roosevelt and the conservatives of his party shouting back and forth at each other, shaking their fists, and each side remaining adamant. Not only were the conservatives angry at FDR over the soaring budget figures and his support for labor, but they also realized that Congress could no longer go along with FDR's social experimentation. In the past the conservatives had relied on the Supreme Court to defend the country from any results that would be too outlandish. But Owen J. Roberts had nixed that possibility for them. The conservatives among the Democrats in Congress would have to do their own fighting. To them it now appeared that Harry Byrd, Carter Glass, and Millard Tydings, who had fought the Court plan from the beginning, apparently had had the right approach all along.

"Cactus Jack" Garner began to make very clear that he at least was no longer part of Franklin Roosevelt's stable of willing lieutenants. How should I vote on this issue? a Democratic senator asked the Vice President about the Court plan in April. "Let your conscience be your guide," answered Garner—not a phrase calling for loyalty to the President.

Still, this message of Congressional unrest was not getting through to the White House and to the President. Early in May, Harold Ickes, concerned about the Court bill's prospects, telephoned Corcoran. The bubbly "Tommy the Cork" assured Ickes there was little cause for concern. He rattled off the names of several senators who, Corcoran said, were certain to vote for the bill. The list still included the names of senators Nye and Shipstead, who were definitely against the bill to the end. Corcoran said most of the trouble lay with Henry Ashurst, claiming that the Arizonan had delayed the bill so much because he enjoyed the publicity he was receiving for holding the hearings. In the telephone conversation, Corcoran tossed off that it might be necessary to force a motion through the Senate to discharge the Ashurst committee from further consideration of the bill in order to bring it to the Senate floor for a vote. Ickes found Corcoran's whole attitude of supreme self-confidence reassuring. Actually Corcoran's comments indicated he had miscalculated tremendously. First, rather than blocking the bill, the committee was by this time anxious to send it to the Senate floor with a scathing report and a recommendation that the Senate disapprove it. Second, his talk of a discharge motion was the fanciful comment of a person who had little conception of the Senate. That institution does at times rebuke one of its committee chairmen but not very often, and only when the committee chairman has been so derelict in his responsibilities as to be contemptuous of the Senate. Whether the chairman might be contemptuous of the President is of little concern to the members of the Senate. Such a move as discharging the Ashurst committee could succeed only if the Senate was almost unanimously behind FDR, and no one thought it was that. No one, that is, who really knew what was going on.

The President's friends among the members of Congress, those who saw him on occasion and could speak with him, were reluctant to do so. There were too many stories circulating in the Senate cloakroom of FDR's taking unkindly to suggestions that his Court plan was in trouble. One senator claimed that he tried to talk reason to FDR but that the President froze up and would not listen to a word about compromise. Another senator, according to a story in the cloakrooms, told the President that his Court plan was searing a line through the Senate, dividing friends, splitting up the Sunday morning golf games, turning pleasant dinner parties into furious debating sessions. Roosevelt responded to this, so the cloakroom story went, by saying that the senator giving him the information was against the Court plan and only saying such things in hopes of defeating it. In this kind of atmosphere, there was not much inclination on Capitol Hill to tell Franklin Roosevelt the harsh truth he needed to know: his original Court bill could not pass.

When Roosevelt came back from his fishing trip to the Gulf of Mexico, the trip with the side visit to Texas, where he stopped off to be photographed with Lyndon Johnson, he immediately should have sensed the Congressional atmosphere. When his train pulled into Union Station, the President was greeted by only a few friends from his private and official families. In 1934, three years earlier, he had returned from a similar trip to be greeted by hundreds of members of Congress anxious to wave to him, to have him know they had affection for him and wanted to stand behind him. This time when he returned, there were no members of Congress on hand. One Republican recorded why, writing: "To them he is no longer the 'tough guy,' who in 1934 came back from

Florida waters and found obsequious houses, ready to enact his slightest whim. Today we are finding an assertion of legislative independence."

Roosevelt appeared not to notice, perhaps did not wish to notice. He was still filled with the account of young Lyndon Johnson's victory and with other stories of popular support for his Court plan. It was at this point that he met with his Congressional leaders and gave them marching orders: the full Court plan and nothing less! Franklin Roosevelt always before had possessed perfect timing, a near-perfect intuitive sense of what could be accomplished. These qualities had left him now. He had become too committed to the Court plan. He could not back down. He could not permit himself to back down. And he was to learn a lesson. Franklin Roosevelt who had taught so many other politicians would now be taught by them that in a duel, as in a war, retreat may be the better strategy even if it is not the better part of valor. "I believe we are going to beat the Roosevelt Supreme Court program," predicted a Republican senator to a friend a few days after FDR had issued his command to Joe Robinson. "It is a close fight," said the Republican, "but it looks better every day."

11

FRANKLIN ROOSEVELT did realize the time had come to take a personal hand in an attempt to fix up his deteriorating relations with Congress. In his usual Machiavellian manner, FDR decided to take an unexpected approach. He would not "strongarm" the recalcitrant congressmen with patronage and power as expected but would instead woo them with smiles, sunshine, beer, and hardshell crabs. His plan was to offer a gigantic three-day picnic at which he would hold court, meeting and chatting with his Democratic "friends." He chose the Jefferson Island Club, a cozy retreat on an island near Annapolis, about fifty miles from Washington. Surrounded by water, the Democrats could relax, patronize the bar, and remove their ties and collars without fear that the press would observe them and report back to their constituencies. The menu included, in addition to the hard-shell crabs, cold meat and potato salad. There was also plenty of beer and a well-stocked bar. FDR himself sat under an apple tree, appearing as casual as his most relaxed guest. He wore an old pair of linen pants, no jacket, and a shirt open at the collar with no tie. He laughed frequently, smiled more often. He seemed to be thoroughly enjoying himself. Even as he laughed and joked with his friends from the Democratic party, however, he was acting still with bad advice.

A few days before the picnic marathon began one of his close political lieutenants had advised FDR: "Rather than agree to a compromise and thereby recognize defeat, find a proper excuse to let the bill go over until next January. This procedure would avoid the long and acrimonious debate that pushing the measure this summer would entail. Then, in my opinion, the opposition will be less vigorous next January after members of Congress have canvassed the sentiment on the ground at home. Furthermore [Roosevelt] will have more time to assist with radio addresses and otherwise between now and January." Of course just the opposite would have been the effect; delaying the bill until January would have permitted more opposition to gather. FDR's only hope of success now lay with going along on a compromise, and the sooner the better. And one reason was the public animosity building up against the Court plan. But Roosevelt, who believed Lyndon Johnson had been elected in the Tenth Congressional District of Texas primarily because the young Texan sensed that the people of his district favored the Court plan, could find other things to believe rather than accept the fact of growing animosity. Again, just before the Jefferson Island picnic, FDR was told about an incident at Mason City, Iowa, in which that state's bar association voted to condemn the President because of his Court plan. The

President was told not to be concerned because "eighty-five or ninety per cent of them are old standpat Republicans who never voted the Democratic ticket in their life and never expect to." Even if that were true, the Iowa Bar Association action and others like it were serious problems because such actions influenced other groups and individuals. This was the shaping of public opinion by the middle class of which William Allen White had written. This and the growing Congressional disenchantment with the man in the White House were the twin evils for Franklin Roosevelt as the three-day attempt at fence mending began.

The three days seemed to go extremely well. Approximately one hundred and fifty Democrats from the House and Senate came to the island each day. They expected to be proselytized. Instead they were entertained. The food was good. The drinks were large. Even the weather cooperated. The days were hot and the sky was clear. The men shucked their jackets and ties and sat around swapping stories, singing songs, and generally making friends with each other. A few of the members of Congress even went into the water for a swim. Not many did, however. Congressmen then tended to be large, slow, and unathletic. Each of the members made the trip to the apple tree where FDR waited for them, his face all smiles and his eyes sparkling behind his sunglasses. The members came to that apple tree braced for a hard sell on the Court plan and other issues, but FDR surprised them by not talking politics. He said he was happy to see them, recalled a funny story from the last time they had met, asked them about an old mutual friend. He talked about anything he could think of, except politics. FDR's purpose of course was to sell himself to the Congressmen. His hope was to reestablish the rapport he believed he once had with Capitol Hill. Never having been a member of Congress, Roosevelt did not understand that members of Congress do not have any rapport with the Presidency. They may fear it, scoff at it, be awed by the leadership of the public it seems to exercise, but they never have rapport with it. By constitutional decree, the members of Congress are in jealous competition with the Presidency. They are its rivals for power.

Still, the picnic appeared a happy occasion. There were even jokes about the lack of political discussion with the President. "Say," said one White House aide, "don't you think the country will be under control by Sunday noon at the latest?" A few members did politic among themselves. "You fellows in the Senate," said one House member, "ought to get wise to yourselves and give us a Supreme Court bill with eleven justices in it. Why not get away from Washington by July 25?"

The "hail fellow" atmosphere of the three-day picnic might have been helpful if it had been coupled with a resurgence of FDR's political strength. But the forces that the President had been anticipating assistance from were not responding, particularly labor and the farmers.

Although union members benefited from the New Deal, union leaders established the organizations' formal positions toward the Roosevelt Administration. Publicly it was difficult for the union leaders to do anything except claim they supported FDR and his program. Privately, when it came to providing the kind of "muscle" that FDR hoped for, the union leaders were less than cooperative. They did not solicit votes for FDR's Court plan in the halls of Congress as he anticipated they would do, nor did they collect petitions or urge their members to write their representatives in Congress. Most of the union leaders did very little, in fact. The American labor movement in the 1930s was deeply split. On the one side were the leaders of the American Federation of Labor, the amalgamation of American labor unions then. Most of the AFL unions were craft unions—the carpenters', the plumbers', and the like. These unions were not particularly anxious to expand their membership. As long as they controlled the size of their memberships, they controlled the number of workmen available for jobs. With a limited number of workmen available, their prices stayed high. To keep up this arrangement the workmen were happy to pay reasonably high union dues to keep their union leaders in a style of their choice. The only possibility of jeopardizing this setup was if a contractor refused to hire union help. The answer to this was the closed shop, forcing an employer to hire only union members. The AFL secured this with the Wagner Act, upheld by the Supreme Court in April, two weeks after Roberts' first switch. After that, the AFL leaders were not interested in what happened to FDR's program other than to pay it lip service. They actually opposed him and parts of his program. The New Deal would result, they feared, in an enlargement of union membership. This, the union leaders' philosophy continued, meant that the individual craftsman could not continue to dictate a high price for his services. The union leaders themselves, accustomed to working with only a relatively small group of men, might not be able to control their membership; might, in fact, get ousted from office. On the other side, opposite these labor Neanderthals, was the crusading spirit of the industrial unions led by John L. Lewis. His approach was to organize all the employees of an industry into one union, not to break them down by their individual jobs. This made the industrial union a more powerful strike weapon. This also demanded that such unions have as wide a membership as possible. The leaders of these unions accepted that their berths as union heads could never be secure unless they worked to hold their positions. This group of union leaders would have backed FDR except that they were wrapped up with their own squabbles with the AFL people, with themselves, with employers, and with anyone else they could find. They were a combative group. Also, John L. Lewis still had not reconciled himself to FDR since their difficulties at the beginning of the year. The two men were growing farther apart. No, the labor unions were not producing for Franklin Roosevelt as he believed he had a right to expect they would.

The farmers did no better for Roosevelt. His refusal to buy their support with promises of specific programs and assistance when tied in with the farmers' innate suspicion of Democrats was sufficient to drive the farm organizations away from the FDR fold. One farm leader, Louis J. Taber, the president of the National Grange, best summed up the conflicting stance of the farmers in relation to the New Deal: accept its benefits but don't support it. "Let us give credit," said Taber, "at the very outset of this discussion to the President of the United States and to the administration for courageous and constructive guidance that has made possible the improved conditions we enjoy and which have helped lift us out of the depression." He then acknowledged that "the farmer's share of the nation's income has increased, farm purchasing power is being restored, wages are advancing, business, manufacturing, and transportation are on the upward march." Magnanimously, Taber then said: "And surely we can give some credit to those in power for this achievement." At that point Taber then announced his opposition to "those in power" over the Court plan because he claimed the success of the Court plan meant ultimately too much federal power. "Who of us wants a federal inspector or bureaucrat," he asked, "to tell us whom we shall employ for school teacher, how we should drain our roads, how we shall repair our bridges . . . ?" And on and on in a like vein with criticisms unrelated to the Court bill. His position was quite clear. It was perfectly acceptable for the federal government to take any action that resulted in an improvement in farmers' income, but it was improper for the federal government to take actions that might result in the improvement of anyone else's income.

Taber actually was a conservative Republican. He and his grange had supported Landon the previous year, and the Administration had not counted on him for a great deal of support. But the other farm groups, the "liberal" ones, did no better for FDR. Some of the leaders of farm groups told Roosevelt they personally favored his plan, but they then sat idly by while their groups went on record against the plan.

These farmers, the labor leaders, Texans like Tom Connally and Republicans like Gerald Nye, were teaching FDR a lesson. He had hoped to forge a great liberal coalition and, in fact, had come very close to doing so in the 1936 campaign. But the President misunderstood the motives of the people behind him. He confused their self-interest with his own national interest. Each of these individuals and the groups they represented, and the others like them, had given support to the New Deal as long as there was something specific they wished out of the New Deal. Once they had achieved their aim, they were no longer interested in the New

Deal. Franklin Roosevelt had a vision of the United States as a great integrated unit. He realized that the farmers could not hope to continue to enjoy a rising prosperity unless the city dwellers also had a rising prosperity with which to purchase the farm products. He understood that Texas was not an economic unit complete within its borders, that it must deal with a viable national community if it was to be prosperous. Franklin Roosevelt well appreciated the difficulties under which the labor unions were operating; he also knew that the gains they had made could be eliminated quickly if a conservative form of government returned to Washington. But his national view was a unique perspective in 1937. The economic minority groups from which he expected support had spent decades fighting for their gains. Now that they had them, or were on the verge of receiving them, their leaders were lighting up fifty-cent cigars and forgetting about the other guy. The liberal coalition was breaking up; each member had gotten his.

12

A TREND BUILDS up its own momentum. When things go well, it seems nothing can break the spell of success. But when things start sliding downhill, nothing can break the fall. So it happened with FDR's Court plan. After a while, it seemed that nothing the Administration did was right or helpful.

Jim Farley actually started the decline early in March when he delivered a speech at the University of North Carolina. His subject before the Carolina Political Union, a student nonpartisan organization, was party responsibility. Should a member of a political party oppose that party at times? Farley's answer, the natural answer of a political professional, was "No." His remarks were not particularly strong or surprising. But they gave the opponents of the Court plan a great opening. Senator Rush D. Holt, a Democrat from West Virginia and an opponent of the Court plan, was asked to speak before the same forum two weeks later. Because Farley had talked of party loyalty in connection with the Court plan, Holt was perfectly justified in answering in kind. He took the theme of Farley's remarks and built on it. Said Holt: "The report has gone abroad that recognition and patronage will be taken from members of the House and Senate simply because they dare to differ with the President and Mr. Farley on this great question. . . . The President and Mr. Farley, by cracking the party whip on this subject, are not appealing to the wisdom of the proposal but to the force that they desire to possess to push it through." Holt then conceded to his audience that patronage has a strong meaning to members of Congress. But he insisted that "there never has been and never should be enough patronage to sway an honest member of either branch of Congress from his duty and from the right as he sees it." The senator approached the crescendo. "We have now reached the time," he said, "when men must make the sacrifice of patronage. It is well worth making now."

What Holt had neatly done was to give senators a moral reason for opposing the Court plan. Be brave! he was saying to his fellow members of the Senate. Show courage! Vote against the Court bill and reveal yourselves as men who dare the strength of the Presidency, perhaps even risk not being reelected, to do what is right. Every member of the Congress likes to think of himself, at least once in his political career, as a statesman who rose above the pushes and pulls of the daily political life. Holt's cry for a moral crusade against the Court bill provided such an opportunity.

The next month the morality became stronger. One afternoon, during the Judiciary Committee hearings, a writer named John T. Flynn was testifying in opposition to the Court plan. During Flynn's discussion of the plan, Senator Edward Burke of Nebraska, a Democrat and a Court plan foe, took advantage of a senator's

right to ask a question that contains a hard right hook. Burke's
question went this way:

I was interested also in what you had to say on the subject of
patronage and the control of enormous funds, as bearing on this
question. And if I may lead up to my next question, I will state it this
way: Today, within the last two hours, a person speaking with considerable authority gave the opinion that, within the next ten days or
two weeks, there would come before the Congress a request for one
billion dollars, possibly one and one-half billion dollars additional ap-
propriations to take care of the needy in this country. In spite of the
fact that the emergency is over, in spite of the fact that we are on the
upgrade, there would be this request for an enormous appropriation,
to be turned over to the Executive to use for the very laudable purpose
of relieving distress in this country; and the person with whom I was
talking, and whose name will not be mentioned, asked this question:
"Do you not realize that in the face of one and one-half billion dollars
at the disposal of the Executive, you are fighting a losing fight in trying
to defeat any proposal on the part of one who has that much money
at his control, to do with it as he wishes?" Do you feel that there is
real danger to our democratic processes, under a system that makes
that possible?

Burke had charged indirectly that the Administration was trying
to buy votes for the Court plan with its public welfare appropriation.
This charge also was part of the strategy. Members of Congress
could now claim that they were voting against the Court plan
because "they can't buy my vote." Flynn stumbled for an answer,
and several committee members became angry at the public suggestion made by their colleague Burke that their votes could be
bought. There are some things members of Congress prefer not
to discuss publicly.

Burke refused to identify the Administration official who had
first spoken to him of welfare funds. It had been Jack Garner.
However, the Vice President did not mention the money in an effort
to bribe Burke or coerce him into supporting the Court plan. The
Vice President wasn't doing things like that, even then in April.
He had mentioned the figure as an example of what the problems
were, of how difficult it would be to defeat Roosevelt on the issue

because he would have that money with which to tempt members of the Senate.

This morality issue grew. "They picked off one senator with a judgeship, another with a big plum, and they will undoubtedly pick off more of this sort," snapped one senator. And Rush Holt, the West Virginia Democrat opposed to the Court plan, spelled out this kind of patronage ploy in even more detail one day on the Senate floor. "For fourteen months," he told his colleagues, "I was not even consulted about any appointment in my state. Immediately after the President submitted his [Court] proposal I was called by a high official. . . . He very generously wanted to know if I was interested in suggesting someone for federal judge in West Virginia. He talked about the present administration. He did not say, 'I am going to give you a judge for your vote.' I hope he did not think I was that dumb, but I know what he meant and he knew what he meant. He meant if I went along on the President's proposal, I would get a judge."

Holt had identified the "high official" who approached him as a Justice Department employee. A couple of days later Homer Cummings held a news conference. Part of it was reported in *The New York Times* this way: "The Attorney General also asserted that Senator Holt had done a 'great injustice' to Joseph B. Keenan, Assistant Attorney General, by charging that Mr. Keenan had tried to obtain his vote for the Court plan in exchange for the appointment of a district judge. He declared that Mr. Keenan had merely invited Mr. Holt to testify as to the fitness of the candidate, as is the custom of the Department of Justice."

The morality issue continued in April; this time Burton Wheeler was involved. *The March of Time,* a series of documentary films on contemporary subjects, did a featurette on the Court fight in which Wheeler was quoted: "You can say that the privilege of appointing postmasters will not be accorded to me. You can say that I'll get no more projects for my state. You can say what you please, but I say to you and to Mr. Farley, to everybody else, that I will vote against this proposition because it is morally wrong; it is morally unsound; it is a dangerous proceeding." Wheeler's comments were overly dramatic and obviously designed to appeal for public support by showing the opponents of FDR as being statesmen willing to risk their patronage, but they were not much more than what others were saying. When *The March of Time* came to Kansas, however, some member of that state's Board of Censors, for reasons not fully explained, ordered that speech cut out of the featurette. The censor apparently was a Democrat and thought the editing of that statement would help FDR. Just the opposite happened, of course. Wheeler happened to be in Kansas making some speeches when he heard that his remarks had been deleted from *The March of Time*. He immediately charged that the censoring was done on orders from persons in Washington high places. The Administration, he continued, was afraid to fight him fair and square but was, instead, using underhanded tactics. He actually had a very good case. The role of the censors in Kansas was to delete immoral scenes and lines from movies. Wheeler's comments might have been politically objectionable but they certainly were not immoral. The news stories spread across the nation, repeating Wheeler's charge that the Administration was trying to shut him up. Thoughtful persons realized that the real issue in the Kansas incident was free speech. The censorship of Wheeler's remarks made the talk about FDR's wanting to become a dictator all the more frightening. No one ever found out if the Administration in Washington had been responsible; Wheeler believed it had. When one news story reported that Wheeler had accused Farley of being the mastermind behind the censorship, Farley wrote a letter to Wheeler proclaiming his innocence. Wheeler was willing to grant Farley's innocence. "You would have too much political sense," he said. "But I am afraid that others with no political sense may have advised the action."

There probably was never a time that Burt Wheeler would have backtracked on his Court plan opposition; he had spoken out too strongly for that. But, and this should have been a consideration at the White House, a time might have come when he would be ready for compromise. As adamant as Roosevelt was on one side and Wheeler on the other, both sides should have realized that political warfare is like military warfare—one leaves his opponent an "out," a means of surrendering without losing all honor. To refuse to leave such an out is to seek a battle to the last man, a battle of no compromise, a battle of complete destruction. Such tactics as the censorship of Burt Wheeler's remarks only made it necessary for him not to compromise. Wheeler was being pulled deeper and deeper into a political morass by the Court fight.

Although Wheeler was gaining immeasurably on a national scale, giving rise to talk of him as a Presidential candidate in 1940, he was rapidly losing strength in Montana, his power base. Jim Farley happily sent FDR a letter written by a Democratic politician in Wheeler's home state of Montana and saying, ". . . the Wheeler balloon here is badly punctured." Things were good back home for the men who worked the mines and generally made up the Democratic party's strength in Montana. Copper prices were up, and the miners actually were living in a boomtown atmosphere. "Butte is wide open," reported a young newsman named Richard Neuberger. "Faro games and roulette wheels entice men in from the main streets. Girls have packed the cribs along 'Venus Alley.' Prices are high and men are earning $5.75 a day." The men figured the good times were due to the Roosevelt prosperity, and in return, the people of Montana had given the President a three-to-one majority in 1936. In 1937 these same people did not look happily on Wheeler's challenging FDR. "No, by gosh," said one miner to a friend, "I wouldn't vote for Wheeler for dog catcher. He's sold out labor." At the same time that Wheeler was losing support from the working men he was not picking up any strength from the conservatives in his state who remembered his twenty-year record of progressivism. Said one conservative in Montana when asked if he would switch to supporting Wheeler in view of Wheeler's work against Roosevelt: "No, he's too darn radical." Caught in this kind of pull, Wheeler could not really compromise without being sharply yanked one way or the other. Then an incident occurred that made compromise virtually impossible for Burt Wheeler ever to consider.

"On March 30, Senator Wheeler ordered and paid for 65,000

copies, costing $196.33, of the radio address which he delivered in opposition to the President's Court reform program," read the memorandum the President held before him. "On April 2nd, Senator Wheeler ordered and paid for 200,000 copies, costing $577.82, of his radio address of March 10th, including the remarks made by Representative Lemke of North Dakota in the House of Representatives on March 9th, the latter being titled 'Neither the President nor the Court is Infallible.'" The memorandum continued with additional details describing the speech reprints that Burt Wheeler was buying and the amounts paid "to the Public Printer in cash by Senator Wheeler." And it concluded: "It will be seen that the Senator had had printed 2,308,000 copies of speeches in opposition to the President's Court reform proposal and that these have been or are being broadcast under his frank through the mails of the United States. The total printing bill paid by the Senator is $8,796.72. It would be interesting to know whether the money expended by the Senator comes from his own pocket or what the source of the revenues are; whether he is reimbursed and if so, by whom." Franklin Roosevelt considered the memorandum for a few minutes; he could not know, of course, that the Gannett committee was paying for reprints and their mailing. Then he looked up at those sitting with him and murmured that it might be interesting to examine Wheeler's income tax.

Burt Wheeler usually paid his income tax in Montana; it had never been much of a problem with him because his outside income was not great, consisting of some rentals from a building he owned in Montana and some dividends from a small number of stocks in his wife's name. In 1937, however, he was a little late preparing his tax return so he filed it in Baltimore. A few weeks after that he received a notice from the Internal Revenue Service raising a number of questions about his return. This had never happened to him before. He believed the questions were particularly suspect. He was asked, for example, what basis he used to determine the depreciation of his building. The depreciation rate he used was a standard one. The other questions were of the same kind, suggesting that someone had gone over his return seeking all possible questions in hopes of harassing the senator. Wheeler answered the questions, then wrote to Henry Morgenthau, the Secretary of the Treasury (the Treasury Department was the Internal Revenue Service's parent agency). In his letter to Morgenthau, Wheeler asked: "Are you checking up on the income tax of any other member of the Senate?"

Morgenthau called Wheeler. "I just want to tell you . . . as man to man . . . as long as I have been here," Morgenthau said, "and as long as I stay here . . . the office of the Secretary of the Treasury will never be used to persecute anybody on income tax." Wheeler replied that he had not thought that was the case, that his friend "Henry" wanted to persecute him, "and that's why I sent the letter to you." Morgenthau repeated his assurances that the income tax system was above politics even though "all through the campaign there were suggestions made to me." He also insisted that if anyone in his department did use tax returns for political purposes "he goes out on his ear in fifteen seconds" and if ever "I'm guilty of it I'm willing to quit."

"Perhaps I was overly suspicious," replied Wheeler; then he referred to his run-in with the censorship in Kansas. "What happened in Kansas I felt came from a certain source and then I went out there and then I got this, and in addition to that you know this has been—they've been circulating around and some of these two by four fellows around here, you know that claim to be close advised, kept saying—ah—this fellow will be punished and that fellow will be punished." Morgenthau replied that he held his office too high for such political hanky-panky, and then he insisted: "There's been no request of any kind from across the street [the White House]—I want to tell you that too. . . . No request or no hint of anything." Burton Wheeler never quite accepted that, that the White House had not been involved. As far as he was concerned, the Court struggle had progressed far beyond being a political duel. It was a personal dispute.

The income tax query to Burton Wheeler was another example of the inability of the Administration to do anything right. Another example was Jim Farley; almost everything he said seemed to be the wrong thing. In March he was in Austin appearing before the Texas legislature, which was meeting in joint session. His purpose was to defend the Court plan, as Harold Ickes had done from the same platform a month earlier. But Farley could not stop there. He went on to speak of "those opposed to the measure." He said this group "embraces the standpat Republican members of the Senate, the Liberty Leaguers on the outside, every agency that opposed and combatted the President's re-election." Unfortunately, however, he was speaking before a group that had gone on record against the Court plan. One Democratic member of the Texas legislature who supported the resolution condemning the Court plan said after the Farley appearance: "I was a member of the national committee from my Congressional district and my county raised six times its quota for the [Roosevelt] campaign. I resent being classed as a reactionary, a Liberty Leaguer and part of a stubborn minority." Obviously Jim Farley wasn't making too many friends in Texas.

But the worst Farley did was yet to come. As he emerged one day from a White House session with the President, a reporter for the Washington *Post*, followed by several other newsmen, latched on to him to get a reading on the Court bill, how the votes were lining up. The Postmaster General answered in his usual optimistic manner, a façade that is necessary for politicians. Then the reporter continued by asking how Farley could make such an optimistic assessment when so many Democratic senators appeared to be in opposition. Jim Farley answered with a question of his own. How, he asked the reporters, could Democratic senators—and he specifically named Pat McCarran of Nevada and Joe O'Mahoney of Wyoming—afford not to vote for the bill if they ever wanted anything from the Administration? The remark said a good deal about Jim Farley. He was "Big Jim Farley" boasting of how he was going to take care of those United States senators. He was going to be rough and tough, and they were going to do exactly what he told them to do, or else they were in trouble. But if Jim Farley really had known his politics as he was reputed to know them, he would have known that United States senators cannot permit themselves to be talked to in such a manner. Not only does it hurt their ego, but they cannot go before their constituents unless they appear to be fighting the spirit such words suggest. They cannot go before the voters appearing to be persons cringing before the Administration. Voters like congressmen who appear to have guts.

Farley later claimed his remarks were intended to be off the record. That is, the newsmen were not supposed to report them as having been spoken by the Postmaster General. Newsmen in Washington always have been very reliable about not violating an off-the-record confidence. To do so once means that a good many doors will be closed to the reporter. However, it was naïve to make such comments when several newsmen were standing by, even if an off-the-record restriction had been placed on them, and expect that the words would not be repeated over a drink, at a lunch, on a golf course, until finally one reporter heard them who was not restricted by anything Farley had said to him personally. The situation was comparable to that in which James McReynolds spoke before the fraternity dinner. Both men made controversial and significant remarks which, once the adverse reactions were evident, they claimed were intended to be off the record. The long experience of both men in Washington should have made evident to them that such remarks could not be kept quiet.

Farley claimed that publication of his remarks resulted in preventing McCarran and O'Mahoney from supporting the President. They never would have supported the President anyhow on the Court fight. The remarks did more than that. They speeded up the process going on in the Senate. The senators were drawing toward each other and away from the President. Such threats as Farley's angered the senators. "It is vindictiveness run mad," said Carter Glass. They always feel closer to each other than they do to the members of the executive branch. A display of raw Presidential power gave them another excuse to go before their constituents to justify their position of being against the President. And the senators made the most of it. McCarran, for example, rose from a sickbed to speak before a crowded Senate chamber. "This is the first time for a year and a half that I have attempted to deliver a speech of any magnitude, and I am delivering it now contrary to a doctor's orders," he told his fellow senators. His voice growing stronger, he continued: "But I think the cause is worth while. I think this cause is worthy of any man's life." Jim Farley had given Pat McCarran the opportunity to be heroic, and McCarran was not going to permit the moment to pass unused.

Actually, Franklin Roosevelt was not being vindictive. When all the talk was done, he was not declining to make appointments because of opposition to the Court bill. On June 18, for example, he appointed Representative Frank Le Blond Kloeb of Celina, Ohio, to be a United States District Court judge. "I am very much pleased at the appointing authorities overlooking my stand on the court reorganization question," said Kloeb. "I think it was mighty fine of them." His stand had been against the FDR bill. His appointment was favorably reported by the Senate Judiciary Committee only three days after the White House announced it. And there were several other appointments of persons opposed to the Court bill. The publicity given to these appointments was sufficient to make official Washington understand that, when the oratory was done, there was to be no withdrawing of patronage.

Franklin Roosevelt might not have made so many mistakes with Congress if he had had the advice of the man in his official family who could be the best source of information on the Congress. This was Jack Garner, FDR's Vice President. More than Joe Robinson, the Senate Democratic leader, and more than Speaker Bankhead or Sam Rayburn, the Democratic leader on the House side, Garner understood the Congress. His long experience as a legislator and his conviviality with the members made him a knowledgeable person. He would be presiding in the Senate and motion with a nod of his head to one of the senators. The senator quietly stood and ambled out of the Senate chamber to the small, hidden office known as "the board of education." Garner would shuffle in within a few moments. He would point to the bottle and say: "Go pour yourself a drink and pour one for me." Then, over their bourbon and with their feet up on a desk, the two men would relax and talk. With only a few sessions like this, there was little going on in the Senate that Garner was not aware of. But Garner did not help FDR. He did not wish to.

13

ONCE, WHEN John Nance Garner emerged from a White House session, newsmen besieged him with questions about the meeting with the President. "Don't you know," the Vice President cracked to the reporters, "that I'm deaf, dumb and blind?" As far as Garner's willingness to discuss matters publicly, that was an accurate description. In the presence of reporters and those he suspected of often talking to reporters, he kept quiet. He visualized the Vice Presidency so narrowly that he did not even campaign in 1936. He spoke of his role as being a negligible one—"the fifth wheel" on the government car. But with his long experience in the Congress, rising to become Speaker of the House of Representatives, the most revered position in that body, he could have used the Vice Presidency as a powerful weapon for the New Deal. During the first years of the Roosevelt Administration he did just that. His "board of education," where he and others "struck a blow for liberty" with a drink of bourbon and branch water was much more than an informal drinking club for Garner and some of his old friends. Garner had set up shop in a little room off the Old Supreme Court Chamber, hidden in the bowels of the Capitol. He filled it with a table, a few straight chairs, some shelves, and an ice-water cooler. Much of the Senate business was actually conducted here in the early days of the New Deal. A senator would come to bargain, to object, to be criticized. Here tempers were soothed and wounds in the friendly relations between senators were healed. A few plots were hatched also.

Garner had become Vice President in 1933 through what was a new route. The Vice Presidency had been a sinecure for the hack, or, so it was thought in the case of Theodore Roosevelt, a place safely to bury someone. The job had not produced a President through the elective process for almost a century, not even a serious candidate for the Presidency. The job was being parodied at this time in a George Gershwin musical, *Of Thee I Sing,* in which the Vice President cannot get a library card because he cannot obtain two character references. But Garner had come to the 1932 Democratic national convention as a serious candidate for the Presidency. He was no hack in search of a sinecure. He was the man being offered by the conservatives and southerners in the party. He did not have enough electoral votes to make it. Neither did FDR, but he had more than Garner. When the two men combined on a Roosevelt-Garner ticket, they won the nomination. It was a good ticket in 1932 for many reasons. Roosevelt represented the liberal Northeast and responded to the intellectuals, the writers, the city dwellers. Garner respresented the South and the West. He responded to the farmers, the cattlemen, the segregationists. The combination of these two men made the Democratic tickets in 1932 and 1936 national tickets. At a time when the nation was in deep trouble and sorely divided economically, geographically, and intellectually, it was part of the healing process to have a ticket made up of two men who represented both sides of those divisions. Each side could find comfort in the thought that his own man was at or near the top of the government.

The Vice President went along with FDR, although he felt uncomfortable with the New Deal's liberalism. FDR, so Garner believed, was spending too much money, putting the nation too much in debt, allowing labor unions to make a mockery of law and order with their sit-down strikes. Still, he was a reasonably loyal lieutenant during the first term. When 1936 came Roosevelt had no desire to drop his second man. The Democratic convention still operated under the two-thirds rule. A two-thirds vote of the convention, rather than a majority, was required to nominate; the 1936 convention was the last with this rule in effect. FDR did not wish to risk a convention fight over the question of the Vice Presidency while he still needed so many of the delegates. Also, Garner had been helpful as a liaison man on Capitol Hill. There was no reason not to want him along the second time.

Garner, as the 1936 convention neared, had some reservations about Franklin Roosevelt. "Whatever have been his faults and his errors," Garner said, "Roosevelt has been a good President for the country." Then he added: "He's got too much power. Some power we have granted him is no longer needed. The other can be worked into the framework of the law." The Vice President acknowledged that Roosevelt "has been matured by four years in office. With good administration of the laws we have carried, his second term should be an Indian summer." Garner was thinking of a second term that would consolidate the advances of the first four years, perhaps even eliminate some of them. He had conceded that the depression had required some drastic acts, but in 1936 he believed the time for drastic action, for the liberalism of the New Deal, was at an end. The time was appropriate for a move back toward conservatism.

After the election and the inauguration Garner realized his ideas of what was appropriate in the second term of the Roosevelt Administration did not coincide with FDR's. When Roosevelt refused to condemn the labor strikes, launched his move against the Court, and pressed for a billion-dollar-plus welfare program, Garner realized he was very much out of sympathy with Franklin Roosevelt in the second four years of the New Deal. Mixed with his disappointment at the New Deal in 1937 was his practical estimate of the Court bill's chances. Garner figured the bill could not make it, that it would not be enacted. Even if it passed the Senate, Garner reasoned, the House would block it. Hatton Sumners would bottle the bill up in his Judiciary Committee, and the House members did not appear very anxious to dislodge the bill from his grasp. With his political instincts, Garner realized that party solidarity was being risked in the Court fight. He saw the widening of the gulf between the New Dealers and the southern conservatives, and it greatly troubled him.

The White House was well aware of Garner's attitude, that the Court bill had little chance. "The chief danger," the President said in April to Harold Ickes, was "the defeatist attitude of the Vice President." The President continued that Garner talked so pessimistically at "board of education" meetings about the bill's future that the defeatist air might have been enveloping the bill in the Senate. FDR was afraid the defeatist air created by Garner might persuade Joe Robinson and other backers of the bill to take a compromise rather than press for passage of the complete measure. Roosevelt was greatly concerned by the growing conservatism of Garner and some of the other southerners. He did not like it, believing the shift to the right was almost disloyal. He was not aware of just how disloyal it actually was. It is one thing for a member of an administration to disagree with that administration in the confines of the Cabinet room or the President's oval office. It is another for that person to permit his disagreement to become a matter known to the public. Such an event usually means the dismissal of that person from the administration. It is even worse for a member of an administration to work for the defeat of that administration's program. This is what John Nance Garner was trying to do. His purpose was to build up within the Roosevelt Administration a cabal aimed at cutting back federal spending. At one point Garner suggested to Henry Morgenthau that Morgenthau resign as Secretary of the Treasury in a protest move if spending was not reduced. Perhaps at no other time in American history since the passage of the Twelfth Amendment to the Constitution, which gave the Presidential candidate a voice in the selection of his running mate, has a Vice President so schemed against his President.

Morgenthau, writing of himself in the third person, described the scene this way in his diary on April 27:

Henry Morgenthau Jr. called to see the Vice President this morning. The Vice President told Henry Morgenthau Jr. that as Secretary of the Treasury he has the responsibility of the budget and the time may come when he may have to resign if he does not get the cooperation of the President on "spending." Henry Morgenthau Jr. told him that he does not threaten but if the President does not carry out his promise to stop spending, he will resign.

The Vice President told Henry Morgenthau Jr. that for two months he has laid the ground work for the curtailing of spending but that the President would not listen. He also said, "Henry, frankly, I am talking to the President through you." Henry Morgenthau Jr. replied that he understood.

Henry Morgenthau Jr. asked the Vice President whether he had confidence in him and the Vice President answered, "Henry, I am your friend and I am proud of you. You can always count on me."

By the middle of May, when Franklin Roosevelt had returned from his fishing trip to the Gulf of Mexico and his political sounding journey through Texas, he was ready to have a no-holds-barred session with Garner. The two men met before a Cabinet meeting. "The Vice President looked as if he had had a thoroughly sound spanking," thought Ickes when Garner emerged from the meeting with FDR. "The attitude of the President seemed to me to prove that he had been administering a spanking because on a couple of occasions he went out of his way to bring the Vice President into the discussion just as a father tries to mollify the hurt feelings of a child after he has chastised it," said Ickes. Then he added, significantly: "However, the Vice President was unusually quiet all during Cabinet meetings and gave the impression that something had happened."

At the beginning of the year Garner had visualized a quick session of Congress with little legislation of substance sought by the Administration or enacted by the Congress. This meant for him that Congress would adjourn by June, and he made plans for a June vacation in Texas. He had never before taken a vacation while Congress was in session, never in more than thirty years. Garner said he had "the Boss's" permission to be away from Washington for five weeks. Garner also said he would return at any time, if needed.

Speculation began immediately. The trip appeared to be sudden; few in Washington believed that Garner planned it six months earlier. Actually, whether he had or not was incidental. Trips can be postponed, vacations delayed. They often are by legislators when their presence appears to be needed. Garner's trip to Texas seemed to be notice that he was disassociating himself from his President and his President's program. One prominent Republican wondered aloud if the trip was not Garner's method of saying to the country that he saw little reason for the general reforms that Roosevelt was urging.

The newspapers played up the Garner trip as a signal that the Vice President had broken with FDR, that he had given up on the Court bill. "Why in hell did Jack have to leave at this time for?" grumbled Roosevelt through his cigarette smoke. ". . . This is a fine time to jump ship." Jim Farley, who heard these remarks, wrote to Garner in Texas, suggesting he return. Garner replied, first professing his loyalty and then stressing his disagreements with FDR, and concluding with "I am subject to his call at any moment." Garner also wrote a "Dear Chief" letter to FDR, explaining his opposition to the position FDR had taken on the strikes and spending. And he ended with "I have never kept even as much as a mosquito bar over my soul when I unburdened myself to you. I solicit the same confidence on your part."

Finally, in July, FDR wrote to Garner, asking that he come back. "If Congress does not run wild in the next six weeks or two months," FDR told his Vice President, "you will be glad to know that the budget for the coming year looks like a very definite assurance of a balanced budget. The receipts from taxation are exceeding estimates and the departments and agencies are cooperating in trying to cut their actual expenditures about four hundred million dollars under the appropriation bills." FDR then went on to say the public was "pretty sick of the extremists which exist both in the CIO [the John L. Lewis labor group] and some of the AFL unions" as well as some of the Wall Street tycoons. Roosevelt actually was wooing Garner, telling Garner what he wanted to hear: the budget was moving toward balance, the labor extremists had lost their power. Franklin Roosevelt acknowledged at last that he was facing trouble in the Congress over his Court bill and believed he needed help from Jack Garner to overcome those difficulties. That is why he wrote such a placating letter.

"Cactus Jack" Garner returned from Texas as his "Chief" asked. But Garner did not supply the helping hand Franklin Roosevelt needed. It was too late. The split between the liberal wing and the conservative side of the Democratic party was too wide.

Part Five

Do You Want It with the Bark On or Off, Cap'n?

14

JOHN T. SUTTER was the Associated Press reporter in Washington covering the Supreme Court. For years he had filed stories about the Court's decisions, their meaning and possible impact on various administrations. He had begun his newspaper reporting at age nineteen. Now seventy-one years old, he enjoyed a special relationship with the justices of the Supreme Court. Often he dropped by one of their homes to chat about law, about decisions handed down by the Court. The purpose of such talks was to insure that Suter's stories, which had the greatest circulation in the country of the written accounts of the Court's actions, were accurate and fully representative of the nuances of the law. At the end of such talks, there would be informal discussions between the newsman and the justice as between two old friends. Confidences between the justices and the reporter never were broken. This position of trust paid off handsomely for Suter on Tuesday, May 18, 1937.

At eight o'clock that morning, the telephone at John Suter's home rang. When the reporter picked it up, a voice said: "Mr. Suter, Justice Van Devanter wants to know if you can drop by his apartment on the way to the office."

In a taxi on the way to Van Devanter's apartment, Suter realized there could be only one story that prompted the telephone call: Justice Van Devanter obviously planned to announce his retirement. The implications this act would have on Franklin Roosevelt's Court bill buzzed through Suter's mind as the taxicab came to the 2100 block of Connecticut Avenue, where it pulled to a stop. Once in the Justice's apartment, however, it seemed a story about his retirement or about anything of importance was far from Van Devanter's mind. Dressed for work and puffing on his pipe, the Justice spoke for fifteen minutes about Suter's health. He asked how the reporter was feeling, sympathized with his ailments, suggested some remedies. Finally, he said: "What I really wanted to see you about is that I'm going to notify the President of my retirement." He then handed the reporter a copy of his letter of retirement to the President, stipulating that Suter not make it public until after it reached the White House—which it would do in only a few minutes. "Be sure to visit me on my farm," the seventy-eight-year-old Justice said as Suter rushed out with one of the major scoops of 1937.

The special messenger carrying Van Devanter's resignation arrived at the White House at nine forty-five that morning. The letter was carried up to the Presidential bedroom, where FDR, as was his habit, was conducting his early morning business while propped up in bed. He read the letter quickly. It was almost a form resignation, announcing the Justice's retirement on June 2, the day the current Court session ended. The President picked up a pencil and scrawled a courteous reply, accepting the Justice's resignation, extending "to you every good wish," and inviting Van Devanter to pay a last call at the White House before leaving Washington for the summer.

The Van Devanter resignation appeared to eliminate one of Roosevelt's arguments for the Court bill, that the members were holding on to their seats on the bench so that FDR could not have the opportunity to replace them. Now all that was changed. With his letter, Van Devanter had given FDR an opportunity to make an appointment to the Court. Assuming Owen Roberts stayed with the liberals, where he had been for the past few months, that Roosevelt appointment would give the President a six-to-three majority on the Court rather than the five-to-four lineup he had had since "White Monday." The larger majority is what the Administration had been saying was needed as it pressed to continue the Court fight. Now, it seemed, it had all that it said it needed.

The resignation came as a surprise to many persons in Washington. There had been no hint publicly that any of the justices was contemplating resignation. A year earlier, when he became seventy-seven years old, Van Devanter had been noncommittal: "I'm not saying I will [retire] and I'm not saying I won't; when one gets along in years, as I am, of course anything can happen." But then he had remained silent. Nor did any of the other justices give any indication about such plans. When Chief Justice Hughes became seventy-five years old, on April 11, 1937, he allowed the day to go by without any unusual activity. It was a Sunday and he remained at home in the morning, reading, and took a walk in the afternoon. His pew at Calvary Baptist Church was unoccupied, and his regular automobile ride in the afternoon was passed by. "I will follow my customary itinerary," he said. His associates also stressed that the Chief Justice was in excellent health, never missing a day from the Court's work since his 1930 appointment.

When James McReynolds had become seventy-five in February, two days before the Roosevelt Court bill was announced, the Justice shrugged the day off as "just another day and I'm another year older." After the Court bill had been announced and created its furor, McReynolds continued to make clear his intention to ride out the conflict. "Against my inclinations to seek freedom from the incessant demands on my time and strength," he said in April, "it is not my purpose at present to retire from the bench in the immediate future."

The other justices also gave no indication that retirement was in their future. The rumor that several of the justices planned to retire once their retirement income was assured had continued strong in Washington until March 1, when FDR signed the Hatton Sumners bill into law. This was the legislation guaranteeing that a Supreme Court justice's retirement income could not be cut by Congress, as had happened to Oliver Wendell Holmes. Once the bill became law, however, no justice appeared anxious to take advantage of it. Retirement of some of the justices was publicly urged. "It is now the duty, therefore," said Representative Emanuel Celler the day the Sumners bill became law, "of some of the more virile and younger judges, within the next six months or a year, to persuade their older and less vigorous brethren to retire." But the justices of the Supreme Court were not anxious to suggest that their fellow justices retire. Chief Justice Hughes, about a decade earlier, had explained why.

Once in the nineteenth century an aging justice named Robert C. Grier stayed on the bench too long, according to Hughes's story. A committee of the Court, including Associate Justice Stephen J. Field, approached Grier and asked him to resign because of his age. Field himself then stayed on the bench too long, continuing to sit when age made it difficult for him to give the position the full responsibility it deserved. Associate Justice John Marshall Harlan was appointed by the Court to approach Field to ask him to resign as Field had once asked Grier to resign. As Hughes told the story, Harlan

went over to Justice Field, who was sitting alone on a settee in the robing room apparently oblivious of his surroundings, and after arousing him gradually approached the question, asking if he did not recall how anxious the Court had become with respect to Justice Grier's condition and the feeling of the other Justices that in his own interest and in that of the Court he should give up his work. Justice Harlan asked if Justice Field did not remember what had been said to Justice Grier on that occasion. The old man listened, gradually became alert, and finally, with his eyes blazing with the old fire of youth, he burst out: "Yes! And a dirtier day's work I never did in my life!"

That, explained Hughes, was the end of all attempts to persuade justices to retire.

It had been Charles Evans Hughes who well remembered this story and who had refused to accede to Herbert Hoover's plan to persuade Louis Brandeis to resign early in the Court fight. Nor would Hughes make any attempt or permit any attempt to be made to persuade any of the other justices to retire, even though there were some signs that several of the justices, Van Devanter and George Sutherland particularly, were interested in leaving the bench after their retirement pay was secure. The rumors that had circulated in Washington during the Court fight, that justices would retire as a device to defeat the Roosevelt bill, never had been based on fact.

Although the Van Devanter resignation, when it came at last, was a surprise to many persons in Washington, it was not a surprise to all. Actually it had been well planned. William Borah, the Republican senator who was working without publicity to defeat the Court bill, had long been aware that Van Devanter, a close friend of his, wanted to retire. Borah also knew that Van Devanter would have retired shortly after the Sumners bill had been signed except that to retire in the face of the Roosevelt challenge to the Court would appear to be running. However, Borah persuaded Van Devanter that a resignation while the Court bill was still waiting for a vote, particularly while it was still in the Judiciary Committee, could have a devastating impact on the bill's prospects. With the conniving of Burton Wheeler, the date of Van Devanter's resignation was carefully chosen.

At approximately ten o'clock in the morning of the day Van Devanter resigned, eighteen members of the Senate Judiciary Committee filed into their committee room to vote on Franklin Roosevelt's Court bill. They would adopt a report saying whether they opposed or supported the President's bill and why they did so. William Borah, a committee member, made certain each senator, as he prepared to vote, was aware of the Van Devanter resignation only a few moments earlier. Its meaning, that one of FDR's reasons for seeking the Court bill no longer existed, was evident to each senator. The closed-door committee session began with a series of six votes, all designed to give Franklin Roosevelt something of his original bill. The Administration forces lost each of those votes. Then the committee took up the report being prepared for it by its staff, which each of the committee members knew was the document that was going to be approved. It was, by a vote of ten to eight.

The report began with the President's assertion that the purpose of his bill was to infuse new blood into the Court. The report rejected this, saying that the purpose was to persuade justices over seventy to resign. It continued, lashing out at FDR and his Ad-

ministration for presenting "a needlesss, futile, and utterly dangerous abandonment of constitutional principle" when it sent the
Court bill to Congress. The bill's "ultimate purpose," said the
report, "would be to make this Government one of men rather
than one of law, and its practical operation would be to make the
Constitution what the executive or legislative branches of the
government choose to say it is—an interpretation to be changed
with each change of administration." Rarely—perhaps never—had
a committee of Congress, controlled by the same political party as
the White House, spoken so sharply and so critically of the actions
of the man in the White House. Even then, the report was not done.
Its closing line was without equal. "It is a measure," said the report of the Court bill, "which should be so emphatically rejected
that its parallel will never again be presented to the free representatives of the free people of America."

Arthur Krock summed up the meaning of the committee's action.
He wrote:

Since there were two ways of writing the report, the personal excoria-
tion of the President is accepted by politicians here as a deliberate
choice. And since it was possible to have conceded some merit to
certain parts of the Maverick-Ashurst bill, the fact that none was
admitted is taken for willingness on the part of the seven Democrats
[on the committee who voted against Roosevelt] and those whom
they represent to have a clean break, party-wise with Mr. Roosevelt.
The sum of much experienced Washington opinion is that a large
group of Democratic senators, who oppose the later extensions of the
New Deal, are determined to take back party control in 1940.

Krock had made it a matter of public record: the duel now was not
over the future of the Supreme Court but over the future of the
Democratic party.

The same day that Van Devanter resigned and the committee
voted against the Court bill, Franklin Roosevelt was asked what
impact the resignation would have on the bill. He answered
tersely: "I have no news on that subject today." One of FDR's
closest advisers of this time reminisced many years later about
the Court fight, saying: "The Supreme Court happened to be a

place in which political forces were fighting. The law had nothing to do with it." It seemed one could almost feel the jackals circling the White House, hoping to move in for the kill. "I hope to heaven you boys have got Roosevelt licked on the court thing," William Allen White said about this time to a Republican senator. "That is fundamental. If we are licked on that, we are licked on everything. And on the other hand, if we lick [Roosevelt] there I think we've got him started going."

The curious thing, however, was that FDR actually had won the Court fight. When Owen Roberts switched and when Willis Van Devanter resigned, the Supreme Court had become a Roosevelt Court. Franklin Roosevelt could not claim victory, however. Like Napoleon in Moscow, the city was his but the triumph was not. He still had the challenge within his party, a challenge made more obvious by the committee vote and report. He also knew his American history. His Republican cousin, Theodore Roosevelt, had instituted reforms and various legislative breakthroughs when he was President, only to see them erased when the conservative Republican William Howard Taft became President. Franklin Roosevelt still had to cement his philosophy to the Democratic party. No erasures could be allowed at a later time. So FDR must search for a triumph, not just a victory.

But the triumph must be a somewhat limited one. Joe Robinson finally convinced Roosevelt of that. The portly Senate leader came to the White House for a two-hour session with the President. Robinson was blunt. He had counted the votes; the Administration did not have enough to pass the original Court bill. There were no qualifications, no prospects that that situation would be reversed. Joe Robinson did have an alternative. A compromise was being worked up, he explained, that called for the acceptance of the FDR principle of appointing a co-justice for each elderly justice but would limit the appointments to one or perhaps two a year. That compromise had been kicking around for a few weeks before Robinson presented it formally to FDR the night of June 3. The New Dealers had not taken kindly to it. Tommy Corcoran thought that it actually cut the ground out from under the opposition because it accepted the principle of the FDR plan. To illustrate, Corcoran told the story of the man who goes to the matrimonial agency seeking a wife. The agency pairs him off with an attractive woman. Then one week after the marriage the bridegroom comes storming into the office of the matrimonial agency to complain angrily to the marriage broker that his wife was pregnant when he married her. "Ah," concedes the marriage broker, "but she is only a little bit pregnant."

FDR told Robinson to go ahead with the compromise; he would succeed in having Congress accept his proposal in principle if not in detail, Robinson emerged from the White House that night feeling much better than he had for weeks. He now had the lever, the FDR agreement to a compromise, that, he was confident, could move the Senate into an affirmative vote. He tipped off the reporters waiting for him with this statement: "It is felt that during the last few months some changes have occurred which have modified the situation, but there still exists the necessity for the injecting of new blood into the Court."

The next morning in his news conference FDR conceded that he was willing to accept a compromise. First he said it was "plain silly" to believe that Court reform had been abandoned as some newsmen had written. He insisted that reform "is going to be carried through without question." A few moments later he said, "The desire of the country for court reform is going through. There is no question about that—and that is the forest." A reporter asked: "How about the number of judges as provided for under the original bill?" FDR answered: "That again is trees. You are talking about trees and I am talking about the forest." Now the newsmen were hot on the trail of a story. "There has been some discussion—Senator Robinson last evening gave the impression that a two-addition compromise might be acceptable to the White House." FDR: "Again you are speaking about trees." Reporter: "I beg pardon." FDR: "Trees—I am talking about court reform and you are talking about trees." The meaning of the exchange was clear. Franklin Roosevelt now was willing to compromise on the number of trees (judges) if he could have his forest (the principle of Court reform).

This was a new factor for the opposition. For the past four months, the foes of FDR and his Court bill had been dancing around him, darting in for a blow, jumping back before they could be hit. Quite suddenly the Administration was adopting the same tactics. Joe Robinson had authority to make the best deal he could. A number of Democratic senators, always leery of challenging their party leader, would seize the compromise as an opportunity to come back into the party fold. With just one brief action, the announcement that a compromise was acceptable, the opposition had been disarmed. The votes the opposition thought it had to defeat the FDR bill disappeared before it. The only other tactic available to it was to defeat the bill with less than a majority by a filibuster on the Senate floor. This is a talkathon, the right of the minority in the Senate to block the "tyranny of the majority," as the filibusterers always enjoy announcing, by talking endlessly. A two-thirds vote of the Senate was necessary to end a filibuster. This meant that sixty-four senators (two-thirds of ninety-six) must vote in the affirmative to end the talkathon. The Administration forces believed they had a majority but never did they think they were near a two-thirds count. "I will stand in the Senate until I drop," vowed Pat McCarran, dramatizing the threat of a filibuster. And Edward Burke said there were forty foes of the FDR bill ready to filibuster against it. The prospect was for a long, hot summer.

At the middle of June, Joe Robinson counted forty-five votes "pretty sure pro" and thirty-nine senators "pretty sure no" with the remaining twelve being divided among "unknown" and "unknown, apparently might go along." By the end of the month, with his promise of compromise always on his tongue, he believed he had pulled enough senators to the Administration's side to assure a favorable vote. "I have enough votes pledged to pass it," he said to the Vice President on July 2. "I think I have the most compact organization ever effected in the Senate. . . . If a filibuster occurs of course, I do not know how long or how well the line will hold." He added that "if it were not for Bert Wheeler, the opposition could be pretty well pacified but Wheeler is irreconcilable. I think this is due to his personal antagonism to the President."

But a vote count—and by now Robinson was counting fifty-one votes behind FDR—is only as good as the people doing the counting. Some of the young New Dealers still insisted on believing public pressure would force Gerald Nye, for example, to switch from the "against" to the "for" column before the final vote. He was counted among the "unknowns." He belonged among those "pretty sure no." Joe Robinson also counted Claude Pepper, the young New Deal senator from Florida, among the fifty-one senators expected to vote for FDR's bill. But Pepper, years later, recalled that no one, either from the Congressional leadership or from the White House, ever had discussed the Court bill with him. His opinion is that the leadership assumed, because of his New Deal record, that he automatically supported the Court plan. Actually, Pepper has recalled, he never did make up his mind on the issue until the very last minute, being unsure of how he would vote until the roll call began.

On Friday, July 2, 1937, the compromise bill was formally introduced. It called for the appointment to the Supreme Court of one co-justice for each justice on the Court over seventy-five years of age, but with no more than one co-justice appointed a year. Where FDR wanted immediately as many appointments of co-justices as there were elderly justices on the Court, he would be limited to one a year by the compromise. Also, the compromise defined "elderly" as seventy-five years of age, where FDR had defined it as seventy. Still, the compromise included his original publicly made point that older judges cannot carry on a full share of work and need co-justices to assist them. Its passage would be a triumph for him, perhaps not a full-scale triumph but enough of one for him to be shown once again as the political master who should not be challenged.

"Of course the so-called compromise is a complete illusion," said Erwin N. Griswold, a Harvard law professor, to William Borah. "It is no compromise at all." Griswold then pointed out that FDR still would be able to make three appointments to the Court in less than six months; one to replace the retiring Willis Van Devanter, one co-justice for the year 1937 and a second co-justice for the year 1938. Because of this, said Griswold, the compromise "is just as wrong in principle as the first bill, since its only purpose is the subjugation of the judiciary." And Frank Gannett pled with conservative senators not to surrender before the FDR compromise which, he said, "is no less dishonest, reprehensible, and dangerous than the first bill. Identical in purpose, and only slightly slower in accomplishment than the President's original proposal." He urged the conservatives to filibuster the compromise so that the bill eventually could be defeated "by overwhelming popular opinion." He assured the senators that the American public "will uphold you in a filibuster."

As the political activities appeared to be writing a finish to the Court duel, those persons most immediately affected—the justices of the Supreme Court—were away from Washington. The 1936-37 session had ended June 2, and they had left the city almost immediately. "We'll travel about as the spirit moves us," said Mrs. Charles Evans Hughes. When the Court dispute reached its climax, the Chief Justice and Mrs. Hughes were in Littleton, New Hampshire, living quietly in a small resort bungalow belonging to a local hotel. The hotel clerks, bellboys, and other personnel were instructed to keep other guests away from the Chief Justice. Hughes spent his time reading, walking, taking long automobile trips. Although he ate in the hotel dining room and bowed courteously to his acquaintances, he rarely spoke to anyone. He never indicated he was aware of the actions in Washington that would so affect his future and history's determination of his contribution to his country. Reached once by telephone by an enterprising reporter and asked to comment on the Court situation, Hughes replied tersely. "No."

The other justices also gave no public sign they were aware of the Senate debate. Van Devanter, his resignation in effect, was happily roaming around his 708-acre farm in Ellicott City, Maryland, dressed in a straw hat and old clothes. James McReynolds announced he planned to visit friends in Elkton, a community in Todd County, Kentucky, where he had been born seventy-five years earlier; then he planned to vacation in Europe. Justice Sutherland and his wife also were in Europe that summer. Louis Brandeis went to his vacation home on Cape Cod as he usually did. Benjamin Cardozo vacationed in Westchester County north of New York City. Pierce Butler returned to Blue Ridge Summit in Pennsylvania, about seventy miles from Washington. He had been there the previous summer and found the cool mountain air enjoyable. Owen Roberts spent the summer at his farm in Chester County near Philadelphia. He roamed through his extensive gardens and orchards and tended his dairy herd. Roberts called his farm Bryn Coed. That was Welsh for "the wooded top of the hill." Harlan Fiske Stone and his wife made a quick trip to Mexico, then retired for the summer to Isle au Haut off the Maine Coast, where they had a summer home. There the Justice rowed, fished, and lived as simple a life as possible.

It was not that the justices were unconcerned. They were very concerned. At this point, however, there was nothing more they could do. They no longer were principals in the duel.

On July 3, three days before the Senate debate was to begin, Senator Logan of Kentucky, an architect of the compromise along with Carl Hatch of New Mexico, again emphasized that the struggle was not over the Court so much as it was for the control of the Democratic party. He charged that the conservatives wanted to destroy FDR's power in Congress as a means of challenging his leadership over the party in 1940. Of the compromise bill, Logan insisted there "is no fundamental issue involved." To buttress his argument against the conservatives, Logan revealed that during the committee sessions he had offered numerous compromises—including one to postpone the effective date of the legislation until after Franklin Roosevelt had left the Presidency—but, he said, the conservatives "wouldn't accept anything." Logan said that the Administration forces had the votes of fifty-four senators

(actually the private count was still fifty-one, two over a majority)
and would stand fast behind the compromise. Logan conceded the
possibility of a filibuster but vowed to fight it. "Keeping the Senate
in session twenty-four hours a day is the only way to break a
filibuster," he said. "If it takes that, we are prepared to go through
with it."

A filibuster can last only as long as those wanting to talk can hold
the Senate floor. Round-the-clock sessions meant that opponents
of the President's program must always be present, twenty-four
hours a day, ready to talk at great length. Otherwise, Joe Robinson
could snatch the floor away from them and order a vote. The
usual procedure, and it was the intention of Robinson to follow
this procedure with the Court bill, is to avoid any charges of
wanting to short-change the opposition's right to speak by permitting debate to run on for several weeks before beginning any
antifilibuster move. Only after debate has run on obviously longer
than necessary is the defense against a filibuster brought out. This
is the all-night sessions with their costs in health, energy, good
spirits, and sometimes the lives of members of the Senate.

The debate in the Senate was scheduled to begin at noon on
Tuesday, July 6. That morning two of the principal antagonists,
Franklin Roosevelt and Burton Wheeler, met at the White House.
Acting on information, erroneous as it turned out, that Wheeler
might be in a mood for a compromise, the President invited the
Senator to visit with him. They met in the President's oval office.
Through the glass doors of that office one can see the Washington
Monument, the Potomac River, and the state of Virginia beyond
it. It is a pleasant and peaceful view. It is a view that belies the
the President's office as the seat of enormous and brutal power.
But with all this power available to the President, the patronage and
the pork barrel, a public willing to be led and politicians willing
to follow, this particular President had been unable to budge this
one senator from his opposition. Actually, with all his power
Franklin Roosevelt could not touch Burton Wheeler. Only the
people of Montana could do that. His future was their choice, not
Franklin Roosevelt's. The meeting this morning between the Presi-

dent and the Senator was a clash, in fact, of the two powers: the national and the state. Actually, the American government had developed so that these two powers would clash at times, that one would be a check on the other, that the state would balance the national government's impetuosity and eagerness for power and the federal government would counterbalance the state's inertia and lack of enthusiasm for doing the national job that had to be done. That Franklin Roosevelt and Burton Wheeler met this particular morning, each resolved to be adamant in his stand and each hoping to persuade the other to surrender, indicated that the system of government woven into the American fabric—the system of power as the rival of power—was succeeding.

Roosevelt began the meeting simply, stating in the most friendly and warm tones that he had only intended to modernize the American judicial system and not, as charged, humble or destroy the Supreme Court. Wheeler's reply indicated he did not accept this explanation. He spoke in terms of a Supreme Court which held the status of a religion with most American people and said that the Court should not be tampered with. If he were the President's worst enemy, said Wheeler, only then would he help him pass the Court bill. "But I am your friend," continued Wheeler, "and this will kill your popularity. It is the difference between you coming out as a great President or as a bad one."

Realizing he could gain nothing with that argument, Roosevelt then switched to one of party loyalty. Let the Republicans lead the fight, he said. If you must vote against the bill, at least don't speak against it. Don't organize other senators to vote against it. Don't destroy the Democratic party. As well as did Roosevelt, Wheeler knew that without his leading the opposition, the duel would be recognized as a liberal-conservative clash and FDR might well win. For that reason he could not accede to FDR's request. Also, too much had happened between Burton Wheeler and Franklin Roosevelt for there to be a rapprochement now. Before the Court bill had been introduced, the national Administration had ignored senators like Wheeler, trampling over their power bases, an act suggesting to their home states that they were not men of high repute in Washington. Once the duel had begun, there had been too much—as far as Burt Wheeler was concerned—of the tactics such as the incident in Kansas and the one with his income tax. The old line that politicians were "friendly enemies" who shake hands when the battle is done did not apply to these two men. It often did to politicians who can oppose each other vehemently on the Senate floor, or between the Senate and the White House, and then laugh at it all later over a golf foursome. But not over this issue. The duel had gone on too long, had been too bitter; the wounds, too deep.

And neither man was interested in compromise. Roosevelt believed his men had the Senate votes to pass the Court bill. Wheeler believed he had the strength, by means of a filibuster, to prevent a vote from being taken. At one point Wheeler did say that if Roosevelt dropped his Court bill there would be two resignations from the Court. These would be in addition to that of Willis Van Devanter. For a brief instant there was a flicker of interest from Roosevelt. How certain was Wheeler of that? Wheeler's information had come from William Borah, who had lines of communication to the conservative members of the Court. However, the information still was based on rumor. Roosevelt passed the deal by. The question of whether Wheeler could really deliver two resignations had not been answered satisfactorily for him. Also, the duel had gone beyond the question of who did or did not sit on the Supreme Court; the duel was now over control of the Democratic party. The two men then were at an impasse. Neither would be the first to yield.

At twelve o'clock that day the imperative rapping of a gavel called the United States Senate into session. A total of eighty-four senators, many dressed in summer white suits, answered to their names when the roll was called. The visitors' galleries were packed with troops of Boy Scouts in Washington for a national jamboree, regular tourists, families of senators, and assorted Washingtonians. The chamber had not been so packed since the days when the late Huey Long upheld his title as the filibuster king by holding forth on the glories of "pot likker." The Senate was about to begin one of its great debates, one of its historic struggles. And everyone knew it.

As happens with a "great" debate and a "historic" struggle in the Senate, the debate over the Court bill began with a bit of fluff. The Republican leader in the Senate, Senator McNary of Oregon, rose to ask if the Senate would be in session the next day, Wednesday, July 7. Everyone understood what he was talking about. There was an important baseball game scheduled for the next day, and the senators had hoped to attend. Joe Robinson began in a heavy-handed way, saying: "It is my intention to ask the Senate to be in session tomorrow. I feel that there is no justification whatever for suspending the public business, under the conditions which now prevail, in order that members may have an opportunity of attending a baseball game." Later, of course, Robinson relented, as his colleagues knew he would do. The Senate did meet Wednesday, but only from ten in the morning until one o'clock in the afternoon. That adjournment hour permitted the senators to get to the ball park with time to spare.

The first test for the Court bill was Robinson's motion to make it the order of business before the Senate. Although such a motion is traditional and rarely challenged, it can be a device to defeat a bill even before a debate begins. If a majority of the Senate had voted against making the Court bill the Senate's pending business, the bill would have been dead at that moment. But the opponents of the Court bill did not request a vote. This was interpreted as a sign that they did not control the votes of a majority of the members of the Senate, that Joe Robinson's fifty-one figure for the number of supporters might be as accurate as he believed it was. It also meant, however, that the only way the Administration opponents could defeat the Court bill was by a filibuster, a talkathon lasting weeks or months until the Administration surrendered or enough Administration supporters decided to switch sides just to end the talk.

Robinson, in his role as Senate Majority Leader and spokesman in the Senate for the President, began the discussion of the Court bill. His speech was a stirring defense of the President and his bill.

His voice grew loud in anger, then low in confidence. His right hand sawed the air. His great bulk moved across the Senate floor as nimbly as his arguments darted from point to point. It was a good show. At the end, however, he turned to the real question that was bothering his colleagues—the prospect of a filibuster.

"I am prompted to make reference to the subject of a threatened filibuster," began Robinson. "It would not seem to me appropriate to do so at this time if it were not for the fact that some of my dear friends who are in the opposition have been quoted in the press as saying that they are determined that the Senate shall never be permitted to register its conclusion on this legislation." Robinson then promised that the right of full and free debate would not be hindered, but he also insisted he would not surrender before a filibuster. "Much as it might surprise the members of the Senate," he continued, "I would probably come out of that kind of a test better than those who are in the opposition, at least some of them. I think I could endure it longer than could the Senator from Montana." With that, Robinson turned slightly toward Burton Wheeler.

Amidst the friendly laughter in the Senate chamber, Wheeler replied, "I am in very good physical condition. I have been training for it." He actually had. For weeks he and his wife had been rising early in the morning and playing nine holes of golf.

Robinson seized on the comment. "Oh, yes; the senator warns me now . . ."

Wheeler interjected: "No, I do not warn the senator."

But Robinson continued: ". . . that he is in training for a filibuster. Very well. Before he gets through, he will not feel so confident as he feels today. . . . I think I will know when you turn from a debater into a filibusterer, and then, as the old saying goes, it will be 'dog eat dog.'" There was a kind of nervous laughter then in the Senate chamber. The members knew Joe Robinson's words were true ones. In a filibuster there are few holds barred. But none knew, could possibly have known, that the fate awaiting Joe Robinson would block a filibuster much more effectively than the words he spoke that day.

The debate began in lackluster fashion. Senator Joseph F. Guffey, a Democrat of Pennsylvania and an FDR supporter on the Court bill, reminded his fellow Democrats that "if they are unaware of the fact that this is a political struggle between the two parties, the leaders on the other side are fully conscious of that fact." He then proceeded to congratulate the Republican leaders for managing "to get the maximum of political advantage for [the GOP] by the somewhat novel process of maintaining silence as deep as the grave on this issue." Congratulations were in order. Seldom had a political party been as successful with a technique as the GOP had been with its approach of silence on the Court bill. No matter how much senators like Guffey tried to place the opposition at the Republicans' door, the public had never come to visualize the Court duel as a partisan struggle. The refusal of the Republican leaders to speak out on the issue was the effective tactic. The decision made by Charles McNary, William Borah, and Arthur Vandenberg at the beginning of the duel had been an eminently correct one for the Republicans.

Sherman Minton, the senator from Indiana who had almost let the cat of Court reform out of the secrecy bag in January, attacked the charge that Franklin Roosevelt wanted to pack the Court. "What do senators think Mr. Justice Van Devanter was doing on the Supreme Court the last three years he was on the bench, when he wrote only about two opinions a year?" asked Minton. "He was not working. He was sitting there packing the Court so that President Roosevelt could not appoint his successor."

There was also, as there is during many Senate debates, an occasional laugh. At one point Minton was having a dialogue with a Republican member of the Judiciary Committee, Warren Austin of Vermont. Minton spoke of President Theodore Roosevelt's advocating recall of federal judges by popular vote, a theory—Minton said to Warren Austin—which "makes the hair on the top of the head of the Senator from Vermont curl."

The senator from Vermont shook his bald head and corrected Minton: "If there were any hair there to curl."

But all the arguments had been heard before, many times. What the senators were doing as the debate lurched aimlessly through its first week was making a public record. They were explaining for the benefit of their constituents, for the information of the organized groups that supported them, and also for the knowledge of the lobbyists who frequented their offices, why they held the position they did. No minds were being changed; the Administration forces still held strong, so Joe Robinson believed, at fifty votes approximately. A narrow margin but still a victory margin.

Over on the House side of the Capitol, Hatton Sumners watched with deep misgivings as the Senate debated. He remained adamantly against the Court bill. He also feared that it would pass the Senate and then come to the House side and to his committee. Could he block it? Would the impetus of a Senate victory for the bill encourage enough of his committee members to defy him by bringing the bill out of committee against his wishes? On July 13, when the Senate debate had been running for a week, Hatton Sumners rose on the House floor to ask that the Court reform bill be dropped. He insisted that once that happened, "as soon as we take the lash from above the heads of these judges over there, some more of them will retire. I mean that as a fact." Approximately three hundred House members were present for his speech, most of them giving cheers and applause. The meaning of the performance was clear. Sumners and his friends were claiming that even if the Senate passed the bill, the House might not. This was an added pressure against Joe Robinson. Some of the fifty-one senators he believed were backing him up had come under tremendous pressure from groups like Frank Gannett's committee, the American Bar Association, and other conservative-oriented organizations. They began to feel uncomfortable. They began to look for an out. Why should we fight over this in the Senate? they asked each other in the cloakroom. Why should we struggle, destroy friendships, perhaps ruin ourselves politically if, when we finish, the House refuses to go along?

At the same time the opponents of the Court bill in both the House and Senate began having "confidential" talks with newsmen. A good politician knows how to use the press for his own ends.

He knows the press can be manipulated, can do the politician's work for him. And so the stories began to seep out from the Capitol to the nation's newspapers that the number of FDR supporters in the Senate was beginning to dwindle. A climate was being created, a climate of defeat. No one wants to be with a loser, and so the uncomfortable senators felt even more uncomfortable, wanting even more to pull out from the commitments they had given to Joe Robinson.

In the end, however, it was not Hatton Sumner's opposition or the stories in the newspapers, not the mistakes made by the Administration or the loose headcount made by Joe Robinson that made the difference in the outcome of the duel between Franklin Roosevelt and the Supreme Court, the duel between Roosevelt and the conservatives in his party.

15

ALMOST FROM the beginning of the Senate debate on the Court bill a heat wave had held the eastern half of the nation in its stifling grasp. By Sunday, July 11, the death toll had reached one hundred and fifty persons, twenty-five of them in the New York city area. In Washington the temperature hovered at ninety-five degrees without promise of relief. Two persons died Monday from the heat; one on Tuesday. Thousands of persons slept on beaches or in parks, wherever they hoped to find some relief from the heat.

The heat was a bother to Joe Robinson. Now sixty-four years old and with a heart condition that had lately been giving him difficulty, he was decidedly uncomfortable as the heat wave enveloped his massive bulk. But he ignored it as best he could. He had a job to do and he intended to see that it was done. For fourteen years he had been leader of the Senate Democrats. He was proud of that tenure, proud of his record of party loyalty, proud of his ability to produce the needed votes from the Senate when he must.

Too much of a conservative to be really happy with the New Deal, he still did his best to support the President in the Senate even though he had many misgivings. The day the Court bill debate opened in the Senate, July 6, he was writing to a friend: "It is hard to make our people conscious of the necessity for retrenchment in public expenditures. Sometimes I get very much discouraged. Thousands of Arkansans come here during the year begging, begging, begging! They sometimes try to lift their process of robbing the federal treasury to a high plane by surrounding their projects and plans with a dignity and magnitude that truly are inspiring. It is going to be very difficult to ever get away from this habit of giving out federal favors. You cannot imagine how persistent are the forces of plunder." A few weeks earlier, when FDR had unveiled his 1.5-billion-dollar relief bill, Robinson had countered with an amendment requiring local communities to put up one-fourth of the cost of public works projects. "Gentlemen may laugh about a thirty-six billion dollar debt hanging over the Treasury if they wish to," he said, "but I find it impossible to laugh about such a thing."

Still Robinson continued to interpret his role of Senate Democratic leader as that of bringing into force the policies of the Democratic party as enunciated by its leader—the man in the White House. Having the Court bill thrust upon him, as it was in February without advance warning and without being asked to give any advice on its chances for passage, was an unpleasant experience for Robinson. But he assumed the job of the good lieutenant and proceeded to try to push it through. After the White House meeting early in June, Joe Robinson lost his misgivings, however. That was the session in which Franklin Roosevelt agreed to accept the best compromise that Robinson could work out. The result was the Marvel Logan-Carl Hatch bill with its provision for the appointment of one co-justice a year, a proposal that Robinson did not find too onerous. Also, he relished being once again the leader able to make compromises, to wheel and deal in search for votes. As the debate began, Joe Robinson was riding pretty high. He had the votes, he believed, to pass the compromise. But quickly he realized the opposition was unyielding. Its threat of filibuster was growing more serious each day.

The usual gentlemanly debate in the Senate at times grew bitter. "If the opponents of the bill had the votes to defeat us," Robinson told the Senate one day, "they would take the vote tomorrow. Do you not all know you would?" When Burton Wheeler tried to interrupt him, Robinson snapped back: "Oh, yes; do not answer or you will discredit yourselves; you know you have not the votes, and, therefore, you are starting out with a threatened filibuster."

At another point Senator Burke from Nebraska charged that Robinson was basing his talk of a threatened filibuster on newspaper speculation. Robinson, perhaps never speaking more harshly to a colleague, replied: "Yes; I have been reading the newspapers; I have been reading the interviews—the ill-considered, unwise interviews—by my good friend the Senator from Nebraska. If he would talk less and do more, my judgment is we would have a shortening of the debate."

To cut the impact of a filibuster and to shorten it, Robinson directed that seldom-used rules of the Senate be invoked. These rules limited a senator to speaking only twice on one subject during a single day. Then the word "day" was interpreted to mean a legislative day. By the parliamentary tactic of recessing at the end of each calendar day, rather than adjourning, the legislative day can continue indefinitely. The rules then were a means of limiting each senator to only two speeches during the whole Senate debate. But Robinson's foes would not let him off so easily. Working with a full-time research staff of lawyers supplied by the American Bar Association, the opponents of the Court bill were preparing dozens of amendments to the Court bill. Each of these amendments, although some were obviously trivial and not offered seriously, was a new subject according to parliamentary procedure. The introduction of each one provided an additional opportunity then for each senator to make two additional speeches, to consume more time, to stretch out the filibuster.

The debate itself was taking its toll on Robinson. It was his responsibility as the leader, he believed, to make most of the speeches in behalf of the, Court bill, to answer the criticisms. But as he spoke, the opponents swarmed around him like snapping animals. They jumped to their feet with questions, points of order, nasty comments. Robinson, his beefy face reddening, his big jaw moving angrily, threw out his answers to them. But it was a tiring process. One day, after a particularly long siege on the Senate floor, Joe Robinson turned his weary body toward Senator Burke, who said: "I should like to ask the senator another question."

"No," answered Joe Robinson. "I am through."

"No more questions?" persisted an unbelieving Burke.

"No more questions today," answered Robinson, his voice somewhat faint. "The senator may reserve them until next week." And then a curious word: "Goodbye." With that, old Joe Robinson turned away from his surprised colleagues and moved slowly out of the Senate chamber.

Most of the members of the Senate were aware that Joe Robinson was ill and that he should not overtax himself in the Court debate. During one strategy session with his fellow Democrats, Robinson asked each of his party members to speak in favor of the bill. When he came to Henry Ashurst he said, "Henry, when will you speak?" Ashurst answered, "My physician will tell me when I may speak and you, Joe, should not speak unless your physician permits." Senator Royal Copeland, the New York Democrat who early in the dispute had permitted his mail to persuade him to go against Roosevelt, was also concerned over Robinson's health. Copeland was a physician, the only one in the Senate. He remembered that after one lengthy speech by Robinson, the Senate leader sauntered over to Copeland's desk and chided the New Yorker for his concern about Robinson's health. Copeland recalled telling Robinson that he was indeed concerned and bluntly informed Robinson that he was playing with death by straining himself; Copeland told Robinson that the Court bill was not worth the price of his life. "Go slow" was Copeland's advice to Robinson, advice the Senate leader was not interested in taking.

There was another reason for Robinson's willingness to go along so wholeheartedly with FDR now, a reason that went beyond the merits of the Court bill compromise. This was Robinson's ambition to cap his public career with a seat on the Supreme Court. It was an ambition well known in Washington, so well known in fact that most persons in Washington assumed that as soon as a vacancy occurred, the appointment of Robinson to the high bench would follow immediately.

The day Willis Van Devanter sent his resignation to the White House, Joe Robinson's colleagues considered his appointment as a replacement a sure thing. So did Robinson. He came into the Senate chamber that afternoon with a wide grin on his face and feeling almost jubilant. His fellow senators of both parties, who were also his old and warm friends, swarmed toward him to congratulate him, shake his hand, slap him on the back. Some even called him "Mr. Justice." This situation, the high probability that Joe Robinson would be named to the Court, was one of the reasons Robinson had been able to secure pledges to support the Court bill compromise. His colleagues assumed that the appointment to the Court would be forthcoming as soon as Joe Robinson delivered passage of the Court bill. Some senators, wavering on judicial reform, had decided to go along as a favor to Robinson. They had much affection for him and wanted him to achieve his ambitions.

FDR, however, although aware that Robinson was expecting the appointment, had some reservations. The day Van Devanter resigned, Roosevelt refused to talk about whom he would name as a replacement. A couple of days later a reporter jokingly asked: "Do you intend to confirm the Senate nomination of Senator Robinson to the Supreme Court?" And a second reporter chimed in with "Get out your rubber stamp." But FDR, joining in the laughter, insisted that "I have not considered the Supreme Court vacancy at all. . . . Anything you write," he told the reporters, "should be headed 'Surmise Number Twenty-three.' "

The trouble was that Robinson would be sixty-five years old

on August 26 and his appointment would cause much merriment in Washington after Franklin Roosevelt had begun his attack on the Court on the basis of age. Also, Robinson was believed to be basically a conservative. Once on the Court he could not be touched by FDR; he would be free to rule against the New Deal. Robert Jackson, the assistant attorney general, advised Roosevelt against naming Robinson. "I think it would be a great mistake for you to pack the court and accept additional memberships on it, if you have got to make Joe Robinson one of them. There is only one excuse for packing the Court and that is to change it. You're very likely not to change anything and you will have all the odium of having packed it and being laughed at besides." But Roosevelt believed he owed the first appointment to Robinson, and he did not see any way to avoid making it, particularly if Robinson pushed the Court bill through the Senate.

Still, the President vacillated on the decision of whether to appoint Robinson. About a week after Van Devanter's resignation, Roosevelt was cruising on the cutter *The Potomac* along the river of the same name with some friends. It was after ten o'clock on a beautiful moonlit Saturday night. The other members of the party had retired to cabins below until only the President and Henry Morgenthau, Jr., his friend and a Cabinet member, sat together on the deck. "If Brandeis resigns," speculated the President, "whom do you think I should appoint to succeed him—Landis or Frankfurter?" The first reference was to James M. Landis, a brilliant young New Dealer, and the second was to Felix Frankfurter of the Harvard Law School who had been a philosophical mentor to the New Deal.

Morgenthau replied that he considered Landis the better choice.

"Frankfurter would rate a more popular opinion."

Morgenthau agreed, saying: "Yes, I suppose he would, but I believe that the public would have more confidence in Landis."

"Well," said the President, "I think I would have a terrible time getting Frankfurter confirmed." Morgenthau agreed, commenting that "one of the troubles with Frankfurter is that he is over-brilliant."

A few moments later Morgenthau brought the conversation from the realm of speculation to the immediate problem, the retirement of Willis Van Devanter and the expectation that Joe Robinson would succeed him. "What," he asked the President, "are you going to do about Joe Robinson?"

"I cannot appoint him," announced the President.

"Why not?"

"Because he is not sufficiently liberal."

"I am certainly glad to hear you talk that way," said Morgenthau. "The things that you have done and talked to me about the last ten days have encouraged me tremendously because after all I am a reformer."

Several moments later the President returned to the question of appointing Joe Robinson. "If I had three vacancies, I might be able to sandwich in Joe Robinson." But he continued that he had no idea of who was going to resign after Van Devanter, or if anyone would.

Meanwhile, however, Robinson acted as if his appointment were cinched. At the beginning of June he told a friend, "Without a single dissenting view [his fellow senators] have expressed themselves as favorable to my succeeding Mr. Justice Van Devanter." He discounted opposition from "braintrusters" in the White House, saying they were as enthusiastic for his appointment as were conservative senators.

Jim Farley was the one who sealed the appointment finally. At a meeting with Roosevelt he urged the President to agree to naming Robinson, explaining that it would create a great deal of good will between the President and the senators, at a time when the amount of good will between them had been dwindling rapidly. Farley recalls that Homer Cummings was at that meeting and endorsed the appointment of Robinson. At this point the President agreed. Farley called Robinson the next morning and began the conversation by calling the senator "Mr. Justice." Farley then suggested that Robinson not do anything to upset things—that is, that he deliver on the Court bill—and all would be okay with his appointment. Among professional politicians such a discussion amounts to an ironclad agreement.

In his pursuit of success with the Court bill Joe Robinson played by a set of practices that might seem curiously unethical outside the Senate. One of Robinson's aides was a young man named Leslie Biffle. Frequently during the months in which both sides had been pulling and hauling for votes, Biffle called up Wheeler to tip him off as to which senators were lined up in which column. Wheeler believed that Biffle could not have engaged in that extracurricular activity without Robinson's knowledge and blessing. Also, Robinson did not hesitate at times to express sympathy with the opposition. The day the Senate debate opened and Burt Wheeler returned from the unsuccessful session at the White House, Joe Robinson asked him, "How'd you make out?" When Wheeler replied that he had not made out well at all, Robinson said: "You keep at him. I can't do anything with him."

Although it may have appeared that Robinson was "double-crossing" the side he was supposed to be supporting or that he did not really favor Roosevelt's side of the issue, this was not true. He did realize, however, that once the Court bill was disposed of, however it went, the Senate would have to work on other issues and would have to overcome any animosities created by the Court bill. One who knew Joe Robinson well in those years and who was a part of the Court fight explained Robinson's activities this way: "The Senate and the senators did not like to engage in a war where communication with the enemy is treason." Not much information was divulged by Biffle to Wheeler. Some senators were known to support FDR; others obviously did not. There were no secrets about these. There were the "swing" senators, those whose position either was not known or could change. But they were known in the Senate also. All that Biffle was doing, as was Robinson with his camaraderie, was keeping lines open between the two sides so that, once the Court duel had ended, members of the United States Senate could still talk with each other.

But the process was an arduous one. The whole Court struggle had been difficult for Joe Robinson. He had been so exhausted at one point that he had to take a two-week rest. Although the duel now was obviously coming to an end, it still continued, for him, to be extremely difficult and sapping of his strength. On Monday, July 12, Robinson posed for an artist who was painting his portrait. The artist, S. J. Woolf, later recalled of that sitting: "As he leaned back in a great leather chair, [Robinson] spoke of the things which were happening in the Senate chamber. . . . He seemed strong, vibrant and vital. His mind worked with startling keenness and his body seemed physically fit." But, conceded Woolf, Robinson did complain of not feeling well.

Monday, July 12, was a bad day for Robinson. He was talking with Henry Ashurst in the Senate reception room adjacent to the private cloakroom when he complained of a sharp pain in his chest. "I immediately dispatched two colored boys to give him hot water and common soda which appeared to relieve him," said Ashurst. Robinson apparently felt better because that night he went to the movies with a friend from Little Rock, a man named Homer Adkins.

On Tuesday, Robinson stayed away from the Senate chamber except to attend a few strategy conferences. At one time Alben Barkley saw Robinson quickly leave the Senate chamber. Barkley followed him out and found his friend sitting on the Capitol portico. Joe Robinson said he had "a little flurry" in his chest about where his heart was located and asked Barkley: "Do you think I ought to see a physician?" Barkley suggested he see one immediately. Robinson said he would do so and also that he was going home to rest.

Home in Washington for Joe Robinson was a five-room apartment on the fourth floor of the Methodist Building, directly and conveniently across from the Capitol. He was alone in Washington this week; Mrs. Robinson happened to be in Little Rock. He did not look well that Tuesday evening. The elevator boy in the Methodist Building asked Robinson if he perhaps would like someone to stay with him that night. Robinson replied that it would not be necessary, that he was feeling quite all right. Dressed in his pajamas, Robinson sat up in his bed reading by the light of a bed lamp. His reading material was the bible of government officials in Washington, the *Congressional Record,* the daily journal and record of what happens and is said on the floors of the House and Senate.

The next morning, Wednesday, July 14, Mary Jasper, the Robinsons' maid, arrived at the apartment. She let herself in and went into the kitchen to make breakfast for the Senator. Joe Robinson had regular habits, and when he did not appear for his breakfast a few minutes before eight o'clock, the maid became concerned. She knocked on the door of his bedroom. There was no answer. She turned the knob and entered. The electric light by the bed was still burning. The bed obviously had been slept in but was empty. Beyond the bed the door to the bathroom was open; that room appeared empty. The maid rushed out of the apartment and summoned the boy who ran the elevator. Had he seen the Senator leave? she demanded. No, said the boy. He had not seen the Senator since the previous day when the Senator had come to his apartment. The elevator boy and Mary Jasper entered the apartment together. They went into the Senator's bedroom, went farther into the room than the doorway and finally saw Joe Robinson.

The great Democrat who had manfully shouldered the burdens of his party for many years, the loyal party member who had tried to save the Presidential candidacy of Al Smith from the anti-Catholicism of the 1920s, the willing Senate leader who had dutifully followed political orders even when they challenged his own philosophical beliefs—this man now lay dead, sprawled out on the floor. A heart attack had claimed him in the early hours of the morning. By his right hand, where it had fallen when he dropped it, lay the *Congressional Record,* the journal of the institution he loved and to which he had devoted his life.

16

THE FIRST CALL to the White House asking Franklin Roosevelt to drop the Court bill because of the Robinson death came from Bernard Baruch, the financier, the advisor to Presidents, and the associate of southern conservative Democrats like Robinson. Baruch had been scheduled to sail to Europe that morning, but when he heard the news about Robinson's death, he got off the ship and canceled his passage. His message to the President was simple: Stop the Court duel before any additional senators are killed. Roosevelt's reply was that it was not the bill that was killing anyone but the filibuster against it.

Burton Wheeler was one of the next to call on the President to end the Court duel. His request was public. "Joe Robinson was both a political and personal friend of mine," he told newsmen, continuing: "Had it not been for the Court bill he would be alive today. I beseech the President to drop the fight lest he appear to fight against God." He was answered by Eleanor Roosevelt, the President's wife. She had stayed out of the Court duel, saying very little, but Wheeler's comment seemed to her too much of an attack on her husband. "The gentleman," she said of Burton Wheeler, "seemed to feel that he was so receptive to information from the Almighty that he knew the reason for whatever might happen on this little planet of ours."

Whatever course FDR chose, it was obvious that his Court bill was in difficulty because of the death of Joe Robinson. "Robinson alone could have marshalled the support of three or four senators who were his close friends who were not committed and whose votes were absolutely essential for success," Jimmy Byrnes recalled later. It was true, at least it was widely believed, that a few of the votes that had given Joe Robinson his tight majority were pledged to him personally, payments for old favors he had rendered or simply because some of the senators wanted him to deliver on the Court bill so he could achieve his ambition of a seat on the Supreme Court. With Robinson dead, those votes probably were lost to the Administration.

Roosevelt, almost immediately after the Robinson death, had a vivid glimpse of how shaky was the Administration majority. During the Senate debate, prior to the Robinson death, a group of four young Democratic senators decided it was time to discuss the Court bill with the President. The four were Prentiss M. Brown of Michigan, Edwin C. Johnson of Colorado, Charles O. Andrews of Florida, and Guy M. Gillette of Iowa. Of the four, Gillette was known to be an opponent of the Court bill. Andrews also was suspect. He had his own version of how best to reform the Court. He would have the Supreme Court increased to ten members and picked on a basis of geography. (Robinson had opposed that approach because there would have been no opening in the foreseeable future for him on the Court; he was from Arkansas and that mid-south region was well represented on the Court.) The other two senators, Brown and Johnson, were expected to go along with the Administration when the Court bill came to a vote.

The meeting of the four senators with the President took place on Thursday, July 15, one day after Robinson's death. The accounts of the meeting differ. According to newspaper stories of the time, the four senators advised FDR that his Court bill was finished and that he would do well to withdraw it rather than continue to press for its passage. Continuing with the bill, the four reportedly told the President, would only increase the bitterness in the Senate. According to an account written a few months after the meeting, the four senators met with Roosevelt for an hour, with the President doing most of the talking. He told the senators, according to this account, that all Democrats must support him as did Joe Robinson and that only archconservatives and enemies of the Party would oppose him. But, this account continues, the senators broke in and bluntly told the President they could not go along on the Court bill.

The meeting had taken place on Thursday, July 15. That Saturday, Edwin Johnson, one of the four senators at the session, wrote this note to the President:

> Our conference Thursday seems to have been terribly misunderstood. Last week Senator Brown suggested that Senators Andrews, Gillette and I join him in a visit to you for a frank discussion of the Court matter, Senator Brown to make the appointment. I was glad for such an opportunity. So many wild stories and rumors were being told that I desired to find out first hand your position on a constitutional amendment and on the so-called Hatch substitution as well as your opinion upon the urgency for action at this session on the whole Court plan. Of course, I had no thought of issuing anything in the nature of a mild senatorial ultimatum to you, or of making an implied demand or even a strong suggestion. I wanted your viewpoint.

Whether the meeting with the President was as blunt as the first two accounts claim or as mild-mannered as the Edwin Johnson letter suggests, the session obviously demonstrated that there was a considerable amount of wavering among the Administration forces in the Senate. That point would be hammered home to the White House again and again in the next few days.

After lying in state at the Capitol in Washington, Robinson was to be buried in Little Rock. A special funeral train of ten Pullman cars carrying his body and his friends left Washington Saturday. Aboard the train were thirty-eight senators, the men who had stood with Joe Robinson in the Senate for many years. They had drunk with him, joked with him, fought with him at times, but always thought of him as a comrade. Now they came to his hometown to bury him. There were also twenty-three members of the House of Representatives and Jim Farley, the Postmaster General, as well as Bernard Baruch, Robinson's friend. Vice President Garner, finally back from Texas, was at the funeral, representing the President. The Senator's body lay in state at the statehouse, then was taken to the cemetery for the burial. The coffin was to be lowered into the ground beneath the spreading boughs of four oak trees. As the cortege approached the cemetery the sky was crossed with peals of thunder and flashes of lightning. The hundreds of spectators

glanced nervously at the cloud-laden skies. The rain, a hard down-
pour, came just as the flag-covered casket was poised above the
grave, ready to be lowered into the ground. Many of the spectators
ran for shelter, but a large group of the Senate Majority Leader's
old friends stayed, becoming drenched by the rain, until the casket
had been lowered and the final word of benediction said. It was a
curious group that remained standing in the rain. Back a little, but
still able to witness the ceremony, were a number of Negro dirt
farmers. Many of them had known Joe Robinson fifty years earlier
when he had worked the fields beside them. Others had come to
know him through the years because of his consideration for them
and his generosity. Closer to the site of the ceremony were the Vice
President of the United States, John Nance Garner; Bernard Baruch, one of the wealthiest men in the nation; and a collection of
some of the most important politicians, government officials, and
statesmen in the state of Arkansas and the United States.

That all these stood in the rain that day was a commentary on
Joe Robinson's life. In his closing years he had become one with
the powerful and the rich. But in doing so he had not lost the love
and respect of the humble and the poor. To few men can such a
tribute be paid as was paid to Joe Robinson that day.

Politicians are such that politics never can be dismissed from
their lives. At almost every waking moment, and even some of their
sleeping ones, politics dominates their thoughts and their actions.
It is not that they are callous persons. Rather, it is that politics is
so demanding that it becomes not a vocation but, instead, a jealous
mistress that will not permit its captive time or energy for other
pursuits, that will not permit its captive any respite. For this reason
those politicians who rode the special funeral train from Washington to Little Rock and then back again assumed that politics would
preempt their mourning. The sadness of Joe Robinson's death,
they knew, would be placed aside as they took up the problems they
faced in their tomorrows.

That is exactly how it was. As the train pulled out from Little
Rock, Vice President Garner established his "board of education"
in a drawing room. He shucked his coat and armed himself with

some bourbon and branch water. During the trip to Washington, Garner spoke with every senator on the train, to ascertain how they felt and would vote on the President's Court bill. The sentiment decidedly was shifting against the President, and then came another event—totally unexpected—that made the shift against FDR a complete rout.

In New York, Herbert Lehman had continued to oppose the Court plan as he had in February when he had written a private letter to FDR. But he had otherwise kept his opposition to himself. Unaware of how the votes were shifting against FDR, Lehman, then Governor of New York State, believed he should take some action, in a public fashion, against the Court plan. His opposition would be symbolic; he had no vote in the Senate. But it would be an important symbol. If Herbert Lehman, one of the most respected and courageous liberals of the 1930s, came out against the Court bill, certainly he would influence a number of other liberals to do so also. His public opposition would give some wavering liberals a perfect "out." If a liberal like Herbert Lehman is against the Court bill, these waverers could explain to their liberal supporters, then don't be angry with me for opposing it.

"I thought we were getting to the critical point," Lehman said later, "and unless I released the letter it would be useless for me to do anything." The letter he was referring to was one Lehman had written to Senator Robert Wagner of New York, expressing opposition to the Court plan. "I believe that the orderly and deliberate processes of government should not be sacrificed merely to meet an immediate situation," Lehman wrote to Wagner. Any gain from such action, Lehman continued, would "be far more than offset by a loss of confidence in the independence of the courts and in governmental procedure." Then, even before Senator Wagner received the letter, Governor Lehman released it to the press in New York. It was the first public break between Lehman and Franklin Roosevelt. The news reached the Robinson funeral train when it stopped briefly at Chillicothe, Ohio, on its way back to the nation's capital. The foes of the Court bill were ecstatic. "That is the complete and final blow to the Administration's court reorganization project," said Senator Burke. And Senator Vandenberg announced that "Governor Lehman's intellectual honesty has driven him to a courageous and invincible conclusion. All that remains to be done is to call the coroner." Jim Farley, publicly, tried to shrug off the letter as being of not much importance. Privately, however, he was seething. In Washington it was reported that the White House considered the Lehman letter "a stab in the back."

And Roosevelt was having other troubles also. The death of Robinson meant that the position of Senate Democratic leader was open. Although it is traditional for the President to maintain a hands-off policy about the selection of a senator to fill that position, it also was obvious to Roosevelt that if the Robinson replacement was not a senator who would support the Administration down the line, the New Deal was in trouble. The choice appeared to be between two Democrats, Pat Harrison of Mississippi and Alben Barkley of Kentucky. Barkley was then assistant majority leader and, because of that, might have a good chance of replacing Robinson. But Harrison seemed to have the greater support among the Democrats, primarily because he was more independent of the White House than was Barkley. Actually both Harrison and Barkley had good pro-Roosevelt voting records, but Harrison's sympathy with the New Deal had always been suspect. The belief was that he went along only because political realities compelled him to do so. Roosevelt's task then was to secure the election of Barkley as Robinson's replacement.

His first move was to write a "My Dear Alben" letter to Barkley, calling on him to continue leading the fight for the Court bill. The letter was made public even before the Robinson funeral, and FDR was accused of trying to capitalize on the Robinson death by appealing to the senators' sympathy for their dead colleague. Roosevelt denied that was his purpose. He explained, when Farley personally complained to him about the letter, that he wrote the letter to stress that he was not giving up the Court fight as was rumored and reported in the newspapers immediately after Robinson's death. FDR continued that he could not have written to

Garner, who then still was in Texas. He wrote to Barkley because, FDR said, he was acting leader.

The Democratic senators, however, believed—and were probably very close to the mark—that Franklin Roosevelt was trying to interfere with the inner workings of the Senate by influencing the outcome of the leadership election. The members of Congress are jealous of their powers and always look with suspicion on the executive branch of the government. Rightly or wrongly, the members fear the President is trying to usurp their powers. They were particularly suspicious of Franklin Roosevelt because, it seemed to them, they had lost so much of their power, position, and public respect since he came to the Presidency. If Roosevelt had better understood the Senate, or if his aides who were advising him had had more respect for that institution as well as a better understanding of it, FDR never would have sent the Barkley letter and so taunted the Senate. But Franklin Roosevelt's understanding of the Democrats in the Senate was that they were a group to be commanded. He did not see the Senate as part of a coequal branch of government but as part of a less equal branch. And this was something the senators never could accept.

In the election for the leadership position there was much backstage politicking between the Barkley and Harrison forces. Pressures mounted on both sides. The Administration, according to one story, persuaded William Dieterich of Illinois to go along with Barkley by the use of some judiciously placed telephone calls to prominent Democratic politicians in Chicago. On the other side, freshman Senator Harry Truman had pledged his vote to Barkley but then asked to be released from his pledge because the pressure on him was so intense. Some of the votes were cast on the basis of settling old scores. In 1923, for example, a federal district judge named Edwin R. Holmes had sent a Mississippian named Theodore G. Bilbo to jail for ten days on a contempt of court charge. As life often works out, Bilbo had a chance for revenge. He became a United States Senator and Judge Holmes was recommended for promotion to the Circuit Court of Appeals, a federal appointment. Bilbo, remembering his ignominious jail sentence more than a decade earlier, opposed the appointment. Mississippi's senior senator, Pat Harrison, however, supported it, and Holmes was confirmed in the new judgeship position much to Bilbo's chagrin. Bilbo never forgave Harrison for that. In the contest for the leader's post between Harrison and Barkley, Bilbo supported Barkley. This was at variance with a tradition in the Senate that junior senators support the senior senators from their state in whatever actions they take or positions they seek.

Claude Pepper, the young liberal from Florida, was naturally expected to side with Barkley. But Pepper had an old relationship with Harrison. Pepper's former law partner, more than thirty years earlier, had worked for Harrison when Harrison was a member of the House. When Pepper had come to the Senate, Pat Harrison had been kind to him, given him advice on how to get along in the Senate, introduced him to some of the more important members. Pepper voted for Harrison.

The Democrats met the morning of July 21, Wednesday, in the office of Vice President Garner in the Senate Office Building to decide between Pat Harrison and Alben Barkley. The real question was whether they would pick their own leader—Harrison— or whether they would pick a Roosevelt lieutenant—Barkley. While inside Suite 201 the Democratic senators voted by secret ballot on their next leader, the halls outside were crammed with reporters, newspapermen holding their notebooks, photographers with their cameras, and radio men with their portable broadcasting units. It was a dramatic moment. The senators had marched into Garner's office silently. Carl Hayden of Arizona had left a sickbed to cast his vote for Harrison. Senator John H. Bankhead of Alabama sent a proxy vote for Harrison.

Most of the newsmen's bets were on Pat Harrison, but there were no heavy odds given. All knew the contest would be a close one. Inside the Vice President's office, the suspense of that closeness was almost unbearable. After the Democrats had cast their secret ballots, tellers counted the votes aloud. As the tallies mounted Barkley and Harrison never were more than one or two votes apart, first one was ahead and then the other took the narrow lead. Finally, as the Democrats sat in complete silence, the seesaw count evened out at 37 to 37. One vote was left.

The teller read the last ballot. "Barkley!" he cried.

The senators came out of Garner's office in twos, not speaking. When the newsmen heard that the Kentuckian had won by thirty-eight-to-thirty-seven vote, one cracked: "At least thirty-eight of them can claim credit for the deciding vote." Inside Garner's office Senator Barkley was receiving congratulations, including a kiss from a woman. "Some member of the Barkley family," explained a Senate staff member to a visiting newspaper reporter. The staff member paused for a moment. "At least," he said of the woman who kissed Barkley, "I hope it was a member of his family."

Meanwhile, Garner had visited with Franklin Roosevelt. It was their first session together since Garner had canvassed senatorial sentiment on the funeral train. "How did you find the Court situation, Jack?" asked the President.

"Do you want it with the bark on or off, Cap'n?"

Roosevelt replied: "The rough way."

"All right," answered Cactus Jack. "You are beat. You haven't got the votes."

There is no dispute over what Roosevelt said next. He directed Garner to make "the best settlement possible." But there is a dispute over how Garner carried out that order.

Actually, whether the Administration did not have the votes after Robinson's death was as questionable as whether it did have the votes while Joe Robinson was alive. Robert Wagner of New York, for example, told Harold Ickes that even with the loss of Robinson the Administration still had forty-nine votes, enough to pass the bill. From other sources Ickes heard that the count was actually fifty-three senators for the Court bill. But these counts included people like Claude Pepper of Florida, who would not make up his mind until the last moment. It included George Norris, the Nebraskan senator who preferred to be called Independent rather than either Republican or Democrat; but he was away from the Senate the month of July, ill from an attack of acute indigestion. He could not vote on the Court bill; even if he had, he might have voted against it. Also on the list of senators expected to support FDR was Morris Sheppard of Texas. His opposition to the Court bill had not changed.

In a tight contest on controversial legislation, it is impossible to predict the outcome. Too many senators will not make up their minds until the last minute. Too many senators will indicate they lean one way when they really are inclined in another direction. Too many senators can be moved by a last surge of public pressure. Too many senators are responsive to the party leadership.

The Party leadership, in the case of the Court bill, was not very demonstrative. Garner had received the assignment to make the best deal he could. Admittedly, it was a tough job. Shortly after the meeting between Garner and FDR a group of senators met in Prentiss Brown's office. Brown was the freshman senator from Michigan who had arranged the meeting of the four senators with the President shortly after Robinson's death. There were nine senators at the meeting in Brown's office; with only one exception they agreed to oppose the Court bill. Some of them already had been against it. Some were leaning against it although they were being counted as Administration supporters on the issue. That meeting in Brown's office did cost the Administration some votes, exactly how many is unknown; enough certainly to destroy any illusion that the Administration still held a majority.

If Garner, acting on behalf of the White House, had put a last effort into bringing those senators behind the Court bill, would they have returned to the Roosevelt fold? Could Garner have stopped the rout? That was the real question hanging over the last lingering days of the Court fight.

Garner did not put forth any such last effort. He did check in the Senate on sentiment but did not try to influence it. He made a routine offer of a compromise with Burton Wheeler—to limit the enlargement of the Court to a total of two new justices. As expected, Wheeler turned him down. There was no effort being made, as far as Wheeler could tell, by the Administration to save the Court bill. Wheeler did not see any reason for him to make such an effort.

Then Garner talked to Alben Barkley, the new majority leader. Armed with FDR's directive to make the best deal possible, Garner insisted that the Court bill could no longer pass and it was harmful to the Democratic party to pretend any longer that it could. Barkley responded to this by agreeing with Garner to junk the bill. Then they called in Henry Ashurst. Garner telephoned to the chairman of the Senate Judiciary Committee, saying: "Important." By the time Ashurst arrived, senators Wheeler, Harry Byrd of Virginia, and Josiah Bailey of North Carolina also were present. These last three were, of course, opponents of FDR's Court bill.

"The Vice President," according to Ashurst, "said that the time had come to render a great service; that the President's plan to reorganize the Judiciary was now a plague to the country, to the Senate and to the Democratic Party, and that it ought to be within the resources of my committee's statesmanship to bring in a bill for judicial reform and relief without increasing the membership of the Supreme Court of the United States." More than five months earlier, when Franklin Roosevelt had unveiled his Court bill, John Nance Garner had stood in full view of his Senate colleagues holding his nose and pointing his thumb down to indicate his displeasure with the bill. Now that sentiment was having its impact. He was directing that the bill be destroyed.

Under this circumstance there was nothing for Ashurst to do. He agreed to call a meeting of his committee for the next morning at which Garner and senators Barkley and Wheeler could speak on the future of the Court bill. Ashurst was another who would not survive the Court fight with any laurels. His game of playing both ends—publicly appearing to support the bill while actually working against it by delaying it so long in his committee— was publicized that day. A local newspaper ran a story revealing Ashurst's delaying tactics, saying that the Arizonan should be credited with effectively blocking passage of the bill because he had stretched out the hearings until the original impetus for the

Court bill had been lost. That night the "friendly voice" from the White House, which Ashurst always refused to identify, telephoned "advising me that Eff Dee's opinion that my attitude during the judicial reorganization contest was fatal to his bill had been confirmed." In his diary Ashurst underlined the word "confirmed."

The next morning at the committee meeting Garner was blunt. "My loyalties are in this order," he said, "first, to my country; second, to my party; third to my President." He then proceeded to demonstrate that, as he said, his loyalty to his President's program came far below his loyalty to what he considered the best interests of the Democratic party. The Court bill is dead, he said. "There is no use kidding yourselves," Garner told the committee members as an approving Burton Wheeler looked on. "No matter what your ideas are, everybody with any sense knows that all proposals with reference to the Supreme Court are out of the window." And it is better dead, he continued. "This thing has split the party and has the country turned upside down," he said. "We must have party harmony for the country's good," he told the Democrats, continuing: "You are saying mean things against each other which you shouldn't be saying." Party harmony meant a great deal to John Nance Garner. Born dirt-poor sixty-eight years earlier in Red River County in Texas, Garner had had limited educational advantages. He had managed to study a little law and was admitted to the bar. This title of "lawyer," however, was the key that enabled him to become a member of the ruling clique of the Democratic party. The party then and for many years later was very much like a club with a few people running it, forging its policies, choosing its candidates, A bright young man with a little legal training who was willing to work hard within the Democratic party of Texas could go far in the world beyond Texas and succeed beyond the expectations of most youngsters born in Red River County. Garner was such a man. Soon he was in the state legislature, then the Congress in Washington, finally becoming Speaker of the House—the most revered position in the House of Representatives. And, after he had been in Congress thirty years, the Democratic party made him Vice President of the United States. This Democratic party then had been the source of Garner's fame and fortune. It was the center of the circle around which his life revolved to the exclusion of almost all other interests. The Democratic party was both a house of pleasure and a church to John Nance Garner.

To Franklin Roosevelt the Democratic party had another meaning. For him it was a vehicle to be used to advance the liberal philosophy he subscribed to. In the past he had combined with liberals who were not Democrats, and he would do so in the future. The Democratic party was not his religion; liberalism was. This is why he and Garner could not understand each other on the Court issue. The two men had different faiths.

Garner was willing to inter the Court bill with as little additional insult to Roosevelt as possible; the act of burying the bill would be sufficient. But Burt Wheeler was riding high. The meet-in Prentiss Brown's office had been publicized as meaning the "death knell" for the Court bill. Wheeler had held a council of war with his supporters, and they had agreed on a strategy of toughness. Rather than as little insult to Roosevelt as possible, there would be as much as possible.

There were several ways of disposing of the Court bill. One was to bring it to a vote and permit it to be voted down. Neither side, the Administration's or Burt Wheeler's, would accept this. The Administration did not wish to take a clear-cut defeat like that. Wheeler's forces did not wish to take a chance that, by permitting a vote to be held, the Administration might make a last burst of effort and secure enough votes for passage. A second way of disposing of the bill was simply to leave it to languish on the Senate calendar, never debate it again and never call it to a vote. This is what the Administration forces preferred. They could always claim the bill had only been postponed. It would be a weak face-saver but a face-saver nevertheless. This the opponents of the Court bill did not permit. They insisted on a third means. They wanted the Court bill to be recommitted to the Senate Judiciary Committee with instructions that it be redrafted to exclude any reference to enlarging the Supreme Court and leaving only some minor provisions about reforming the lower federal courts. The emasculated version then would be resubmitted to the Senate. Directing the committee to strip the provisions about enlarging the Supreme Court would be a clear message to the nation that Franklin Roosevelt had been beaten.

Garner, Barkley, and the others agreed; there was nothing else they could do. Also, Garner seemed ready—if not anxious—to go along with the insult to Roosevelt. The best the Administration forces could secure was a pledge that the motion to recommit would be done without a record vote. This would avoid placing the Democrats in the embarrassing position of publicly voting against their President. It would also avoid revealing the strength of the forces opposed to Roosevelt and how badly they were whipping him. Another pledge the President's men secured was that the words "Supreme Court" would not be mentioned on the Senate floor. All that the two pledges would do was avoid a little embarrassment for the President, blunt somewhat the sharp edge of his defeat.

Even this, however, was not to be.

Part Six

The Supreme Court Is Out of the Way?

17

THE VOTE in the Senate of the United States came at two fifty-five in the afternoon of Thursday, July 22, 1937. According to the agreement that had been reached in the meeting of the Senate Judiciary Committee that morning, Senator Marvel M. Logan, one of the authors of the one-judge a year compromise, rose and informed the presiding officer of the Senate that he wished "unanimous consent" to move that the judicial reform bill be returned to the Judiciary Committee. "I might say by way of explanation," said Logan, "that, after a very full and free hearing this morning, the Committee on the Judiciary directed me to make this request, with the understanding that it would be instructed to report a bill for the reform of the judiciary within ten days, if the motion should prevail. I ask unanimous consent that I may be authorized to make the motion at this time."

With those words, Logan was announcing to any senator not aware of the deal that an arrangement had been made; the members of the Senate were to sit quietly while the deal for a nonrecord vote—unanimous consent—went through. But the Republicans did not feel they could sit by idly and watch the Democratic President escape that easily. After five and one-half months of watching and maneuvering from the background, the GOP dashed to the front. Wisely they chose to make their move on a point of parliamentary procedure. No onus would fall on the GOP. The public would not understand and would quickly forget the maneuver, but the public would appreciate the impact of the maneuver.

Before the Senate could quickly grant Logan's request, Charles

McNary of Oregon rose. McNary was the elected leader of the Republican senators, the minority party's counterpart of Joe Robinson and his successor Alben Barkley. Now sixty-three years old and finishing his second decade as a United States senator, McNary had risen to his leadership position through his ability to make the right decision at the right time and to persuade his fellow Republicans just how right it was. He was the one who had insisted that the GOP stay in the background during the Court fight. Now, he decided, was time to step out from the shadows. "I usually try to follow the Chair," he said to the Senate, "but that cannot be done now. I am willing to grant unanimous consent that the motion may be made, but not that the bill may go back to the committee." Translated from the parliamentary language of the Senate floor, McNary's words meant that he would permit Logan only to offer his motion that the judicial reform bill be recommitted to the Judiciary Committee without a vote, but that McNary would insist on a record vote on the motion itself.

So the first pledge would be broken. The Republicans did not feel bound by any agreements Burton Wheeler might have made that morning in the Judiciary Committee. They had used him well. Now they discarded him.

Logan then made his motion to recommit the bill. Before the record vote could be held, however, and that first pledge broken, old Hiram Johnson of California rose to break the second one, that the Supreme Court not be mentioned in the Senate debate. The motion made by Logan directed the Judiciary Committee to redraft the bill to permit "judicial reform." The understanding was that the redrafted bill would make no mention of enlarging the Supreme Court. But that understanding, while explained in the Senate cloakrooms, was not spelled out in the Logan motion. Hiram Johnson, the old progressive and now conservative Republican, could not let that pass.

"I desire to know," he asked, "what the judicial reform refers to. Does it refer to the Supreme Court or the inferior courts?"

An embarrassed Senator Logan answered, "I may say to the Senator from California that the Committee on the Judiciary this morning had an understanding that we did not think it was proper to embrace in the motion what it should refer to. The senior Senator from Wyoming [Joseph O'Mahoney] wrote out what we had before us in the Committee on the Judiciary. It was a statement of what had been said, I believe, by the leader," and he added for emphasis, "and some others, and that did not refer to the Supreme Court. That was not to be considered at all, I may say."

The words had been mentioned on the Senate floor. The second pledge had been broken. Still this was not enough for Hiram Johnson. "The Supreme Court is out of the way?" he insisted on knowing.

A defeated Marvel Logan acknowledged: "The Supreme Court is out of the way."

Hiram Johnson raised his arms to the skies and his eyes to the galleries. "Glory be to God!" he shouted. As if on cue, the spectators in the galleries responded with applause; and also for many years after, commentators were able to add that the nation said "Amen" to Hiram Johnson's prayer that the duel had been ended with Franklin Roosevelt's defeat.

There was nothing left then except the formal roll-call vote and the knowledge of how badly the President was beaten. Any thoughts that there might be a breaking away, that the Democrats might become angry at Charles McNary's and Hiram Johnson's double crosses and rally to their President, were destroyed when early in the vote Henry Ashurst, the chairman of the Judiciary Committee, who never had changed his public position of Presidential support, and Alben Barkley, the Presidential choice for Senate Democratic leader, cast their votes for recommital. This was a signal to the other Democrats that there would be no valiant but doomed attempts to rescue the President from the ignominy of a crushing defeat. The only desire in the Senate now was to finish up the business as quickly as possible. As the roll call proceeded, the embarrassed Administration Democrats cast their votes in such low voices they could barely be heard, much to the amusement of spectators in the galleries. Soon it was obvious that the defeat for Franklin Roosevelt would be even greater than anticipated. The "ayes" sending the Court bill to its death came with greater frequency, each one appearing to be a nail in Roosevelt's political coffin. At the end the count was seventy senators in favor of recommitting the bill and ending the Court duel with FDR's defeat. Only twenty were against the recommittal motion. Of the seventy in favor of recommitting, fifty-three were Democrats, members of Roosevelt's own party; sixteen were Republicans, and one was a Farmer-Laborite. Only eighteen Democrats, joined by one Progressive and one Farmer-Laborite, gave Franklin Roosevelt a supporting vote. It was a crushing defeat. Almost.

Actually the results were mixed. Franklin Roosevelt had lost his bill but made his point, and then lost his political party.

The next morning Roosevelt was holding a regular news conference when a reporter asked: "Do you plan any further campaign with regard to the Supreme Court?" FDR, who did not enjoy defeat, replied: "Further campaign? . . . I haven't made any campaign; I sent a message to the Congress." Pressed further, however, the President began a rambling talk that showed he was aware that he had not lost everything. He said:

I think it goes back, just for background, to fundamentals and objectives just the same way we talked about right along. There were, as you know, certain original objectives. . . . There was a lot of feeling back in T.R.'s [President Theodore Roosevelt's Administration] time about the need for judicial reform and it took the form, in the 1912 campaign, of the Progressive Party asking for all kinds of things like recall of judges and overriding of decisions by popular vote. Well, the interesting thing was that for about fifteen or twenty years that demand on the part of a very large group of Americans had an enormous effect on the courts, as you all know. Even as late as 1924 the older Senator LaFollette and Senator Wheeler, on the LaFollette-Wheeler ticket, ran on a platform that demanded all kinds of drastic things. And, during those years when there was agitation for judicial reform, there were some pretty effective results. The courts listened and they legislated. . . .

The President joined in the laughter at his use of that word, then continued to more laughter:

I mean they decided, it is the same thing. They made their decisions more on judicial lines than on legislative lines and of course later on, when the cry had died during the Coolidge Administration and the Hoover Administration, there was a great deal more in the way of legislative action on the part of the courts. Of course, the people of the country have always realized that courts should be judicial and not legislative.

The same thing had to be done again this year. The result was a message for the improvement of the whole judicial system and it is rather interesting that a large, a good part of that objective has already been obtained, temporarily. I say "temporarily," but I hope permanently. I was getting a rather interesting check on what has happened, a comparison between what has happened and this past term of the Supreme Court.

Then the President went down a memorandum he had showing how the Court had reversed itself since February, when he had sent his message calling for judicial reform to the Congress. Originally the Court had called the Agricultural Adjustment Act unconstitutional and, in doing so, placed constitutional limits on the federal government's spending power. After February 5 the Court upheld the Social Security Act, a decision which, in effect, overruled its earlier adverse ruling on the AAA. Before February 5 the Court had knocked down the Guffey Act; that decision was overruled when the Court, after February 5, upheld the Wagner Act granting certain privileges of striking to labor union members. Involved in those two decisions, more than the labor union members' right to strike, was the question of how far the federal government could enter the realm of interstate commerce. With the second decision the Court seemed to say there were no limits. Prior to February 5 the Court had called minimum wage laws unconstitutional; but then, with the Owen Roberts switch, it reversed itself on that.

"The net result," the President continued to the reporters, "is that we have obtained certain objectives, talking in the large. The country still wants assurance—I put it this way—assurance of the continuity of that objective, and the country, of course, wants a better judicial mechanism of giving maximum justice in minimum time."

He conceded that as far as his proposal to enlarge the Supreme Court was concerned, "There is nothing more that I can say." Then he added what is a customary defense by Presidents who face recalcitrant Congresses. "It is the duty," Franklin Roosevelt said, "of the President to propose and it is the privilege of the Congress to dispose."

It was impossible that morning, the first after Franklin Roosevelt's defeat in the Senate, to know whether the recent espousal of liberalism by the Supreme Court would continue or not. Beginning with Owen Roberts' switch, each tactic and decision by the Court was viewed by the Administration with suspicion. Was this permanent? Was it temporary? Were the decisions, pointing to an obvious liberal direction for the Court, only a device to lull the American people into believing that Court packing was unnecessary? Or had the Court finally realized that it must shift its outlook?

Helped by Roberts' switch and the retirement of Willis Van Devanter, replaced on the Court with Senator Hugo L. Black of Alabama, who proved himself a liberal, the Court did continue as a liberal institution. The basic issue before the Court had been whether the Presidency, when authorized by Congress, can enter into the national commerce and the national economics to do what it believes proper for its constituency. Unlike other constituencies, this Presidential constituency is all—rather than only segments of—the American people. Harry Truman, after he had been President himself, explained it this way: "It is only the President who is responsible to all the people. He alone has no sectional, no occupational, no economic ties. If anyone is to speak for the people, it has to be the President." This philosophy was seconded by another successor of Franklin Roosevelt's, Dwight D. Eisenhower. "Because your President, aside from the Vice President, is the only governmental official chosen by a vote of all the people," said Eisenhower, "he must make his decisions on the basis of what he thinks best for all the people. He cannot consider only a district, a state or a region in developing solutions to problems. He must always use the yardstick of the national interest."

In the realm of economics, the concept that the Presidency is the advocate of the interests of the mass of people had not been a vital one, perhaps, until the twentieth century. Before then only the wealthy appreciated the value of governmental assistance. Those with wealth understood they benefited when the government built the canals to carry their commerce, provided the military might to protect their exploitation of foreign countries, and gave them wide swaths of land for the building of railroads.

In this period the individual without wealth did not understand how he could use his government. He remained tied to his farm, his small community, still not comprehending or understanding that the economic factors that so greatly influenced his life were determined by others. The so-called "radicals" of the nineteenth century did understand that economic power was a most compelling power in the United States and that its control lay with the wealthy. They also saw, these bearded and much criticized radicals, that only when the individuals massed together and acted through the national government could they be strong enough to counter the power of the few persons with control over the nation's economy.

In the twentieth century the arguments of these radicals became the liberal cause. Beginning with Theodore Roosevelt and continuing in the administration of Woodrow Wilson, this liberal cause moved toward becoming a Presidential—a national—policy. In Franklin Roosevelt's New Deal this liberalism did become synonymous with national policy. The over-all impact of all the New Deal's alphabet agencies was to use the federal government to create a balance to the power of those few with economic strength. Because of the federal government, individual employees could form into unions and bargain with their employers. The small investor had protection against the stock market manipulator; the bank depositor knew that his funds were secure. The farmer was not gouged by manipulated prices that forced him to buy high and sell low. The small businessman was protected from exorbitant interest rates and sharp movements in his market. All these things, and many others like them, the individual could not do himself. Before Franklin Roosevelt insisted that the federal government, specifically the Presidency, act in the name of these people, the individual was at the mercy of forces too strong for him to counter. But when all the "forgotten men," to use Franklin Roosevelt's phrase, joined together behind the President, they became themselves a powerful force.

The New Deal then was a revamping of the purpose of national government. Using the tools a democracy offers to its leader, Franklin Roosevelt had persuaded a suspicious Congress to support him in this revolution. When the Supreme Court not only refused to join this revolution but worked to stop it, Roosevelt was forced to begin the duel which would have an ever-widening impact in American history.

Most White House aides, both at the time of the duel and years later, believed FDR would have won some enlargement of the Court if it had not been for Joe Robinson's death. The closeness FDR came to victory made a strong impression on the Court. Never again in the years following the duel with Franklin Roosevelt did the Court so bluntly, callously, and consistently deny the public's opinion as it had by rebuffing the New Deal. Led by a number of Roosevelt-appointed justices who came in subsequent years, the Court never again ventured out so long from what Charles Evans Hughes in the 1920s had called the Court's "fortress in public opinion." As one New Dealer said of the Supreme Court justices: "They subdued the rebellion against their Constitutional dogma by joining it."

But if Franklin Roosevelt had won one part of the duel by making the Supreme Court as responsive to the needs of the American people as were the President and much of the Congress, he appeared to lose the second part of the duel, and to lose it disastrously. This was the duel for the leadership of the Democratic party, the duel to determine in which direction the party would move in the future. To FDR the question was a personal one: to have a political party created in his image. It was also, however, a philosophical and political question: to insure that the Democratic party, under another leadership, did not at a later date junk the New Deal approach and return to conservatism. Franklin Roosevelt believed just that had happened to the Republican party when William Howard Taft replaced Theodore Roosevelt in the White House.

With his victory over the Supreme Court, Franklin Roosevelt had guaranteed that he could impose a New Deal liberalism on the federal government. But his apparent defeat by the conservatives in his party suggested that he could not hold his party to the New Deal banner in the future.

When the voting ended in the Senate that hot July afternoon, most members of Congress talked as if the fighting were all over and everyone would be friends and political cronies once more. This, however, was not to be. Burton Wheeler spoke magnanimously as he gloated over Roosevelt's defeat. "All in all," he told reporters, "the Court bill fight has been a wonderful thing. The agitation brought the people to a study of the fundamentals of their government, gave them a veritable lesson in elemental civics. The fight has done the judiciary good too. Courts had become arrogant, and sometimes disrespectful of the rights of the public— particularly the federal courts. Can anyone look at the record already available and say that what has happened recently has not been beneficial to the courts themselves?" If Roosevelt had won, he could have said the same thing. There was nothing about the President in Wheeler's remarks. But Burton Wheeler felt very strongly about Franklin Roosevelt. Many years later, as he sat in his law office overlooking the world of political Washington that had been his world for many years, Burton Wheeler, now in his eighties but with his convictions and his mind still strong and clear, recalled the time he had dealt Franklin Roosevelt the worst political defeat of the President's career. Said Wheeler: "If he'd got away with that, God only knows what he would have done."

The political victory that the conservative Democrats had won meant that the grand political coalition Franklin Roosevelt had formed out of a group of dissident economic groups, state political organizations, religious, racial, and ethnic blocs was breaking up. The Democratic party was disintegrating, returning to its previous method of politics by brokers—a method where the leaders of the different groups and blocs bargain together for what they want. This is the fragmentation of power, a system which accomplishes very little. Under this system the liberalism of the twentieth century is sacrificed on the altar of expediency. Under this system, too, the New Deal came to an end. Many of the bills passed after the Court fight were gutted or were the product of the kind of political bartering in the backrooms of Congress that Franklin Roosevelt had not before engaged in. The farm bill and the wages and hours act of 1938 are two examples. The program for executive reorganization, which FDR had proposed even before the Court bill, remained stymied. Worse, when the nation moved into an economic recession in 1938, Franklin Roosevelt, realizing his political strength was ebbing from him, floundered around in search of a solution. Too many enemies were sniping at him from too many directions to permit the adoption of any one course and expect it to win Congressional approval. Danger built upon danger. With the recession continuing, the American people grew increasingly disenchanted with the President. And because of this disenchantment, members of Congress felt emboldened to increase their opposition to the President's policies.

For Franklin Roosevelt the problem was clear. He must do something to reassert his personal strength, to tie his party together again, to assure its allegiance to the banner of liberalism.

In 1938 Roosevelt attempted to purge some of the conservative Democrats who had opposed him. It did not work. Often all a Congressional candidate needs to win an election is the belief by his constituents that the President does not like him. The voters immediately assume that the Congressional candidate must be independent-minded and courageous enough to defy the White House. That assumption can be enough to elect the candidate. Rather than reassert FDR's strength, the 1938 purge attempt further aggravated the split between the White House and the Congress. The members on Capitol Hill tend to draw together when their own are under attack.

There was only one other thing then that Franklin Roosevelt could do, he believed. Only one technique remained available to him to bind up his party and turn its members back to the liberalism of the New Deal from the path of self-interest that had recalled them. This was a third term as President of the United States.

Prior to Franklin Roosevelt's Presidency there had been a tradition that a President serve only for eight years. This meant, to many politicians, that a President lost much of his power in his second term. Since the man in the White House would not be running again, so went this argument, then whether he endorsed or refused to endorse Congressional candidates, whether he made speeches in their behalf, or whether he gave them the benefit of his political coattails was no longer important. The Congressional candidates did not have to patronize the man in the White House. From their point of view it was much more valuable to patronize the man who sought to be his successor.

Franklin Roosevelt understood this feeling. Early in the Court fight he commented angrily that "some of our Democratic 'friends' do not at all like the idea that I may keep on making speeches and radio talks for the next three and a half years. They think that a second term President should be duly grateful and retire into innocuous desuetude." Jim Farley recalls that at one point in the Court duel he gave FDR a rundown on the Democratic senators who were splitting away from the President. Farley remembers Roosevelt saying, almost to himself, "This comes from telling them I would not be a candidate again."

There often was talk of support for Roosevelt for a third term, but few took it seriously—except, that is, Roosevelt himself. The Supreme Court duel had so sharply revealed to him how tenuous were the ties that bound the political fragments into the Democratic party. Roosevelt eventually came to believe that in 1940 only he could force the party to continue on the liberal path mapped out by the New Deal. This became more evident to him because of the other Presidential possibilities he saw as being available if he were not. One was Jim Farley, who by this time had drifted away from FDR in an effort to fulfill his own ambitions to become President. Farley was not a political liberal, nor was he a political conservative. He was, instead, a political professional to whom the practice of politics was more important than the philosophy of politics. Another possibility was John Nance Garner, who sought his party's nomination in 1940. He even asked Burton Wheeler to run with him. But FDR never forgave what he considered Garner's conservatism or his transgression in the Court struggle. When he had sent the Vice President up to Capitol Hill to make the best settlement possible, the President believed either that part of his Supreme Court enlargement approach could be salvaged, or, if it must be junked in its entirety, that it would be junked with as little embarrassment to the President as possible. The opposite outcome, FDR believed, was due to Garner's being too willing to surrender to Burton Wheeler. After that July, 1937, vote, Franklin Roosevelt never again spoke to John Nance Garner except when protocol and a minimum courtesy demanded it. The split between the two men, begun because one was a liberal and the other a conservative, was complete.

By the time of the 1940 Democratic Presidential convention political realities as well as Franklin Roosevelt's own ego combined to convince him that liberalism and FDR were synonymous, that without Franklin Roosevelt in the White House the gains of the New Deal in the previous eight years would be wiped away. So Roosevelt chose the only alternative he believed available to him. He ran for a third term and was elected. Then, in the midst of a world war, he ran for a fourth term although his health was failing. He died in office before that term was three months old.

He did not fulfill his purpose. He did not bind his party together again. He did not assure its liberalism. With Franklin Roosevelt's third term came the threat of American involvement in a world war and the war itself. Domestic legislation was forgotten in the desire to get on with what was the more immediate and more important job. When peace did come in 1945 and Harry Truman was President, he tried to revive the Roosevelt liberalism with his Fair Deal, an attempt to expand the social welfare programs of the 1930s. But Truman soon became embroiled in the cold war with Russia and then a shooting war in Korea. And this too meant that the federal government was not so concerned with domestic legislation as it had been in the 1930s. This lack of concern with welfare programs during war years is not because the government officials are too callous of the public's problems or too busy to think of them. Rather, wars cure many domestic problems. The rush for armaments creates factory jobs. The high salaries paid make such things as the need for an expanded Social Security program seem far off. The demand for able-bodied men to fight means the dropping of certain racial barriers.

And then, too, there was another development. When the southern Democrats and midwestern Republicans—these were the conservatives of both parties—joined together to fight the Court bill, they found the old saying that in unity there is strength is true. They could provide the needed margin of votes that secured passage of legislation they favored while blocking passage of legislation they opposed. Through use this coalition became stronger and stronger. After the Second World War, in its most elemental form this coalition worked to block civil rights bills, legislation that the southerners opposed, and to keep farm price supports high, subsidies which the midwesterners wanted. It also worked effectively to block any expansion of the New Deal. In the peace years of the 1950s this coalition reached its high point. In the White House was a President, Dwight Eisenhower, who agreed with the conservatives of both political parties that "the welfare state," as they called the results of the New Deal laws, had gone far enough. The liberal wing of the Democratic Party in this period, however, remained active, if not successful.

Proposals were developed in the spirit of the New Deal to extend the role of the federal government. Medical care payments for senior citizens, aid to education, aid to depressed areas, job retraining programs—these were all the products of the 1950s. If the southern Democratic–conservative Republican coalition, working with a President who subscribed to their philosophy that enough is enough, succeeded in defeating these proposals on the floors of Congress in the 1950s, it could not stop the support for these programs from slowly building up in the nation.

When John F. Kennedy, who had been twenty years old when

the coalition was formed, became President in 1961, the nation was ready to reconsider favorably the philosophy of the New Deal. He understood this and capitalized on it. With that as his basic strength, he worked to break up the coalition. Using a combination of flattery, courtesy, bribery, restraint, and political muscle on occasion, he succeeded. He won his first points at the beginning of his administration when he destroyed the power of the House Rules Committee, which had been the coalition's chief weapon. The final victory came early in November of 1963 when the Attorney General, Robert F. Kennedy, who had been eleven years old when the coalition was formed, persuaded Representative Charles Halleck, one of the coalition's architects, to turn his back on his old southern cohorts and announce his support for the strongest civil rights bill Congress ever had considered.

The victory over the coalition meant that the way was then free for a continuation of the philosophy of the New Deal. The hiatus of a quarter of a century was perhaps a good thing. The New Deal shifted the whole focus of American government, from the wealthy to the poor, from the few to the many. No matter how valuable such a shift is, no matter how right it may be, it is not a good thing to make such a startling shift abruptly. The pause in the enactment of the New Deal, from the 1930s to the 1960s, gave the American people the time to consider what they had done, to evaluate it, to determine if they wished to proceed with it. The pause provided the opportunity for the American people to protect themselves against their own impetuosity, from their own political extravagance. It gave the American people the chance to consider the New Deal not only in the framework of an immediate economic disaster such as the depression of the early 1930s but also in the calmness of the prosperity of the 1960s.

That the American people proceeded with the philosophy of the New Deal then, that they did not turn their backs on the reforms fought for and instituted by Franklin Roosevelt—this signifies the real victory of Franklin Roosevelt.

Sources

I wish to express my appreciation for their assistance to former senators Burton K. Wheeler, Gerald P. Nye, and Claude D. Pepper; and to former Governor Alf M. Landon; and to Carl McFarland, an associate of Attorney General Homer S. Cummings during the Court duel; and to Benjamin V. Cohen, a Presidential assistant in the same period. I wish also to thank several other persons who were involved in the Court dispute and who shared their memories and their documents with me but whom I am not identifying because they requested anonymity. I was most fortunate in being given access to the private papers of a Republican prominent in the Court dispute. These papers provided an insight into the Republican strategy and also detailed the machinations of former President Herbert Hoover. I was asked not to quote directly from these papers and not to identify the source of my information; I have honored that request.

The Franklin D. Roosevelt Library at Hyde Park, New York, granted me permission to quote from the Roosevelt papers there. John Morton Blum granted me permission to quote from the diaries of Henry S. Morgenthau, Jr., and the family of Senator Carter Glass allowed me to quote from the Senator's papers. I am most appreciative of those privileges.

Much has been written about the New Deal period, and many private collections of papers pertinent to that period exist. In the following bibliography, however, I have listed only those sources from which I quoted directly or in which I found a specific point of information.

Alsop, Joseph and Catledge, Turner, *The 168 Days,* Doubleday, Doran & Co., Inc., Garden City, New York, 1938.

Ashurst, Henry Fountain, *The Diary of Henry Fountain Ashurst* (on microfilm), The University of Arizona, Tucson.

Bargeron, Carlisle, "Justice Van Devanter Speaks," *Nation's Business,* July, 1937.

Barkley, Alben W., *That Reminds Me,* Doubleday & Co., Inc., Garden City, New York, 1954.

Bickel, Alexander M., "Is the Warren Court Too Political?" *The New York Times Magazine,* Sept. 25, 1966.

Borah, William E., "The William E. Borah Papers," a collection in the Library of Congress.

Byrnes, James F., *All in One Lifetime,* Harper & Brothers, New York, 1958.

Celler, Emanuel, *You Never Leave Brooklyn,* The John Day Co., New York, 1953.

Chase, Stuart, "The Stuart Chase Papers," a collection in the Library of Congress.

Childs, Marquis W., "The Supreme Court Today," *Harper's,* May, 1938.

Congressional Record, various volumes as cited in Notes.

Cope, Alfred Haines and Krinsky, Fred, *Franklin D. Roosevelt and the Supreme Court,* D. C. Heath & Co., Boston, 1952.

Corwin, Edward S., *Constitutional Revolution, Ltd.,* Claremont College, Claremont, Cal., 1941.

Creel, George, *Rebel at Large,* G. P. Putnam's Sons, New York, 1947.

———, "Roosevelt's Plans and Purposes," *Collier's,* Dec. 26, 1936.

Cummings, Homer S., "Addresses," Vol. II (bound transcripts), The United States Department of Justice Library.

Dorough, C. Dwight, *Mr. Sam,* Random House, New York, 1962.

Farley, James A., *Jim Farley's Story,* McGraw-Hill Book Co., New York, 1948.

Gerhart, Eugene C., *America's Advocate: Robert H. Jackson,* The Bobbs-Merrill Co., Inc., Indianapolis–New York, 1958.

Gilbert, Stirling Price, *James Clark McReynolds* (privately printed), 1946.

Glass, Carter, "The Carter Glass Papers," a collection in the Alderman Library, University of Virginia.

Hughes, Charles Evans, "Autobiographical Notes," a typewritten manuscript in the Library of Congress.

———, "The Papers of Charles Evans Hughes," a collection in the Library of Congress.

———, *The Supreme Court of the United States,* Garden City Publishing Co., Garden City, New York, 1936. (This is a published version of a series of lectures Charles Evans Hughes delivered in 1928.)

Ickes, Harold L., *The Secret Diary of Harold L. Ikes,* Vols. I and II, Simon & Schuster, Inc., New York, 1954.

Inaugural Addresses of the Presidents of the United States, Government Printing Office, Washington, D.C., 1961.

Jackson, Robert H., "Addresses," Vol. I (bound transcripts), The United States Department of Justice Library.

———, *The Struggle for Judicial Supremacy,* Alfred A. Knopf, New York, 1941.

———, *The Supreme Court in the American System of Government,* Harvard University Press, Cambridge, 1955.

Johnson, Claudius O., *Borah of Idaho,* Longmans, Green & Co., 1936.

Keenan, Joseph B., "Addresses" (bound transcripts), The United States Department of Justice Library.

Keller, Morton, *In Defense of Yesterday,* Coward-McCann, Inc., New York, 1958.

Lief, Alfred, *Democracy's Norris,* Stackpole Sons, New York, 1939.

MacColl, E. Kimbark, "The Supreme Court and Public Opinion—A Study of the Court Fight of 1937," a doctor's thesis for the University of California, Graduate Division, southern section, 1953.

McKenna, Marian C., *Borah,* The University of Michigan Press, Ann Arbor, 1961.

McMahon, Brien,, "Addresses" (bound transcripts), United States Department of Justice Library.

Mason, Alpheus Thomas, *Brandeis: A Free Man's Life,* The Viking Press, New York, 1956.

———, *Harlan Fiske Stone: Pillar of the Law,* The Viking Press, New York, 1956.

Michelson, Charles, *The Ghost Talks,* G. P. Putnam's Sons, New York, 1944.

Morgenthau, Jr., Henry S., "Diaries" (on microfilm), The Franklin D. Roosevelt Library, Hyde Park, N.Y.

Murrow, Edward R. (ed.), *Talks,* Columbia Broadcasting System, New York, 1937.

Neal, Nevin Emil, "A Biography of Joseph T. Robinson," a doctor's thesis for the University of Oklahoma Graduate College, 1958.

Nevins, Allan, *Herbert H. Lehman and His Era,* Charles Scribner's Sons, New York, 1963.

Neuberger, Richard L., "Senator Wheeler's Plight," *Current History,* Aug., 1937.

New York Times, The, various issues as cited in the Notes.

Norris, George W., "The Papers of George W. Norris," a collection in the Library of Congress.

Padover, Saul K. (ed.), *Thomas Jefferson On Democracy,* The New American Library, New York, 1946.

Pearson, Drew and Allen, Robert S., *The Nine Old Men,* Doubleday, Doran & Co., Inc., Garden City, New York, 1937.

Perkins, Frances, *The Roosevelt I Knew,* Harper Colophon Books, New York, 1964.

Pfeffer, Leo, *This Honorable Court,* Beacon Press, Boston, 1965.

Pittman, Key, "The Papers of Key Pittman," a collection in the Library of Congress.

Pusey, Merlo J., *Charles Evans Hughes,* The Macmillan Co., New York, 1952.

———, *The Supreme Court Crisis,* The Macmillan Co., New York, 1937.

Roosevelt, Franklin D., *F.D.R.—His Personal Letters 1928–1945* (Elliott Roosevelt, ed.), Vols. I and II, Duell, Sloan & Pearce, New York, 1950.

———, "The Franklin D. Roosevelt Papers," a collection in the Franklin D. Roosevelt Library, Hyde Park, N.Y. (This highly organized collection of papers is collected in several ways. There are the press conferences in bound volumes; references to these in the Notes are identified by PC and the appropriate volume and page numbers. There is the official file, identified in the Notes as "of [with the number of the appropriate folder], such as of 41. There is the President's personal file, identified in like manner— ppf and a folder number. Finally, there is the President's secretary's file, identified as psf and the subject matter of the particular file.)

———, *Public Papers and Addresses,* Vols. IV, V, VI, Random House, New York, 1938.

Roosevelt, James and Shalett, Sidney, *Affectionately, F.D.R.,* Harcourt, Brace & Co., New York, 1959.

Rosenman, Samuel I., *Working with Roosevelt,* Harper & Brothers, New York, 1952.

Ruetten, Richard T., "Burton K. Wheeler of Montana: A Progressive Between the Wars," a doctor's thesis for the University of Oregon, Graduate School, 1961.

Salter, John Thomas, *The American Politician,* The University of North Carolina Press, Chapel Hill, 1938.

Smith, Rixey and Beasley, Norman, *Carter Glass,* Longmans, Green & Co., New York, 1939.

Stern, Max, "The Little Red House," *Today,* May 19, 1934.

Swisher, Carl Brent (ed.), *Selected Papers of Homer Cummings,* Charles Scribner's Sons, New York, 1939.

Timmons, Bascom N., *Garner of Texas,* Harper & Brothers, New York, 1948.

Tourtellot, Arthur Bernon, *The Presidents on the Presidency,* Doubleday & Co., Garden City, New York, 1964.

Truman, Harry S., *Memoirs,* Vols. I and II, Doubleday & Co., Garden City, New York, 1955.

Tully, Grace, *F.D.R. My Boss,* Charles Scribner's Sons, New York, 1949.

United States Congress, "Composition and Jurisdiction of the Supreme Court, Hearings Before a Subcommittee of the Committee on the Judiciary, United States Senate, 83d Congress, second session, on S. J. Res. 44," United States Government Printing Office, Washington, 1954.

————, "Reorganization of the Federal Judiciary, Hearings Before the Committee on the Judiciary, United States Senate, 75th Congress, first session," United States Government Printing Office, Washington, 1937.

Vandenberg, Arthur H., "The Biography of an Undelivered Speech," *The Saturday Evening Post,* Oct. 9, 1937.

Washington Post, The, various issues.

Westin, Alan F. (ed.), *An Autobiography of the Supreme Court,* The Macmillan Co., New York, 1963.

————, (ed.), *The Supreme Court: View from Inside,* W. W. Norton & Co., Inc., New York, 1961.

Wheeler, Burton K. with Healy, Paul F., *Yankee from the West,* Doubleday & Co., Garden City, New York, 1962.

White, William Allen, "The Papers of William Allen White," a collection in the Library of Congress.

Williamson, Samuel T., *Frank Gannett,* Duell, Sloan & Pearce, New York, 1940.

Wolfskill, George, *The Revolt of the Conservatives,* Houghton Mifflin Co., Boston, 1962.

Notes

The sources abbreviated in the following notes are identified in full in the preceding bibliography. In these notes a citation of several pages may be used to identify a brief quotation in the text. Where this is so, the citation provides not only the quotation but also other information pertinent to that section of the text in which the quotation appears.

PART ONE

Chapter 1

P. 3 "Why are you," Ashurst, pp. 560–62.
"I regret this," Dorough, pp. 260–61.

P. 4 "I am bursting," Cummings memo to FDR 12/22/36, FDR "Papers," Box 52.

P. 6 "If we can," FDR letter to Charles R. Crane 2/8/37, FDR, "Papers," ppf 462.

P. 7 "into which Henry," Ashurst, pp. 560–62.

P. 8 "Boys, here's where," Alsop, pp. 67–68.
"infamous" and gave it "Hell," Early memo to FDR 2/8/37, FDR, "Papers," Box 52.
"It will fall," Ashurst letter to FDR 2/19/36, Ashurst, no page reference.
"Father Time, with," Ashurst, pp. 560–62.
"Dear Henry, here," FDR note to Ashurst 2/5/37, FDR, "Papers," of 41.

P. 9 "a large sum," Wolfskill, p. 250.
"Give me ten," Ickes, II, 64–66.

P. 10 "When I retire," *N.Y. Times,* 2/28/37, p. 1.

P. 12 "He insisted that," Ickes, II, 74–75.

P. 13 "If that's the," author's interview with Carl McFarland, Cummings' assistant 4/18/66.

P. 14 "the most destructive," confidential source.

P. 14 "My task is," Robinson letter to Horace Chamberlain 3/2/37, quoted in Neal, p. 445.

"President Roosevelt, during," Ashurst, p. 503–4.

P. 15 "The subject," Early memo to FDR 2/5/37, FDR, "Papers," Box 114.

"and don't anybody," FDR "Papers," PC, 130–47.

P. 16 "I made notes," Timmons, p. 218.

P. 17 "Can you tell," FDR "Papers," PC, IX, 130–47.

Chapter 2

P. 20 "The Democrats cheered," *N.Y. Times,* 1/7/37, p. 1.

"found myself yelling," Ickes, 32–33.

P. 21 "I knew from," Truman, Vol. I, p. 154.

"We were shocked," Celler, p. 14.

"Wouldn't you have . . ." A memorandum of this conversation between Speaker Bankhead and Representative Lindsay C. Warren of Washington, North Carolina, is on file in the Warren Papers in the Southern Historical Collection at the University of North Carolina Library. The memorandum consists of a single page, typewritten and single-spaced.

P. 22 "The President would," Robinson letter 3/2/37, quoted in Neal, p. 445.

"more than once," Farley, p. 73.

"I think that," *N.Y. Times,* 1/19/37, p. 1.

P. 23 "The White House," *N.Y. Times,* 1/20/37, p. 9.

"Can you tell," FDR "Papers," PC, IX, 102.

"If, in the," Borah, Box 621.

P. 24 "it would seem," J. Reuben Clark letter to Borah 1/30/37 and Borah reply 2/1/37, Borah, Box 415.

"I was flabbergasted," Wheeler, p. 321.

P. 25 "As I look," Wheeler, p. 297.

"My dear Burt," FDR letter to Wheeler 10/23/36 and Wheeler reply 10/24/36, FDR, "Papers," ppf 723.

P. 26 "If you knew," confidential source.

P. 27 "a cheap politician," author's interview with former Sen. Wheeler 9/28/66.

"Listen to this," Williamson, p. 177.

P. 28 "it is now," *N.Y. Times,* 2/6/37, p. 1.

"I feel that," Nevins, p. 190.

"Adroitly President Roosevelt," editorial in Emporia *Gazette,* 2/6/37, reprinted in *Congressional Record,* Vol. 81, App. p. 189.

Chapter 3

P. 30   "They's de grandest," Roy H. Everett letter to Hughes
        11/30/37, Hughes, "Papers," Box 120.
P. 31   "It is well," Hughes to Erwin N. Griswold 12/14/36, Hughes,
        "Papers," Box 111.
        "the Court has," Hughes, *Supreme Court,* p. 24.
        "suffered severely from," Hughes, *Supreme Court,* pp. 51–53.
P. 32   "My personal relations," Hughes, "Notes," ch. 23, pp. 33–34.
        "Politics may make," Ickes, II, 50–52.
P. 33   "It has been," Henry J. Brant letter to Hughes 1/21/37,
        Hughes, "Papers," Box 118.
        "I felt like," Rosenman, p. 144.
P. 35   "He would have," address by Robert H. Jackson before
        Brandeis Memorial Colony dinner 6/23/43, printed in
        Westin, *Autobiography,* p. 236.
P. 36   "justly regarded as," Hughes, "Notes," ch. 23, p. 19.
        "are available for," Hughes, "Papers," Box 118.
        "I gave your," Hughes, "Papers," Box 122.
P. 37   "It was a," J. Edgar Hoover letter to Hughes 2/17/37,
        Hughes, "Papers," Box 121.
P. 38   "Much excitement over," Ashurst, pp. 562–63.
        "The President sent," author's interview with former Sen.
        Pepper 5/3/66.

PART TWO

Chapter 4

P. 41   "all we have," Farley, pp. 78–79.
        "I found that," Celler, p. 12.
        "I've never encountered," author's interview with former Sen.
        Nye 9/1/66.
P. 42   "It was the," Creel, p. 7.
P. 43   "Is the Supreme," *N.Y. Times,* 6/24/36, p. 1.
        "more or less," *N.Y. Times,* 5/27/36, p. 22.
P. 44   "Does any man," speech by Charles L. Dawson, quoted in
        N.Y. Times, 1/26/36, p. 37.
        "This election will," *N.Y. Times,* 2/22/36, p. 37.
        "thought the Constitution," Landon letter to author 7/14/66.
P. 45   "The President was," Landon letter to author 7/14/66.
        "The integrity and," *N.Y. Times,* 6/12/36, p. 1.
        "amendment of the," *N.Y. Times,* 7/3/36, p. 7.

P. 45 "one of the," Sen. Lester J. Dickinson, quoted in *N.Y. Times,* 9/10/36, p. 8.

P. 46 "Why not tell," *N.Y. Times,* 10/31/36, p. 4.

"we are left," *N.Y. Times,* 10/22/36, p. 21.

"The Republicans lost," Jackson, *Struggle,* p. 177.

P. 47 "The President has," Ickes, II, 74–75.

"I do not," Morgenthau, Bk. 55, p. 95.

"Everyone now understands," Sen. Key Pittman to FDR 6/6/32, Pittman, Box 15.

"Even many persons," Ashurst, p. 573.

P. 48 "I wish I," Lippmann column 6/26/37.

"When Chief Justice," Byrnes radio speech 2/17/37, printed in *Congressional Record,* Vol. 81, App. pp. 276–77.

"Would it be," confidential source.

P. 49 "If the Court," FDR, *Letters,* I, 669–70.

P. 50 "smacked of the," FDR, *Letters,* I, 673.

P. 51 "For one, I," Pepper to FDR 12/22/28, reprinted in *Congressional Record,* Vol. 90, p. 2049.

"In a great," FDR, *Letters,* I, 268–69.

"I remember when," Smith interview with Robert C. Albright, Washington *Post,* 8/29/66, p. 1.

P. 52 "I shall continue," Glass to Harry E. Mock of Evanston, Ill., 10/5/36, Glass, Box 380.

"Within a few," Glass to Sen. Millard E. Tydings 10/9/36, Glass, Box 380.

"It is well," Smith, p. 369.

"Apparently [FDR] is," H. F. Byrd to Carter Glass 4/29/37, Glass, Box 345.

P. 53 "I think that," *Congressional Record,* Vol. 81, pp. 3646–47.

"be required, with," Cope, p. 83.

P. 54 "answer to a," MacColl, p. 125.

P. 55 "His peroration was," Ickes, II, 59.

"go over with," Roosevelt, *Affectionately,* p. 292.

"The Child Labor," Chase, Box 2.

P. 56 "inspiring. . . . I feel," LaFollette to FDR 3/5/37, FDR, "Papers," ppf 1792.

Chapter 5

P. 58 "The Chief would," author's interview with former Sen. Nye 9/1/66.

P. 59 "Signs of uneasiness," Borah, Box 624.

"Well, I understand," Morgenthau, Bk. 55, pp. 236–38.

P. 64   "Mr. President, you," Barkley, p. 144.
P. 65   "I suggest you," Rayburn to FDR, undated note, FDR, "Papers," Box 114.
         "quite important for," Bankhead to FDR 2/18/37, FDR, "Papers," Box 52.
P. 66   "I am a," *Congressional Record,* Vol. 81, App. p. 541.
         "I wish to," Ashurst, pp. 565–66.
P. 68   "I replied that," Ashurst, pp. 564–65.
         "There was a," *N.Y. Times,* 2/21/37, p. 1.

Chapter 6

P. 70   "In our federal," Cummings, no page reference.
P. 71   "a justice of," Ickes, II, 87.
         "more distress and," Clarke telegram to FDR 3/14/37, FDR, "Papers," ppf 2927.
P. 72   "Senator Borah is," J. C. O'Laughlin to W. A. White 3/8/37 and White to R. Roberts 3/10/37, White, Box 186.
         "told us yesterday," White, Box 187.
P. 73   "About this man," White, Box 187.
         "to blindly support," U.S. Congress, "Reorganization," p. 686.
         "It is with," Hirth letter to FDR 3/18/37 and FDR reply 3/24/37, FDR, "Papers," ppf 69.
P. 75   "There is no," *Congressional Record,* Vol. 81, p. 1661.
P. 76   "What can you," Borah, Box 621.
         "We understand the," Glass, Box 372.
         "In recent order," FDR, "Papers," of 179.
P. 78   "an independent judiciary," *N.Y. Times,* 2/21/37, p. 24.
         "It was the," *N.Y. Times,* 2/21/37, Sec. E, p. 3.
P. 79   "We thank you," Borah, Box 621.
         "To meet the," Norris, Tray 27, Box 2.
P. 80   "contained representations and," *Congressional Record,* Vol. 81, p. 1658.
         "the most transparent," *N.Y. Times,* 2/23/37, p. 6.
         "The other day," Gannett speech on CBS 2/21/37, text.
P. 81   "If you don't," author's interview with former Sen. Wheeler 9/28/66.
P. 82   "Well, Mr. President," *N.Y. Times,* 2/23/37, p. 1.
P. 83   "You remember the," *Congressional Record,* Vol. 81, App. pp. 493–94.
         "know that [Ickes]," text of Glass speech 3/29/37, printed in Smith.
P. 84   "provide facilities for," *N.Y. Times,* 2/21/37, p. 23.

P. 85 "It looks like," Swisher, p. 153.
"the day after," White, Box 190.
P. 86 "It is important," FDR, "Papers," Box 19.
P. 87 "Farmers, as well," *N.Y. Times,* 3/10/37, p. 1.
"We have no," *N.Y. Times,* 2/17/37, p. 1.
P. 89 "I most emphatically," *N.Y. Times,* 2/6/37, p. 9.
"The [GOP] strategy," Ickes, II, 93.
P. 90 "I hope that," Wolfskill, p. 351.
"If we grant," *Congressional Record,* Vol. 81, App. p. 871.
P. 91 "Unfortunately Landon got," Alsop, pp. 97–98.
"McCormick persuaded Landon," Wolfskill, p. 252.
"No one persuaded," Landon letter to author 7/14/66.
P. 92 "Mr. Roosevelt has," *N.Y. Times,* 2/21/37, p. 23.
"It seems to," Mason, *Brandeis,* pp. 624–25.
P. 96 "I have your," confidential source.
"It seems to," Hoover to White 5/11/37, White, Box 188.
P. 97 "When you have," *N.Y. Times,* 7/20/37, p. 10.
P. 99 "There probably never," Vandenberg, p. 25.
"A small army," author's interview with former Sen. Wheeler
9/28/66.

PART THREE

Chapter 7

P. 104 "two kinds of," Jackson, *Struggle,* p. xii.
P. 105 "In the summer," Rosenman, p. 110.
P. 106 "the present assault," quoted in Pfeffer, p. 220.
"the black flag," Mason, *Brandeis,* pp. 24–25.
"And I have," quoted in Jackson, *Struggle,* p. 183.
P. 107 "has made three," quoted in Pfeffer, p. 271.
P. 108 "I was amused," FDR, *Letters,* I, 265.
"Four Horsemen . . . distinction, Cope, p. 1.
"I know what," Byrnes, p. 65.
P. 109 "suggested to Bert," Keller, p. 256.
"I think there," Shipstead letter to George W. Norris 5/17/37,
Norris, Tray 27, Box 1.
P. 110 "follow some certain," Bickel.
"I can have," FDR letter to B. N. Cardozo, FDR, *Letters,*
I, 307–8.
"your Court tells," Perkins, p. 286.

P. 111   "in certain fields," FDR letter to Norman Hapgood 2/4/36, FDR, *Letters,* I, 561.

         "All you need," Cope, p. 3.

P. 113   "and in a," J. P. Kennedy memo 2/18/35, FDR, "Papers," of 229.

P. 114   "such a marked," H. S. Cummings letter to FDR 5/7/35, quoted in Swisher, p. 130.

P. 116   "Well, if I," FDR "Papers," PC, V, 304–6.

P. 117   "The issue is," FDR, "Papers," PC, V, 335–36.

         "A very long," FDR letter to David Gray 6/17/35, FDR, "Papers," ppf 454.

P. 118   "The absolute theory," printed in Swisher, p. 140.

         "no doubt there," H. S. Cummings memo to John Dickinson 12/18/35, printed in Swisher, p. 148.

P. 120   "greatest human tragedy," Pearson, p. 222.

         "As you well," Pusey, *Hughes,* p. 667.

P. 121   "afflict the Court," Pearson, p. 219.

P. 122   "His emphasis on," Eugene Gressman, quoted by Joseph A. Loftus in *N.Y. Times,* 7/2/66.

P. 124   "They have had," U.S. Congress, "Composition," pp. 8–9.

P. 126   "I want to," J. M. Harlan, quoted in Mason, *Brandeis,* p. vii.

P. 127   "You spoke at," H. S. Cummings to H. F. Stone 1/8/36 and Stone reply 1/9/36, FDR, "Papers," Box 20.

         "The objective of," FDR, *Letters,* I, 548–49.

         "It is plain," Ickes, I, 524.

P. 128   "with all the," H. S. Cummings to FDR 1/29/36, printed in Swisher, p. 149.

         "I am happy," *N.Y. Times,* 5/8/36, p. 2.

         "It seems to," FDR, *Public Papers,* V, 192.

P. 129   "We finished the," quoted in Pfeffer, p. 311.

         "there was a," Ickes, I, 705.

         "It will give," FDR to J. M. Patterson 11/9/36, FDR, "Papers," ppf 245.

P. 132   "The subtle corps," Padover, p. 63.

         "The opinion of," Tourtellot, p. 269.

P. 133   "the position assumed," *Inaugural Addresses,* p. 124.

P. 134   "You know, I," Perkins, p. 249.

         "The judges themselves," Cummings, no page reference.

P. 135   "The Court seemed," Jackson, *Struggle,* p. 187.

         "the superannuated old," Westin, *Inside,* p. 95.

Chapter 8

P. 137   "There has been," *N.Y. Times,* 1/17/36, p. 13.

P. 137   "There has been," *N.Y. Times,* 1/17/36, p. 13.
          "a bold and," J. O. Mahoney to FDR 1/10/36, FDR,
          "Papers," ppf 1200.
          "the Supreme Court," *N.Y. Times,* 1/11/37, p. 9.
          "I disagree with," Murrow, p. 64.
          "it takes twelve," *N.Y. Times,* 1/12/36, p. 22.
P. 138   "You are the," Lief, p. 492.
P. 139   "In the interval," Ickes, II, 139.
P. 142   "If I had," Johnson, p. 469.
P. 143   "Congress with no," Murrow, p. 6.
          "Here, for the," Stern, p. 5.
P. 144   "But I don't," Alsop, p. 71.
          "Before I close," *N.Y. Times,* 4/4/37, p. 33.
P. 145   "a large room," Ashurst, pp. 569–70.

PART FOUR

Chapter 9

P. 150   "If there are," *N.Y. Times,* 3/11/37, p. 1.
          "General, I just," U.S. Congress, "Reorganization," p. 15.
          "We do not," Gerhart, p. 111.
          "If the Constitution," U.S. Congress, "Reorganization," p. 63.
P. 151   "unless there is," John Callan O'Laughlin to William Allen
          White 3/8/37, White, Box 186.
P. 152   "I could win," *N.Y. Times,* 3/28/37, p. 1.
P. 153   "May I ask," U.S. Congress, "Reorganization," p. 702.
          "As the opponents," Hughes, "Notes," pp. 20–22.
P. 154   "You tell your," author's interview with former Sen. Wheeler
          9/28/66.
P. 156   "I don't know," Wheeler, pp. 330–33.
          "Senators, we are," U.S. Congress, "Reorganization," pp.
          485–87.
P. 159   "the author said," *N.Y. Times,* 3/23/37, p. 1.
          "It should be," *Congressional Record,* Vol. 81, p. 2817.
          "We're licked," Wheeler, p. 33.
          "The Hughes letter," confidential source.
P. 160   "This letter appears," Hughes, "Notes," ch. 23, p. 23.
          "I hope that," Hughes, "Notes," ch. 23, pp. 20–22.
          "There was no," Mason, *Stone,* pp. 451–52.
P. 161   "Considering the delicacy," Pusey, *Hughes,* pp. 755–56.
          "I simply cannot," F. Frankfurter to H. F. Stone 4/8/37,
          quoted in MacColl, p. 302.

P. 162   "It was good," Ickes, II, 104.

"When I was," PC, IX, 291–92.

P. 163   "I warmly appreciate," Hughes, "Papers," Box 119.

"Between these society," *N.Y. Times,* 5/14/37, p. 17.

"Off the record," MacColl, pp. 294–95.

P. 164   "The evidence of," *N.Y. Times,* 3/17/37, p. 1.

P. 165   "for a southerner," confidential source.

"of the utmost," confidential source.

"and there was," Ashurst, p. 568.

P. 166   "From the time," Hughes, "Notes," ch. 23, pp. 2–3.

P. 167   "I appreciate your," Hughes letter to W. E. Pulliam of Ciudad
Trujillo, Santo Domingo, 5/4/36; Hughes, "Papers," Box
115.

"so that you," Hughes, "Notes," ch. 23, p. 4.

P. 168   "has never given," Mason, *Stone,* p. 460 (footnote).

"His presentation of," quoted in Pusey, *Hughes,* p. 675.

P. 169   "I am sure," O. Roberts address before the Association of
the Bar of the City of New York, Dec., 1948, printed in
Westin, *Autobiography,* pp. 205–10.

P. 170   "a distinguished jurist," Murrow, p. 68.

"I have no," quoted in Mason, *Stone,* p. 449.

P. 171   "some thoughts on," FDR, "Papers," ppf 2293.

P. 172   "Roosevelt is giving," H. F. Stone to Helen Stone Willard
4/7/37, quoted in Mason, *Stone,* p. 447.

"I go my," H. F. Stone to George Biddle 4/8/37, quoted in
Mason, *Stone,* pp. 449–50.

Chapter 10

P. 174   "the switch in," *N. Y. Times,* June 15, 1937, p. 19.

"Many who had," Jackson, *Struggle,* p. 192.

"Utterly baseless. . . . The," Hughes, "Notes," ch. 23, pp.
30–33.

"no action taken," O. Roberts memo to F. Frankfurter
11/9/45, printed in Westin, *Autobiography,* pp. 241–48.

"when my turn," O. Roberts memo to F. Frankfurter 11/9/45,
printed in Westin, *Autobiography,* pp. 241–48.

P. 176   "fully conscious . . . the," U.S. Congress, "Composition,"
pp. 9–14.

P. 177   "was anxious to," Corwin, p. 76.

P. 178   "This doctrine that," Jackson, *Struggle,* pp. 207–13.

P. 179   "I would like," *N.Y. Times,* 3/30/37, p. 1.

"I, for one," *N. Y. Times,* 4/1/37, p. 10.

"remains to be," Mason, *Stone,* p. 457.

P. 180　"It seems to," Ickes, II, 107.

　　　　"Certainly it cannot," McMahon, no page reference.

　　　　"No matter whether," Farley, pp. 79–80.

　　　　"the enlightened judgment," Cummings, no page reference.

P. 181　"It is not," Swisher, p. 161.

　　　　"We have all," FDR "Papers," PC, IX, 259–62.

　　　　"It's been a," *N.Y. Times,* 4/13/37, p. 1.

P. 182　"I have been," FDR "Papers," PC, IX, 259–62.

　　　　"The thing to," Alsop, pp. 152–53.

P. 185　"I believe every," Judge J. Warren Davis of U.S. Court of Appeals, Third Circuit, to FDR 4/4/37, FDR "Papers," Box 52.

　　　　"There isn't any," Ickes to FDR 3/15/37, FDR, "Papers," ppf 3650.

P. 186　"the country is," Ickes, II, 98.

P. 187　"I could hear," Ickes, II, 78–81.

P. 188　"When Lyndon Johnson," confidential source.

P. 189　"The campaign turned," *N.Y. Times,* 4/13/37, p. 21.

　　　　"with the Court," *N.Y. Times,* 4/17/37, p. 4.

　　　　"Mr. Speaker, I," *Congressional Record,* Vol. 81, p. 4508.

P. 190　"the battle will," *N.Y. Times,* 5/15/37, p. 1.

　　　　"hit them hard," Ickes, II, 141–42.

P. 192　"I think the," Sen. Arthur Capper to William Allen White 2/26/37, White, Box 186.

　　　　"It was encouraging," Sen. Robert LaFollette to FDR 3/16/37, FDR, "Papers," ppf. 1792.

P. 193　"Eff Dee leaves," Ashurst, p. 571–72.

P. 194　"An unfavorable report," *N.Y. Times,* 4/25/37, p. 1.

P. 195　"The plan has," *N.Y. Times,* 4/20/37, p. 2.

P. 197　"Let your conscience," confidential source.

P. 198　"To them he," confidential source.

P. 199　"I believe we," Sen. Arthur Capper to William Allen White 5/25/37, White, Box 188.

Chapter 11

P. 200　"Rather than agree," Secretary of Commerce Daniel C. Roper to FDR 6/21/37, FDR, "Papers," of 11.

P. 202　"You fellows in," *N.Y. Times,* 6/26/37, p. 1.

Chapter 12

P. 206　"The report has," speech by R. D. Holt 3/23/37, printed in *Congressional Record,* Vol. 81, App. p. 674.

　　　　"I have been," U.S. Congress, "Reorganization," p. 915–32.

P. 208   "They picked off," Sen. Hiram Johnson in letter to Frank
          P. Doherty 3/13/37, quoted in Ruetten, p. 229.

          "For fourteen months," *Congressional Record*, Vol. 81, p.
          2837.

          "The Attorney General," *N.Y. Times*, 4/1/37, p. 10.

          "You can say," *N.Y. Times*, 4/17/37, p. 4.

P. 209   "You would have," Wheeler letter to Farley 5/10/37, FDR,
          "Papers," ppf 723.

P. 210   "the Wheeler balloon," Farley to FDR 6/16/37, FDR,
          "Papers," ppf 723.

          "Butte is wide," Neuberger, p. 30.

          "On March 30," FDR, "Papers," of 179.

P. 212   "Are you checking," author's interview with former Sen.
          Wheeler 9/28/66.

          "I just want," Morgenthau, Bk. 68, pp. 184–89.

P. 213   "those opposed to," *N.Y. Times*, 3/25/37, p. 1.

P. 214   "It is vindictiveness," Glass letter to H. F. Byrd 5/17/37,
          Glass, Box 345.

          "This is the," *Congressional Record*, Vol. 81, pp. 7019–27.

P. 215   "I am very," *N.Y. Times*, 6/19/37, p. 8.

          "Go pour yourself," author's interview with former Sen.
          Wheeler 9/28/66.

Chapter 13

P. 216   "Don't you know," *N.Y. Times*, 3/28/37, p. 21.

P. 218   "Whatever have been," Timmons, p. 209.

          "The chief danger," Ickes, II, 108.

P. 219   "Henry Morgenthau Jr.," Morgenthau, Bk. 66, p. 88.

P. 220   "The Vice President looked," Ickes, II, 140–41.

P. 221   "Why in hell," Farley, pp. 84–86.

          "I have never," Garner to FDR 6/19/37, FDR, "Papers,"
          Box 53.

          "If Congress does," Roosevelt, *Letters*, I, 692–93.

PART FIVE

Chapter 14

P. 225   "Mr. Suter, Justice," *N.Y. Times*, 5/23/37, p. 4.

P. 226   "to you every," *N.Y. Times*, 5/19/37, p. 1.

P. 227   "I'm not saying," *N.Y. Times*, 4/18/36, p. 17.

          "I will follow," *N.Y. Times*, 4/12/37 p. 4.

          "just another day," *N.Y. Times*, 3/4/37, p. 23.

P. 227   "Against my inclinations," *N.Y. Times,* 4/3/37, p. 2.

         "It is now," *N.Y. Times,* 3/2/27, p. 1.

P. 228   "went over to," Hughes, *Supreme Court,* pp. 75–77.

P. 230   "a needless, futile," reprinted in Cope, pp. 71–80.

         "Since there were," *N.Y. Times,* 6/16/37, p. 22.

         "I have no," *N.Y. Times,* 5/19/37, p. 18.

         "The Supreme Court," confidential source.

P. 231   "I hope to," W. A. White to Sen. Arthur Capper, 5/28/37, White, Box 188.

P. 232   "Ah, but she," Ickes, II, 126–27.

         "It is felt," *N.Y. Times,* 6/4/37, p. 1.

         "plain silly," FDR "Papers," PC, IX, 407–12.

P. 233   "I will stand," *N.Y. Times,* 6/6/37, p. 37.

         "I have enough," quoted in Neal, p. 456.

P. 234   "Of course the," Borah, Box 626.

P. 235   "is no less," Frank Gannett telegram to W. E. Borah 7/9/37, Borah, Box 624.

         "We'll travel about," *N.Y. Times,* 6/6/37, Sec. 4, p. 8.

         "No," *N.Y. Times,* 7/16/37, p. 3.

P. 236   "is no fundamental," *N.Y. Times,* 7/4/37, p. 1.

P. 237   "Keeping the Senate," *N.Y. Times,* 7/6/37, p. 1.

P. 238   "But I am," author's interview with former Sen. Wheeler 9/28/66.

P. 240   "It is my," *Congressional Record,* Vol. 81, pp. 6788–89.

P. 241   "I am prompted," *Congressional Record,* Vol. 81, p. 6796.

P. 242   "If they are," *Congressional Record,* Vol. 81, p. 6878.

         "What do senators," *Congressional Record,* Vol. 81, p. 6916.

         "makes the hair," *N.Y. Times,* 7/9/37, p. 5.

P. 243   "as soon as," *Congressional Record,* Vol. 81, pp. 7141–44.

Chapter 15

P. 245   "It is hard," Robinson letter to W. T. Sitlington, editor of the *Arkansas Democrat,* 7/6/37, quoted in Neal, pp. 412–13.

         "Gentlemen may laugh," *Congressional Record,* Vol. 81, pp. 5956.

P. 246   "If the opponents," *Congressional Record,* Vol. 81, p. 6797.

P. 247   "I should like," *Congressional Record,* Vol. 81, pp. 6797–98.

         "Henry, when will," Ashurst, pp. 576–77.

P. 248   "Go slow," *N.Y. Times,* 7/15/37, p. 12.

P. 249   "I think it," Gerhart, pp. 116–17.

         "If Brandeis resigns," Morgenthau, Bk. 69, pp. 308–9.

P. 250   "Without a single," Robinson to Dr. M. F. Dickinson 6/1/37,
         quoted in Neal, p. 451.
         "Mr. Justice," Farley, p. 86.
P. 251   "How'd you make," author's interview with former Sen.
         Wheeler 9/28/66.
         "The Senate and," confidential source.
P. 252   "As he leaned," *N.Y. Times,* 7/15/37, p. 1.
         "I immediately dispatched," Ashurst, p. 576.
         "a little flurry," *N.Y. Times,* 7/14/37, p. 12.

Chapter 16

P. 254   "Joe Robinson was," *N.Y. Times,* 7/15/37, p. 13.
         "The gentleman seemed," Ruetten, pp. 240–41.
         "Robinson alone could," Byrnes, p. 98.
P. 256   "Our conference Thursday," E. C. Johnson to FDR 7/17/37,
         FDR, "Papers," Box 53.
P. 258   "I thought we," Nevins, p. 192.
         "That is the," *N.Y. Times,* 7/20/37, p. 3.
P. 262   "At least thirty-eight," Russell M. Roberts to W. A. White,
         undated letter in White, Box 190.
         "How did you," Timmons, pp. 222–23.
P. 264   "The Vice President," Ashurst, pp. 578–79.
P. 265   "My loyalties are," Timmons, p. 224.
         "There is no," Washington *Post,* 7/23/37, p. 1.

PART SIX

Chapter 17

P. 271   "I might say," *Congressional Record,* Vol. 81, pp. 7375–82.
P. 274   "Do you plan," FDR "Papers," PC, X, 58–62.
P. 276   "It is only," Truman, Vol. II, p. 24.
         "Because your President," quoted in Tourtellot, p. 69.
P. 278   "They subdued the," Jackson, *Struggle,* p. vi.
         "All in all," Wheeler, p. 339.
P. 279   "If he'd got," author's interview with former Sen. Wheeler
         9/28/66.
P. 281   "some of our," FDR letter to W. E. Dodd 5/25/37, FDR,
         "Papers," ppf Dodd.
         "This comes from," Farley, p. 82.

Index

Index